In memory of Harold Hall

G+e
29/9/88

Copyright © 1987 Eamonn Rodgers

Paperback ISBN 0 9511956 03

Online Typesetting by Intercontinental Photocomposition, Dublin 17.

Printed by Jack Hade & Company.

FROM ENLIGHTENMENT TO REALISM: THE NOVELS OF GALDÓS 1870–1887

by
Eamonn Rodgers
Senior Lecturer in Spanish
Trinity College
Dublin.

DUBLIN 1987

Contents

Acknowledgments

In preparing this study, I was privileged to receive financial and practical support from various agencies to which I would like to record my thanks. A grant from the Graduate Studies Committee of Trinity College enabled me to visit the British Library to collect primary material on nineteenth-century Spanish literary theory. In 1975, the Royal Irish Academy honoured me with an Exchange Fellowship which enabled me to spend a summer at the Institute for Advanced Studies in the Humanities of Edinburgh University, where I enjoyed much-needed leisure to embark on first drafts of the early chapters. My thanks are due to the secretarial staff of the Institute, its then Director, Professor William Beattie, and the staffs of the National Library of Scotland and Edinburgh University Library, and, not least, to the staff of Trinity College Library. I would also like to thank Michael Doherty, of the Trinity College Computer Laboratory, and David Abrahamson, of the Department of Computer Science, for advice and help in solving various word-processing and printing problems. Printing and publication have been assisted by generous grants from the Trinity College Dublin Trust and the Arts and Economic and Social Studies Research Fund, to which warmest gratitude is also due.

This book has been long in the making, and my indebtedness is correspondingly great. My most incalculable debt is to my wife, Valerie, whose book this is as much as mine, for she has not only provided practical and emotional support, but has been a shrewd and patient reader over my shoulder almost since my academic career began. Many others, both colleagues and students, have contributed, often unwittingly, by initiating trains of thought in discussion, and offering advice, criticism and encouragement. In fairness to them, I should make it clear that I have often preferred to plough my own furrow, and any shortcomings in this book are therefore mine alone. Arthur Terry first suggested, many years ago, that I undertake an extended study of Galdós, and gave unstintingly of his time in supervising my doctoral thesis. When I joined the staff of Trinity College I had the benefit of E. C. Riley's vast literary culture and long experience of grappling with the problems of prose fiction. Nigel Glendinning and Richard Cardwell offered useful advice and information on nineteenth-century Spanish literary theory. Nicholas Saul gave me much-needed guidance on the German Enlightenment and Romanticism. I have also benefitted, on numerous occasions, from long and stimulating conversations on Galdós with James Whiston, Peter Bly, Michael Gordon, Maurice Hemingway,

Geoffrey Ribbans and Jennifer Lowe. To all the above my warmest thanks, but I reserve a special tribute of gratitude and affection to the memory of the dedicatee, the late Professor H. B. Hall, whose wise counsel and breadth of knowledge have often saved me from rushing in where better men fear to tread.

Trinity College, Dublin.   *E.R.*
June 1986.

A Note on References

References to Galdós's writings are generally incorporated in the text and are, except where otherwise indicated, to the Aguilar edition of the *Obras completas* and to the *Obras inéditas*, edited by Alberto Ghiraldo (10 vols., Madrid, 1923–30). References will be given in the form (OC 5, 123) or (Ined 5, 123). It is often difficult to find a set of the six-volume Aguilar complete works made up from the same edition, and since the pagination varies from edition to edition, it is well to specify that in the set to which I had access, vol. 4 is the third edition (1954), and vols. 5 and 6 are the second edition (1950 and 1951). Except where otherwise indicated, translations of quotations are my own.

Introduction

Text and Context

A new contribution to the already extensive bibliography on Galdós clearly stands in need of some justification, especially at a time when literary scholars are under considerable pressure to declare their theoretical and ideological baggage. Let me state at the outset, therefore, that the present study aims to steer a middle course between the panoramic approach pioneered in Joaquín Casalduero's important book of 1943, *Vida y obra de Galdós*, and the detailed study of individual novels.[1] I shall be concerned simultaneously with, on the one hand, historical context, literary tradition, the author's ideological background, and the overall shape and development of his work within a particular period, and, on the other, with individual texts as literary artefacts, their internal logic, and the various effects they might have on a certain type of reader.

My approach therefore attempts to achieve a synthesis of literary history, textual analysis and certain elements of reader-response criticism. Nowadays, of course, a reluctance to commit oneself wholeheartedly to a single ideological or theoretical position is often taken as an indication of cowardice or dishonesty, but in my view any narrow or *a priori* approach always risks doing violence to the complexity of the literary work. I would furthermore argue that a synthesis of the kind I have described provides the only effective antidote to what would otherwise be the infinite diversity of possible reader responses. Faced with the question 'Why should any interpretation be more valid than any other?', one can only recognise that all interpretations begin as the subjective responses of individual readers, and that no interpretation can claim absolute and permanent validity. Nevertheless, an interpretation, however subjective, will approximate to objectivity in the measure in which it is accepted by more than one reader. Such acceptance is more likely to be forthcoming if the interpretation is seen to result from a global consideration both of the internal evidence provided by the language and structure of the text, and external or secondary evidence, such as the circumstances of composition, authorial intention and the tradition of interpretation to which critics' readings of the text have already given rise.

Readers of Stanley Fish's *Is There a Text in This Class?* (Harvard University Press, 1980) will readily recognise how much the argument of the foregoing paragraph has been influenced by his notion of 'the authority of interpretive communities'. Fish endeavours to steer a middle course between the two extremes of, on the one hand, total relativism in interpretation, and, on the other, postulating the existence of a stable core of meaning in the text, which may be uncovered by a sufficiently competent reader. Abandoning the idea of stable meanings does not involve the abandonment of shared standards of judgement, argues Fish, because

> . . . communication occurs within situations and . . . to be in a situation is already to be in possession of (or to be possessed by) a structure of assumptions, of practices understood to be relevant in relation to purposes and goals that are already in place; and it is within the assumption of these purposes and goals that any utterance is *immediately* heard. . . . meanings come already calculated, not because of norms embedded in the language but because language is always perceived, from the very first, within a structure of norms. That structure, however, is not abstract and independent but social; and therefore it is not a single structure with a privileged relationship to the process of communication as it occurs in any situation but a structure that changes when one situation, with its assumed background of practices, purposes, and goals, has given way to another (p. 318).

What I find attractive about this formulation is that it gives an intellectually coherent account of what one instinctively knows actually happens in literary criticism. Reassuringly, it shows that criticism can continue even in a climate of obsessive scepticism about the reality of meaning or about the existence of standards of truth. It liberates us from the objective-subjective polarity by depriving it of much of its point. While demonstrating the possibility of shared judgement, it also establishes that judgements are always provisional, and thereby accounts satisfactorily for the fact that texts are read in different ways by different generations of readers.

There is, then, an implied historical relativism in Fish's theory, the methodological implications of which he has not fully developed. For although at the level of general principle Fish defines the boundaries of his 'interpretive communities' very widely, it is nevertheless clearly implied in his more detailed examples that for practical purposes the interpretive community which matters most is that constituted by university literary critics. In my view, however, it is particularly useful, when studying the literature of the past, to include within the structure of shared assumptions and purposes the author and his original readers. One of my most serious reservations about structuralist and post-structuralist criticism is its a-historical character. The critic who treats the text purely as text rather than as a communication between an author and a community of readers can easily delude himself into thinking that his critical method is value-free and valid for all time. Such a critic is often unaware, however, of the extent to which he is himself conditioned by the current climate of relativism and scepticism. As Dorothy L. Sayers wisely remarked many years ago, 'those preferences which appear to us self-justified out of all argument belong to a period attitude . . . Our successors will speak of "the Neo-Elizabethans" precisely as we speak of "the Victorians", and in the same tone of voice . . . '[2] Modern criticism is as much the product of history as modern literature which, as Erich Auerbach reminded us, arose 'in a Europe unsure of itself, overflowing with unsettled ideologies and ways of life, and pregnant with disaster'.[3] The present tendency to concentrate on structural matters or on the alleged absence of connection between language and meaning does not in principle guarantee that any particular critical interpretation will be specially reliable, scientific, or ideologically impartial. Rather it implies the assumption that since there is no consensus on the existence or knowability of reality, or on the standards whereby we may make judgements, discussion of the relation of the literary work to the world is a waste of time.

This is, perhaps, no great harm when the literature under discussion reflects the same sceptical and relativistic outlook, as is the case with most 'self-reflective' novels of this century. But it can be seriously misleading when applied to the literature of the past, the great bulk of which was written and read by people who took for granted the notion that a work of literature had something to say about the life which author and readers shared. This is particularly true of the realist novel, which, as J. P. Stern has aptly pointed out, is 'programmatically connected with the world outside literature'.[4] Because author and readers assume the existence of the external world and of commonly-accepted criteria whereby that world may be interpreted, they implicitly agree that it is useful and meaningful to talk about it. Though many (perhaps most) realist novelists frequently cast doubt on conventional ways of looking at the world, they do so, in the last analysis, in order to contrast true perception of reality with false perception. It follows that they believe in a system of values which makes it possible for this contrast to be measured.

This description of the realist novel is apt to cause contemporary critics to protest that the claims of realism are being accepted at their own evaluation. But the fact that we may disagree with many of the assumptions of the realists should not prevent us from recognising that these assumptions were part of the intellectual and moral climate in which they wrote. Though nineteenth-century liberals inherited from the Enlightenment a hatred of the injustices of the *ancien régime*, few people today would regard as tenable their optimistic belief in progress, or their frequent complacency about the horrors of industrialisation. That such beliefs were conscientiously held by large numbers of intelligent people is, however, an incontrovertible fact, which any criticism which claims to be scholarly has to take into account. The text, of course, retains primacy of place in the hierarchy of evidence, in the sense that the possible range of meanings suggested by the words on the page usually goes far beyond those directly associated with the circumstances of the work's composition. But because the realist novel is bound to its author, its readers, literary and cultural tradition and the external world in a complex nexus of relationships, it is absurd to exclude from the area of critical discussion any evidence which throws light on these relationships. As Wayne C. Booth wisely remarked,

> What is needed is . . . a repudiation of all arbitrary distinctions among 'pure form', 'moral content', and the rhetorical means of realizing for the reader the union of form and matter. When human actions are formed to make an art work, the form that is made can never be divorced from the human meanings, including the moral judgements, that are implicit whenever human beings act.[5]

Galdós and Modernist Criticism

The issues I have been summarising in the foregoing paragraphs have been raised with particular urgency by one of the most important recent contributions to Galdós scholarship, Diane Urey's *Galdós and the Irony of Language* (Cambridge University Press, 1982). The value of Dr Urey's study is two-fold. In the first place, she has carried to a new peak of thoroughness and precision the analysis of the various ways in which Galdós exploits his linguistic resources to achieve different kinds of ironic effect. Secondly, and more significantly, she has paid more attention than any previous critic to the way in which Galdós not only subverts, by means of irony, the conventional assumptions of the society portrayed in his novels, but extends this process of subversion to the reader's own accepted frames of reference:

> Galdós's novels reveal the subjectivity of both the individual and collective social opinion. Even the most generally accepted, so-called objective, and moral opinion is shown to be as relative as the most blind, insane, or selfish individual prejudice. While the reader may condemn the illusions of Isidora and Rosalía or the materialism of Torquemada, the narrative shows that they are only single instances of delusions at work in the novelistic society as a whole. This society is often associated very closely with the reader's own. We come to see the deceptions . . . perpetrated by [the characters] . . . we may also suddenly become aware of our own faulty interpretations. Like those characters, we may be misreaders of our own capacities for insight (125).

As will be seen from the following chapters of my own study, my views overlap to a considerable extent with those of Dr Urey. One of the main contentions of the present book is that Galdós develops in a very radical and original way the classic realist contrast between illusion and reality. Instead of confining his exploration of this contrast to the study of the behaviour of the seeming-virtuous or those who live beyond their means, Galdós calls in question the whole institutional fabric of Spanish society by presenting politics, law, morality, religion and even love (in the sense in which these concepts are conventionally understood by the mass of humanity) as, in a certain sense, 'fictions', things made, products of a human mind prone to error. Hence his constant critique of clichéd ways of thinking, whether these arise from the debased romanticism of the popular novel, conventional piety or political rhetoric. If, however, the critique of clichéd thinking is to be effective, the reader has to be prevented from making the same errors as the deluded characters whom Galdós depicts, and it is therefore essential to Galdós's purpose that the reader should, as Dr Urey rightly implies, be made to observe and criticise his own reading, and be kept aware of the problematical nature of fictional narrative. This is why, as I hope to show, Galdós devotes so much attention to such things as Anselmo's role as narrator in *La sombra* and to the influence of popular fiction in *La desheredada* and *Tormento*.

Where I part company with Dr Urey is in seeing Galdós's ironic presentation of fiction-making as a means to an end, rather than an end in itself. For Dr Urey, irony is much more than saying the opposite of what is meant, or juxtaposing two contrasting statements or patterns in order that the juxtaposition will cause one of them to be called in question. At the very outset, she defines an ironical situation as 'that which exists between an observer and an observed who is not aware of being observed. The narrative situation of the reader and that which he reads, for example, can therefore be seen as *intrinsically* ironic' (p. 1, my italics). Dr Urey, in short, defines irony in such a broad way that she is able to present it as something so pervasive and corrosive in Galdós's work that it dissolves the possibility of his making any meaningful statement about the world: 'Words', she declares, 'create reality, or rather they supplant it by their superimposition upon a reality which can never be known, if it exists at all' (85); *Torquemada en la hoguera* 'is a text which demands constant re-interpretation because it ironizes all attempts at interpretation' (121); 'Galdós' novels . . . contrive to make of language a signifying process incapable of absolutely capturing any object but itself' (123).

In order to substantiate this claim, however, it would be necessary to demonstrate that Galdós is equally ironic about everything, and, as I hope to show in the body of this study, the evidence does not support any such contention. Far from indicating a disbelief in any reality except perception and literary process, Galdós's irony arises from what Leopoldo Alas aptly called 'the clarity, frankness and practical sense . . . revealed in his works'.[6] As we shall see, Galdós's approach to novel-writing was shaped initially by the notion, derived ultimately from the Enlightenment, of progress through the breaking-down of prejudice and the spread of understanding. This idea, current to a limited extent in eighteenth-century Spain, was revitalised in the mid-nineteenth through the influence of an eclectic variety of post-Kantian idealism associated with the minor philosopher Krause. Through being exposed to the influence of what came to be known as *Krausismo* Galdós came to believe that serious literature had a central role to play in educating the reading public and thereby raising the moral and intellectual tone of society. His early output therefore consists principally of historical novels, in which he strives to give his contemporaries a true understanding of their recent history, or novels in which current issues like religious and political intolerance are explored. In the 1880s, Galdós's interests develop in the direction of a denser and subtler presentation of economic and social realities, but his overriding aim remains that of moral scrutiny and judgement. Realism, for Galdós, is as much an ethical as a literary matter, and he therefore deliberately chooses irony, not to undermine the possibility of meaning, but to suggest to a society pervaded by flawed vision and the worship of false gods alternative and more cogent 'meanings' (i.e., values, standards, insights) which that society needs to acknowledge in the interests of its own well-being.[7] In other words, Galdós's irony is not infinitely and destructively self-reflexive, as Dr Urey and other modern critics often suggest, but points away from itself, and, indeed, in a sense, away from the text, towards the folly and triviality of Spanish society and of human behaviour in general, and, beyond these, to the standards of which such behaviour falls short.

A Historical Approach

It is for this reason that I have chosen to place the discussion of individual Galdós novels within a historical framework. Even to a non-Marxist, the Marxist emphasis on social and historical context can illuminate the study of realist fiction in a very helpful way. The Enlightenment–Realism polarity of my title has, indeed, been suggested by the chapter on Balzac and Stendhal in one of the classics of Marxist literary criticism, Georg Lukács's *Studies in European Realism*.[8] Lukács argues that although the two writers are apparently similar in the authenticity with which they mirror society, their perspectives are fundamentally different. Stendhal reveals himself as a disciple of the Enlightenment in his tendency to rely on the personal biographies of characters to sum up the atmosphere of an epoch, particularly through the confrontation between individual ideals and the corruption of the society which emerged from the Napoleonic Wars. Though he represents the defects of this society with an accurate and unromantic eye, he retains sufficient belief in progress to hope that in about fifty years (i.e., by 1880), society will have been changed by the spread of enlightenment. Furthermore, though his protagonists are defeated by the prevailing climate of mediocrity, they retain a certain integrity by their refusal to compromise and by their final withdrawal from life: the execution of Julien Sorel in *Le Rouge et le noir* can be seen as a kind of suicide, and Fabrice in *La Chartreuse de Parme* retires to a monastery. For Lukács, Balzac, on the other hand, mirrors his epoch more accurately than Stendhal, because he is less concerned with individual lives than with the way in which the character of the age is being shaped by social forces, especially the growth of capitalism. Though these social forces are not blind and impersonal but are embodied in the lives of individuals, Balzac nevertheless emphasises not the unique qualities of his characters but what Lukács calls their social 'typicality'. By this he means that there is an organic connection between the life of the individual and the life of society: though Balzac presents vivid and memorable characters rather than 'a lifeless average' (p. 6) they are always seen in their social roles, and as part of a network of relationships and interests.

Lukács's distinction between the Enlightenment approach to fiction-writing represented by Stendhal and the Realist one associated with Balzac provides a convenient frame of reference for our discussion of Galdós, though, as we shall see, it does not enable us to account for all the characteristics of Galdós's literary practice. We shall find, in the first place, that the concept of 'Enlightenment' needs to be redefined to take account of the impact made by Krausism in the specific circumstances of Spain in the 1860s and 1870s. Secondly, we shall not be able to trace a steady progression in Galdós's novels away from a Stendhalian perspective to a Balzacian one, for both the Enlightenment commitment to progress and the Realist awareness of the complexity of social forces may be found in his work from the outset. It is more a matter of these elements being combined in different proportions at different periods: when most acutely aware of the need for reform (e.g., in the 1870s), Galdós wrote with a more explicit sense of educational purpose, but in the calmer climate of the 1880s, he was prepared to examine issues from a larger number of angles. Thirdly, Galdós's sense of reforming social mission sprang from a certain practical patriotism which made him somewhat resistant to following slavishly European fashions in the novel. We shall therefore have to take account of the ways in which his understanding of his literary vocation was influenced by his awareness of native Spanish literary tradition.

My approach is therefore somewhat different from that adopted in two recent books on Galdós which cover much the same ground as my own study. Jacques Beyrie's three-volume *Galdós et son Mythe* (Paris and Lille, 1980) is a mine of information on the novelist's early years, especially on the influences which moulded his liberal consciousness. Insofar as he discusses the novels in relation to their historical context, however, he sees them as reflecting, at specific moments, Galdós's political opinions, and the impact of contemporary events. Galdós's understanding of the relation of literature to the contemporary context, however, was deeper and more organic than Beyrie appears to suppose, for his works derive their entire *raison d'être* from the urge to make literature an instrument of moral and political regeneration. This 're-generationist' perspective is emphasised in Stephen Gilman's *Galdós and the Art of the European Novel: 1867–1887* (Princeton University Press, 1981): Galdós's purpose is 'nothing less than the redemption of his readers' (p. 110), and his works constitute a kind of 'national psychotherapy' (p. 52). Gilman correctly identifies Krausism as the source for the notion that literature can be a means of education and reform, but he does not document exhaustively the connections between Galdós's literary theory and that of the Krausists. He does not, for example, provide a sustained analysis of Galdós's key essay 'Observaciones sobre la novela contemporánea en España' (1870). Furthermore, though he is clearly right in general terms to see the notion of regeneration as closely connected with historical flux, he exaggerates, in my view, the representativeness of some of the characters and situations which Galdós portrays. The protagonist of *La desheredada*, for example, is described in quasi-allegorical language as 'a representation of the Spain of her time', undergoing a 'civic identity crisis' in which the original nineteenth-century reader, deceived as he is by the political oratory of the Restoration, is involved (p. 113). As we shall see, however, Galdós, at this period, was interested above all in individual moral reform: collective enlightenment would, he believed, follow as a consequence of this.

A more serious shortcoming of Gilman's study, however, is his tendency to undervalue much of Galdós's early work because he does not judge it on its own merits, but sees it primarily as a preparation for the great masterpiece of 1886–7, *Fortunata y Jacinta*. Indeed, two-thirds of his book is taken up with discussion either of that novel or of the anticipations of it which Gilman professes to see in certain works of the early 1880s. Though considerable attention is given to *La Fontana de Oro* (1871), *Doña Perfecta* (1876) and *La desheredada* (1881), the five novels between *La desheredada* and *Fortunata y Jacinta* are dealt with in little more than a dozen pages. This is unfairly dismissive, for as I hope to show, some of these novels, especially *El amigo Manso* and *Tormento*, are among the most sophisticated and interesting that Galdós ever wrote. Moreover, even the novels of the 1870s, flawed as they often are by sentimentality, vehemence and melodrama, sometimes reveal unexpected strengths, if they are approached with an open and sympathetic mind. In any case, the reasons for their shortcomings are themselves complex and interesting, because they reflect the conflicting pressures to which Galdós was exposed at that stage of his literary career.

The chronological balance of my own study is therefore very different from Gilman's. Though for reasons of space it has not been possible to discuss all Galdós's writings in the same detail, I have attempted to give a reasonably comprehensive account of the development of his literary career from its inception around 1870 to the publication of *Fortunata y Jacinta* in 1887. Clearly, Galdós continued to produce important masterpieces after that date, but concentration on his formative period and the early part of his mature career enables one to appreciate the connections between his search for an authentic literary voice and his evolving conception of his responsibility as a writer to the world around him. Moreover, by placing the discussion of *La desheredada* at roughly the mid-point in my study, I have tried to bring out the significance of the shift in Galdós's style and interests which takes place around 1880. My critical strategy will be determined in the first place by the nature of the questions raised by the texts themselves. Each of the novels I have chosen for detailed examination is, in one way or another, a fictional experiment which marks a stage in the development of Galdós's understanding of the novelist's craft. At the same time, however, I have attempted to relate Galdós's literary activity both to his sense of reforming mission and to the various traditions of literary theory on which he was able to draw.

Notes to Introduction

1. Distinguished recent examples of work in the Casalduero tradition include José F. Montesinos, *Galdós*, 3 vols. (Madrid, Castalia, 1968–73), and Stephen Miller, *El mundo de Galdós* (Santander, Sociedad Menéndez Pelayo, 1983).
2. Intro. to her translation of Dante's *Purgatorio* (Harmondsworth, Penguin Books, 1955 and subsequent reprints), p. 45.
3. *Mimesis*, tr. Willard Trask (Garden City, New York, 1957), p. 487. First English ed., Princeton University Press, 1953. First German ed., Berne, 1946.
4. *On Realism* (London, 1973), p. 39.
5. *The Rhetoric of Fiction* (Chicago University Press, 1961), p. 397.
6. *Galdós* (Madrid, 1912), p. 26.
7. As has been well said, Galdós's 'strategies in point of view . . . not only depict meaning but qualify that meaning primarily in moral terms' (See Harriet S. Turner, 'Strategies in narrative point of view: On meaning and morality in the Galdós novel', in B. Brancaforte, E. R. Mulvihill and R. G. Sánchez, eds., *Homenaje a Antonio Sánchez-Barbudo* [Madison, University of Wisconsin, 1981], p. 62).
8. London, 1950.

Galdós and the Krausist Enlightenment

Krausism and Spain

The Peace of the Pyrenees in 1659 marks a decisive stage in Spain's decline from the position of dominance in European and world affairs which she had occupied in the reign of Philip II. For the remainder of the seventeenth century, cultural and political hegemony in Europe was to belong to the France of Louis XIV. In 1713 Philip of Anjou, Louis's grandson, succeeded to the throne of Spain, ushering in a century in which the influence of things French on the cultural and intellectual life of Spain was more profound than at any other period of Spanish history. French administrative practices were adopted in central government affairs, and French standards of taste left a marked imprint on the whole way of life of the ruling class, influencing styles of dress, architecture and literary convention, even to the extent of bringing about, in 1765, the prohibition of the traditional allegorical religious drama, the *auto sacramental*.

This adoption of external trappings made members of the educated classes even more acutely aware of the cultural and economic backwardness of the country, and in the second half of the century, especially during the reign of Charles III (1759–1788), attempts were made to modernise political institutions and to tackle the problem of rural poverty. At its deepest level, however, Spanish intellectual and political life was affected only to a limited extent by developments in France. The notion of progress in France was associated primarily with the desire to free human reason from the tyranny of religious superstition and monarchical absolutism, and this gave the French Enlightenment a critical, sceptical and iconoclastic character which was ultimately inimical to traditional religious belief. In Spain, by contrast, Catholic orthodoxy was very deep-rooted even among the educated classes, and was vigorously defended by a still-active Inquisition. Besides, the Crown was not an obstacle to reform and modernisation but, most notably during the reign of Charles III, the principal instigator of change. Both these factors, the character of the monarchy and the general resistance to atheistic and materialistic philosophies, caused eighteenth-century Spanish intellectuals to set limits to their exploratory and investigative activities. Episodes such as the prosecution by the Inquisition of the Marqués de Narros for defending the views of d'Holbach, Voltaire and Rousseau[1] intensified what was already a strongly rooted tendency towards self-censorship. Thus, for example, the Duque de Villahermosa mentions in a letter to Bernardo de Iriarte (20 February 1771) that he knows that the Duque de Medina Sidonia has a copy of d'Holbach's *Système de la nature*, but that he cannot persuade him to admit that he possesses it.[2] To such circumspect readers, the cataclysmic upheaval of the French Revolution seemed the realisation of their worst fears, and even leading reformers like Jovellanos were driven into more conservative positions. When, for example, Jovellanos drew up, in 1790, a new syllabus for the Colegio Imperial de Calatrava, he urged that the pupils be taught to refute the errors of 'impious' people such as deists and materialists.[3]

This suspicion of French rationalism on the part of the governing elite was compounded by the upsurge of popular and conservative nationalism which accompanied the Napoleonic invasion and the War of Independence. Henceforth, even those members of the educated classes who took an informed interest in French culture and literature regarded the country with a mixture of fascination and resentment, and the pejorative word *afrancesamiento* ('Frenchification') was frequently used in the nineteenth century to deplore what was perceived as the continuing cultural dominance of the neighbouring country. *Afrancesamiento* was a favourite target of *costumbrista* writers such as Mesonero Romanos, and also of literary critics and literary historians. For example, José Joaquín de Mora, in his preface to Alberto Lista's *Ensayos literarios y críticos* (1844), complained bitterly of the 'humiliating servility' which characterised Spanish letters.[4] For Cándido Nocedal, speaking in 1860, the Royal Spanish Academy's defence of the Spanish language against the inroads of French influence was an attempt to hold 'the last bulwark of Spain's independence'.[5] José Amador de los Ríos, in the first volume of his *Historia crítica de la literatura española* (1861–5), lamented the pervasiveness of 'Gallo-classical influence'.[6] Even in 1879, an anonymous contributor to the *Revista Contemporánea* could still declare that Spaniards had been turned into a 'nation of copyists and imitators'.[7] As late as 1891, Fr. Blanco García could still express his Francophobia in immoderate language:

> Los vientos de la literatura transpirenaica nos trajeron copiosos gérmenes de destrucción, esterilizaron las aptitudes de más de un ingenio, corrompieron la vida moral e intelectual del pueblo español, que nada apenas le debió de sólido y fecundo en compensación de tan graves daños.[8]

> *(The literary winds from across the Pyrenees brought us innumerable seeds of destruction, sterilized the abilities of more than one person of talent, corrupted the moral and intellectual life of the Spanish people, and gave us nothing solid or fruitful to compensate us for such grievous injuries.)*

It would, however, be a mistake to suppose that all Spaniards were afflicted with systematic xenophobia. For most educated Spaniards, the desire to preserve what was traditional and authentic in Spanish culture was not incompatible with openness to influences from abroad, though these influences were more likely to be welcomed if they came from countries other than France. It was Germany which, throughout the nineteenth century, was to play a key role in the gradual opening of Spain to European intellectual currents. Through his translation of *Don Quixote*, Ludwig Tieck had brought Spanish literature to the attention of A. W. Schlegel, and as early as 1803, Schlegel had begun to translate Calderón's plays. From 1814 on, when Juan Nicolás Böhl de Faber translated Schlegel's essay on Calderón, Spanish men of letters became increasingly aware of the growing interest in Spanish literature among German scholars. The first history of Spanish literature ever published was written by a German, Friedrich Bouterwek.[9] C. A. Dohrn's four-volume collection *Spanischen Dramen* appeared in Berlin between 1841 and 1844, Emanuel Geibel's translations of Spanish ballads in 1843, and the first volume of Schack's history of the Spanish theatre in 1845.[10]

The fact that German men of letters were, like the Spaniards, striving to resist the pervasive influence of French classicism, and turning to Spanish and other literatures in search of models reinforced the sympathetic openness towards things German which was to be characteristic of liberal intellectuals in Spain throughout the nineteenth century. It is against this background that we must understand the curious cultural phenomenon which came to be known as *Krausismo*. Karl Christian Friedrich Krause (1781–1832) was a pupil of both Fichte and Schelling, though he distanced himself from his teachers, preferring to combine certain elements of post-Kantian idealism with an older, mainly Protestant-Pietist tradition represented by Leibniz and Wolff. The aspects of Krause's thought which were later to be most influential in Spain were: faith in the underlying harmony of the universe, the belief in a metaphysical and religious dimension to reality, the notion of progress as moral perfectibility, and the consequent interest in education. For Krause, a person did not discover truth either by looking into his own heart or by purely empirical analysis, but by applying his intellect to experience in accordance with universally valid laws. Krause rejected what he regarded as Schelling's pantheism, preferring something to which he gave the name 'panentheism', or 'all things in God'. By this Krause meant that all the fragmented aspects of human experience and human thought form part of a divinely pre-ordained harmony. This harmony is temporarily eclipsed because man erroneously pursues partial and illusory views of reality. Harmony can, however, be re-established if man follows the rule of reason, and devotes his life, first to his own moral improvement, and then to the betterment of his fellow-men.

Krause's 'harmonic rationalism', as it came to be called, has, therefore, despite its often abstruse metaphysics, an active, reformist character, and it was precisely its practical implications for various areas of personal and social life that attracted the interest of most of Krause's pupils and followers. Heinrich Ahrens and Carl Röder were mainly interested in Krause's philosophy of law, Hermann von Leonhardi, his son-in-law and editor, in his philosophy of history, Tiberghien in his philosophy of religion, and Hohlfeld in his ethics. Among those who adopted Krause's system because of its educational and reformist potential was a young Spaniard, Julián Sanz del Río. In 1843, when a Progressive government was urgently seeking to reform Spanish higher education, Sanz del Río was appointed acting professor of philosophy in Madrid University, on condition that he spent two years in Germany bringing his philosophical knowledge up to date. On his way to Germany in 1843, Sanz del Río visited Heinrich Ahrens in Brussels. Ahrens had studied under Krause in Göttingen in 1831, and he advised Sanz del Río to take up residence in Heidelberg, where Leonhardi and Röder, also former pupils of Krause, were teaching. Sanz del Río remained in Heidelberg from the autumn of 1843 until the end of 1844, during which time his interest in the philosophy of Krause crystallised in the conviction that of all existing philosophical systems, Krausism was the one most likely to facilitate the cultural and intellectual development of contemporary Spain. As he wrote to José de la Revilla in 1844,

> Escogí aquel [sistema] que . . . encontraba más consecuente, más completo, más conforme a lo que nos dicta el sano juicio en los puntos en que éste puede juzgar, y, sobre todo, más susceptible de una aplicación práctica.[11]

> (I chose the system which I found most consistent, most complete, most in accord with the dictates of sound judgement, so far as that extends, and, above all, most capable of practical application.)

This concern for practical relevance is the keynote of the future development of Krausism in Spain. Though Sanz del Río retained until the end of his life the ambition to form a select group of pupils who would dedicate themselves to the arduous task of studying Krause's difficult metaphysical writings, his immediate concern on his return to Spain in 1844 was with Krause's ethics, and with their potential for the moral and intellectual regeneration of the country. Consequently, when in 1860 Sanz published his translation and commentary on Krause's *Urbild der Menschheit* (Dresden, 1811), he took the liberty of adapting Krause's views to make them more applicable to contemporary Spain. Furthermore, Sanz del Río's own pupils and followers, somewhat to his displeasure, soon turned away from metaphysical concerns in favour of the practical implications of Krausism. As a result, what became known as *Krausismo* ultimately stood at several removes from Krause's philosophy. In its early stages, it was essentially Sanz del Río's interpretation of Krause's thought, but before long it had detached itself even from the person and teaching of Sanz del Río, becoming what Juan López-Morillas has aptly called 'a means of stirring up people's minds rather than a system of thought'.[12] The word *Krausista* was not generally used in nineteenth-century Spain by the followers of Krause themselves, but by those outside the movement, and it denoted, not merely philosophers engaged in reformulating and elaborating Krause's system (though in the case of professional academic philosophers like Sanz del Río it could mean that), but, more commonly, someone whose conduct of his private and public life was influenced by the generalised belief in human perfectibility and the consequent aspiration for reform which those philosophers had transmitted in their teaching. It is in this latter and wider sense that I shall use the terms 'Krausist' and 'Krausism' in this study.

The Krausist Opposition

Given the conditions of political life in Spain in the 1860s, it is hardly surprising that this diversification of Krausism took on political overtones. Though Isabella II functioned, at least in legal principle, as a constitutional monarch, effective political power was restricted to an oligarchy drawn from the aristocracy and the *haute bourgeoisie*, consisting of an 'amalgam of speculators, industrialists, landowners, together with the prosperous lawyers and ennobled generals who were its political voice'.[13] Below this oligarchy stretched the larger middle class, consisting of the medium and lower reaches of the bourgeoisie (government officials, small traders, teachers, journalists and the like). Unlike the working class, which as yet lacked both organisation and a political programme, the petty bourgeoisie was politically self-conscious enough to resent its exclusion from power, and articulate enough to express its views. The Progressive liberals appeared to offer some hope of fulfilment of lower-middle-class aspirations, but Isabella persistently refused to give the Progressives a share in political power. In protest, the Progressives, from 1863 on, boycotted political life, and this *retraimiento*, as Carr has shown, was probably the most important single factor which would, in 1868, push the Progressives towards revolution.[14]

The task of articulating liberal opposition to the Isabelline regime fell largely to Krausist intellectuals. In the same year in which Sanz del Río published his version of Krause's *Urbild der Menschheit*, under the title of *Ideal de la humanidad para la vida* (1860), one of his pupils, Francisco de Paula Canalejas, wrote an article in which he spelt out some of the political implications of Sanz's ideas on the reforming mission of education, which then became the subject of lively debate in the Madrid intellectual and literary club, the *Ateneo*. Though in some respects Canalejas's views coincide with the political programme of the Progressives, and even with that of their more radical allies, the Democrats (for example, in respect of freedom of expression and education), the main thrust of Canalejas's argument is that society can only be transformed gradually by the spread of enlightenment, tolerance and intellectual and religious freedom.[15]

If Krausism had political implications, then, it was not because the movement advocated a specific programme for changing the distribution of power, but because in the conditions of intellectual life in nineteenth-century Spain, the issue of freedom of conscience was highly contentious, and this was why the Krausists' mild and gradualist reformism aroused such virulent hostility. Although the neo-Catholic party which came to prominence after 1856, as a result of the revival of popular piety, was regarded as an extremist minority by the reigning Moderates, the neo-Catholics' assumptions about the traditional religious unity of the nation and about the proper relationship between Church and State exercised considerable influence on political life, and, more particularly, on the personal opinions of the Queen, whose confessor, Father Claret, had been prominent in fostering the popular religious revival of the 1840s. In this situation, Krausism was bound to be regarded as subversive because it advocated an inward and personal spirituality and, above all, because it questioned the right of the Church to exercise control over all areas of life.

For both Krausists and neo-Catholics, the most important sphere of influence was education, which was, both before and after the Revolution of 1868, one of the principal battle-grounds on which conservative and liberal forces confronted each other. Krausism would probably not have been perceived as such a threat to traditional assumptions had it not gained a solid foothold in the educational system, particularly after 1854, when Sanz del Río was appointed to a chair in the Central University in Madrid. It was through lecturing and writing that Krausism was disseminated among students, many of whom were in turn to become teachers, or leaders of political and intellectual life. Sanz himself was well aware of the potential of the university for exerting a reforming influence in society as a whole: when he was called upon to give the discourse for the official opening of the 1857–8 session, he chose as his subject the role of higher education in the intellectual and moral regeneration of the young. It was precisely because of its power of attraction for young minds that Krausism became the object of a vituperative campaign which began in 1865 in the neo-Catholic journal *El Pensamiento Español*. In the course of this campaign, the Bishop of Tarazona wrote an open letter to the Queen, in which he warned of the 'impious' and 'pestilent' teaching being received by university students, and demanded that textbooks be submitted to the bishops for examination. He further urged that those professors who 'deny everything spiritual, revealed and divine, destroy Catholicism and pervert youth' should be dismissed.[16] This kind of pressure eventually led, in 1867, to several Krausist professors being expelled from their chairs and others resigning in solidarity. Further resignations were provoked in 1875 by a similar demand that course content conform to orthodox Catholic teaching.

Insofar as traditionalists foresaw some of the social and political consequences of Krausism, their anxieties were perhaps understandable, but they were wide of the mark in equating the dissenting views of the Krausists with hostility to religious belief as such. Though Krause's thought is rationalist in respect of its dialectical method, the goal towards which this method tends is not the elaboration of a mechanistic view of the universe but the attainment of rational knowledge of God. Christianity, to be sure, is seen as a stage on the way to fully rational knowledge, to be superseded in due course, but the transcendental idealism which characterises Krause's system encouraged Spanish Krausists to believe that his philosophy, at least as they understood it, was fully compatible, if not with traditional orthodoxy in the full sense, with what they called rational Catholicism. By this they meant a Catholicism shorn of dogmatism, mystery or belief in miracles, but retaining the essentials of Christian ethics, and a vaguely religious understanding of the universe. Consequently, as José Luis Abellán has pointed out, many Krausists saw themselves as attempting to liberalise and reform Catholicism from within. Francisco Giner de los Ríos, one of Sanz del Río's most distinguished pupils, and the acknowledged leader of the second generation of Krausist intellectuals, appears to have remained a regular churchgoer until the mid-1860s. However, the promulgation of Pius IX's *Syllabus of Errors*, and the encyclical *Quanta Cura* (1864), which condemned the separation of Church and State, and anathematised all those who held that the Church should reconcile itself to 'progress, liberalism and modern civilisation', put a severe strain on the loyalty of men like Giner to the religion into which they had been born. The decree of the First Vatican Council defining the doctrine of Papal Infallibility (1870) finally convinced many liberal Catholics that membership of the official Church was incompatible with their personal convictions.[17] This is well illustrated by the career of another of Sanz del Río's followers, Fernando de Castro, a former Franciscan friar who transferred to the secular clergy, becoming a court preacher and eventually Royal Chaplain. Though in his posthumous *Memoria testamentaria*, published shortly after his death in 1874, he described official Catholicism as 'a force for misgovernment and perversion', he had continued to exercise his priestly ministry in public until 1870, and wore clerical garb until the end of his life. Though he condemned official Catholicism in the *Memoria*, he did so 'with a sense of regret that the kind of Christianity practised in my country has not purified itself from the Romanist leaven by which it is corrupted'.[18]

Galdós and the Ideology of Krausism

The precise means whereby Galdós became acquainted with Krausism remains to some extent obscure. We do not know, for example, whether he actually attended Sanz del Río's lectures. What is certain is that he retained throughout his life a special regard for Castro, who taught him history during his years at the Central University, which he entered in 1862 to study Law. In 1868, Galdós paid affectionate tribute to Castro in terms which leave little doubt of Galdós's personal commitment (at least at that date) to the ideals by which Castro lived:

> No basta estudiar y orar, perfeccionarse intelectual y espiritualmente: es preciso mirar un poco hacia el pobre prójimo que vegeta a un lado ignorante y pecador: es preciso practicar la más noble misión del apóstol y

del sabio; es preciso descender del razonamiento y de la contemplación
para ocuparse en la enseñanza; y ninguno practica con más entusiasmo y
fervor este caritativo sacerdocio.[19]

*(Study and prayer, intellectual and moral perfection are not enough. We
must have some regard for our poor neighbour who vegetates in ignorance
and sinfulness at our side. We must practise the noblest mission of the apostle
and the thinker, and come down from the realm of rational speculation and
contemplation to take part in education. No-one practises this charitable
priesthood more fervently or devotedly [than Fernando de Castro]).*

The most likely channel of Krausist influence on Galdós, however, was the
Ateneo, which he joined in 1865, precisely at the time when Canalejas's mildly
politicised variety of Krausism was being hotly debated, and when Francisco
Navarro Villoslada's campaign against the Krausists in *El Pensamiento Español*
was gathering momentum. It can scarcely be a coincidence that in the same
year, Galdós began a series of articles in the Progressive liberal newspaper *La
Nación*, in which he displayed passionate commitment to the politicallly
reformist ideas of Canalejas. To a large extent, then, Galdós, in his journalistic
activity in the 1860s, became the spokesman of those who hoped for the
overthrow of the Isabelline monarchy, at least insofar as the strict censorship
laws would allow him to be (*La Nación* was actually suppressed for eighteen
months, from June 1866 to January 1868). Galdós, indeed, was involved in the
political turmoil of those years not only as a journalist, but also as a private
citizen. As a student, he took part in a demonstration on St. Daniel's Eve, 10
April 1865, in protest against the sacking of a Madrid University professor who
had published an article attacking the Queen Mother over a financial scandal.
The police charged the demonstration with drawn sabres, several people were
killed, and about a hundred injured (OC 6, 1655).[20] In June 1866, Galdós
witnessed a bloody pitched battle around the San Gil artillery barracks, when a
group of sergeants mutinied and shot their officers. The rising was swiftly
suppressed, and on the following day Galdós watched 66 non-commissioned
officers and privates being taken away to execution (OC 6, 1655–6).

In keeping with his Krausist-derived ideology, Galdós does not offer a
concrete political programme in his *La Nación* articles, but concentrates
instead on the need to get rid of a corrupt and archaic regime, to establish
intellectual freedom, and to stamp out moral corruption. The articles often
make lively reading, because of the trenchancy with which Galdós expresses his
impatience with the immobility of the Isabelline regime, a tone reminiscent, in
some respects, of eighteenth-century political satire. The members of the ruling
oligarchy are

Graves como todo lo impotente, revestidos de esa cómica seriedad que
caracteriza a los anticuarios, parecen cadáveres embalsamados, que en
virtud de una influencia galvánica se agitan y procuran mover la petrificada

lengua para hablar de los días en que vivieron; son recuerdos que viven de la tradición; razones trasnochadas que apelan al incontestable criterio de lo histórico (OC 6, 1541).

(Grave with the gravity which only ineffectualness can confer, invested with that comic solemnity characteristic of antiquarians, they seem like mummified corpses which only an electric shock can galvanise into movement. They try to use their petrified tongues to speak of the time when they were alive. They are throwbacks, living on tradition, stale minds which can only appeal to the unanswerable criterion of antiquity.)

Given Galdós's commitment to intellectual and religious freedom, it is scarcely surprising that his most mordant invective was reserved for the neo-Catholics, the hated *neos*: they are 'la plaga nea que hoy invade, corroe, apolilla, destruye, pudre, descompone las sociedades donde inocula, como la culebra, su mortífero veneno' (OC 6, 1535) (the *neo* plague which now invades, corrodes, eats away, destroys, rots and decomposes societies which, like the serpent, it injects with its mortal poison). Nevertheless, like Castro and other Krausist intellectuals, he opposed the neo-Catholics primarily because of their political pretensions and the hypocritical ostentation of their religious practice. Genuine Christian commitment based on inner spiritual strength he admired and respected, as may be seen from the warm tribute which he paid, in this same series of articles, to the courage and dedication of those priests who ministered to the victims of the cholera epidemic of October 1865 (OC 6, 1536). Though Galdós was later to declare in a letter to the neo-Catholic novelist José María de Pereda that he was totally lacking in religious faith, and although he acquired a well-merited reputation as an opponent of clerical interference in political and social life, he not only retained a belief in spiritual values but frequently expressed that belief in traditional Christian language. When, for example, the eponymous Catholic heroine of *Gloria* (1877) is hounded to death by religious bigots, and her Jewish lover Daniel later dies insane, still searching vainly for the ideal unifying religion of the future, Galdós writes that Daniel will surely find what he is seeking 'in that place where someone waited for him, finding perhaps little joy in Paradise until he came' (OC 4, 682).

In addition to their frequent attacks on the *neos*, Galdós's *La Nación* articles reveal a deep concern with moral corruption in society. Indeed, precisely because the Krausists lacked any clear political programme, other than the generalised aspiration for greater freedom (especially intellectual freedom), they saw the regeneration of society almost exclusively in terms of the moral regeneration of the individual. Already, in his 1857 *Discurso*, Sanz del Río had spoken of the moral consequences of materialism as a disease spreading through the whole social organism,[21] and Galdós's journalistic writings of the 1860s reflect the same concern. His constant attention to the theme of financial speculation, for example, arises from the fact that he sees this area of activity as giving rise to acute ethical problems. As Carr has shown,[22] the underlying basis of the Spanish economy in the nineteenth century was fragile. Although fabulous fortunes could be made, almost overnight, by speculation in railway concessions or government contracts, such large-scale operations usually had to be financed by expensive credit, and often ended in notorious disasters. Though Galdós had little specialist knowledge of the workings of the economy, he regarded the 'improvisadas fortunas' of certain individuals as unsound and morally dubious. Furthermore, the contrast between the outward appearance of wealth and the fragile foundation on which certain fortunes rested often prompted him to reflect on the falsity of the values of Isabelline society. For example, in an article on the Carnival season of 1865, Galdós remarks that there is another Carnival, lasting 362 days, which begins where the official one leaves off. In this year-round Carnival, nearly everyone wears some sort of moral mask:

> Aquí la vanidad se disfraza de modestia; la desvergüenza, de desenfado; el robo, de agiotaje; el pedantismo, de filosofía; la fanfarronería, de valor; el egoísmo, de desinterés; lo grosero, de ideal; la materia, de espíritu. Hay un prurito de evocar todas las formas de la virtud pasada para cubrir el vicio presente de usar las palabras amor, honradez, abnegación, para expresar ideas de lascivia, de engaño y de odio (OC 6, 1505).

> ([In this other Carnival,] vanity passes for modesty, impudence for casualness, robbery for speculation, pedantry for wisdom, boastfulness for courage, selfishness for disinterestedness, what is vulgar for what is ideal, matter for spirit. There is an urge to evoke every kind of past virtue to cover up the present-day vice of using the words love, honesty, and self-sacrifice to express the ideas of lust, deceit and hatred.)[23]

Galdós's concern with the general wellbeing of society then, is essentially an extension of his preoccupation with individual morality. Although in common with most Krausist-influenced intellectuals Galdós looked forward with keen anticipation to the revolution, he did so in the hope that the disappearance of the old regime would remove those obstacles which had hitherto inhibited the development of individual human potential, the most important of which was the absence of freedom of conscience. It is the evolutionary and individualist basis of Galdós's political thinking which enables us to account for the fact that his reformist optimism survived the failure of the 1868 Revolution, albeit in a more sober and realistic form.

In order to set this in context, it would be useful to give a brief account of the course and outcome of the Revolution. As Carr has pointed out, the Revolution of 1868 was largely the work of Progressive and Liberal Union generals, whose intention from the beginning had been to confine the revolution within moderate bounds, and replace the quasi-absolutist regime of Isabella II with an English-style constitutional monarchy. Their aim was essentially that of widening the political nation to include the middle and lower-middle classes, but emphatically not to create a democracy in the full modern sense. It is true that the provisions of the Constitution of 1869 included universal (male) suffrage, but this was simply an index of the degree to which the revolutionary coalition, in order to ensure success, had had to make concessions to the demands of the Democrats, a loose grouping of radicals and crypto-republicans who, despite the vagueness of their political programme, were the only party to enjoy a substantial working-class following. Once in power, the Progressives had to confront the hostility of former supporters who felt that the revolution had been betrayed, and there were outbreaks of rioting in provincial towns in the summer and autumn of 1869. In December 1870, General Prim, the architect of the Revolution, was assassinated. This event was the final blow to the already tottering revolutionary coalition, and it doomed Prim's experiment in constitutional monarchy to failure before it had got properly under way. The Carlists (the absolutist faction who supported the Pretender Don Carlos, Isabella's cousin) seized the opportunity created by the prevailing uncertainty, and a civil war, which was to last four years, broke out in 1872. Internal feuding among the various political parties created a climate of instability which made orderly government impossible, and which eventually provoked the abdication of the new constitutional King, Amadeo, in 1873. A Republic was established, but it lasted less than a year. Indiscipline in the army rendered the new government powerless either to prosecute the war against the Carlists, or to contain extreme federal republicans who were striving to fragment Spain into a confederation of small cantons. Eventually, the leftward drift of the Republic was countered by a military coup in January 1874, and a year later the Bourbon monarchy was restored in the person of Isabella's son, Alfonso XII.

Not surprisingly, these events, together with the revolutionary upheaval of the Paris Commune in 1871, drove Galdós and most of his liberal contemporaries into increasingly conservative positions.[24] Yet this response was entirely consistent with his Krausist-derived ideology, with its avoidance of extremes, its rationalist optimism, and its belief in the self-evident superiority of ideas over force. Nowhere does Galdós show himself so clearly to be the intellectual heir of the Krausists as in his political articles in the *Revista de España* during 1871 and 1872. Looking back in January 1872 over the events of the previous year, he recalled how the survival of the revolutionary coalition had been threatened by an unholy alliance of Carlists and Federal Republicans:

> Los agrestes clérigos de las montañas, los almibarados y maliciosos neo-católicos de las ciudades, los soñadores de la república federal, y los detestables soldados de una escuela que más tarde había de reducir a pavesas los monumentos de la primer [sic] ciudad del mundo [i.e., Paris], formaban juntos una fuerza formidable. Pero ¡cuán inútiles fueron las tentativas de la coalición contra una mayoría que representaba la libertad, el derecho y la fuerza nunca vencida de las ideas![25]

(The uncouth priests from the mountains, the smooth-tongued and ill-intentioned neo-Catholics from the towns, those who dreamt of a federal republic, and the detestable followers of a movement which would later reduce the first city of the world [i.e., Paris] to ashes, all of these formed a redoubtable force. But how useless were the efforts of this coalition against a majority which represented freedom, right and the invincible strength of ideas!)

This confidence in 'la fuerza nunca vencida de las ideas' was what enabled Galdós to cope with the frustration of the hopes which he and other liberals had reposed in the Revolution. His political writings over the next twenty years display an insistent desire to convince himself and his fellow-countrymen that despite the curtailment of the hard-won freedoms (especially freedom of religion) enshrined in the short-lived Constitution of 1869, some political progress had been made. Though he deplored the persistence of political backwardness and corruption, he was prepared to advocate a working compromise with the Restoration settlement.

That settlement was the work of the Conservative politician Antonio Cánovas del Castillo (1828–97). A strong admirer of the English two-party system of government, he nevertheless believed that because of the low level of political education in Spain, the operation of democracy would in practice have to be curtailed if the country were to avoid the excesses which had vitiated the revolutionary experiments of 1868–73. He therefore evolved the system of the *turno pacífico*, the peaceful and artificial alternation in power of the two main parties, Conservative and Liberal. A change of ministry could take place when expediency demanded it, and even on occasion at the price of fabricating a bogus crisis. If it became necessary to hold elections, voting could be rigged by the local notabilities, the *caciques*, who acted as election agents for the Ministry of the Interior. This process manufactured a majority for the party whose turn it was to govern next, and the country enjoyed the illusion of taking part in political decision-making. To our modern democratic way of thinking, Cánovas's system seems a hollow sham, and there were those at the time, including Galdós, who would have agreed. But as Carr has pointed out, these mechanisms enabled effective government to take place in a situation where neither party could hope for a decisive majority in a genuine election, and also ensured that neither party could exercise a monopoly of power.[26] Factitious as it was, the Canovite settlement gave Spain nearly a quarter of a century of relative peace and prosperity. Although the Restoration consensus evolved in the context of widespread and genuine fear of a relapse into violence and chaos, there was no return to the immobility of Isabella's reign. Freedom of expression was more secure than before, and, most significantly of all, political power passed decisively to the elected Cortes: the monarch retained a veto over the decisions of Ministers, but in practice never used it.

In keeping with his reformist tendencies, Galdós frequently expressed his dislike of many features of Restoration political life: the rigged elections, with their accompaniment of 'the smallest possible number of voters, a good few resurrections of the dead, and not a little violence and abuse' (Ined 3, 20); and *caciquismo*, that 'congenital herpes' on the body politic (Ined 3, 295). But he had great respect for Cánovas's intellectual and political gifts. 'Before him', he wrote in 1886, 'there were no conservative governments in Spain, only authoritarian ones' (Ined 3, 182). He even shared many of Cánovas's reservations about the efficacy of free elections, which, he believed, would produce 'what is commonly known as a "centipede", in other words, a Chamber which would make any government impossible' (Ined 3, 124).[27] For all his reservations about the system, he collaborated with it to the extent of allowing himself in 1886 to be elected Liberal deputy for Puerto Rico, without setting foot in the constituency.

It would be unfair to dismiss this as political opportunism, for however much Galdós disliked the shoddy compromises of the Restoration, he hated and feared disorder more. For nearly two decades after the turbulent events of 1868–73, Galdós remained convinced that any undermining of the delicate balance of the Canovite settlement would be an open invitation to the forces of Carlist reaction or Republican irresponsibility. Revolution was all very well as a response to tyranny, but the more deep-seated problems of Spanish society, such as *caciquismo*, could only be overcome by a long and slow process of political education (Ined 3, 295). Fragile as institutions might be, they were sounder and more liberal than at any previous period of Spanish history. Given that constitutional machinery existed for remedying grievances, resort to violence revealed not only criminal irresponsibility, but a gross lack of political realism:

> Emplear la violencia cuando la legalidad ampara a todo el mundo, cuando la tribuna garantiza todas las opiniones y la Prensa goza de amplia libertad, es criminal y contrario a toda sana política . . . Nuestro país . . . cada vez se paga menos de relumbrones, detesta el romanticismo político, la fraseología hueca y las promesas locas, y sabe sentir la realidad. El sentimiento de la realidad es la gran conquista (Ined 3, 120–21).

> (*To resort to violence when the laws protect everyone, when freedom of political debate guarantees that all opinions can be expressed, and when the press enjoys an ample measure of liberty, is criminal and goes against every sane political consideration. Our country is less and less satisfied with the tawdry and flashy, it detests political romanticism, empty phraseology, and wild promises, and has a firm grasp of reality. The sense of reality is the great conquest [it has made].*)

The Novel and National Regeneration

I have dwelt at some length on Galdós's evolutionary liberalism because I want to suggest that there is a close connection between his reformist political ideology and his literary theory. At first glance, the terms 'political romanticism' and 'sense of reality' appear to be used in the above passage in a purely conventional sense, but in Galdós's work as a whole the literary and political associations of these words often overlap to a much greater extent than they do in common parlance. There is, for example, a striking similarity in emphasis between the foregoing piece of primarily political commentary, and certain parts of his most important essay on the theory of the novel, 'Observaciones sobre la novela contemporánea en España' (1870):

> El lirismo nos corroe . . . como un mal crónico e interno, que ya casi forma parte de nuestro organismo. Somos en todo unos soñadores que no sabemos descender de las regiones del más sublime extravío, y *en literatura como en política*, nos vamos por esas nubes montados en nuestros hipogrifos, como si no estuviéramos en el siglo XIX y en un rincón de esta vieja Europa, que ya se va aficionando mucho a la realidad (*my italics*).[28]

> (*Lyricism wastes us away, so to speak, like a chronic internal disease, which has almost become part of our organism. We are in every respect dreamers who cannot come down to earth from regions of the most sublime extravagance, and* both in literature and in politics, *we go round in the clouds mounted on our hippogryphs, as if we were not in the nineteenth century, and in a corner of old Europe, which is fast developing a taste for reality* [my italics]).

Galdós, in short, believed that just as public life was bedevilled by the quixotry which led Spaniards to seek after utopian dreams, and prevented them from taking a sober look at things as they actually were, so also the novel had been prevented from becoming a mature and serious art form by escapism and over-indulgence of the imagination. In writing novels, therefore, he saw himself as furthering progress by raising the general intellectual and moral tone of society. If he portrays life truthfully, it is not solely in the interests of vividness or authenticity, but primarily because he is aiming to re-educate his fellow-countrymen towards a proper appreciation of reality. Although, as I shall be trying to argue in the remainder of this study, the predominantly ethical focus of the early novels is increasingly overlaid by a denser and more complex depiction of social and economic forces, concern with individual ethical choices, and with the wider question of the efficacy of literature for the task of national regeneration, are never absent. Looking back on his career in old age, Galdós declared:

> Creo que la literatura debe ser enseñanza, ejemplo. Yo escribí siempre, excepto en algunos momentos de lirismo, con el propósito de marcar huella. *Doña Perfecta*, *Electra*, *La loca de la casa*, son buena prueba de ello. Mis *Episodios Nacionales* indican un prurito histórico de enseñanza.[29]

> (*I believe that literature should constitute teaching, example. Except in a few moments of lyricism, I have always written with the intention of making a*

point. Doña Perfecta, Electra, La loca de la casa, *are clear proof of that.*
My Scenes from National History *display the urge for instruction in the*
historical field.)

It is for this reason that I have chosen to use the word 'Enlightenment' in my
title, though it will now be clear, I hope, that I am using it in a non-standard
sense. When used to refer to European intellectual movements of the
eighteenth century, the term usually connotes rational scepticism and a secular,
empirical and utilitarian cast of mind, and, as I have argued in this chapter,
such a mentality made little headway in eighteenth-century Spain. Moreover,
Krause's thought, with its eclectic blend of dialectical method and transcendental idealism, does not belong to the mainstream of the Enlightenment, but to
the transition between the late Enlightenment and early Romanticism at the
turn of the eighteenth and nineteenth centuries. I would argue, however, that
it is not entirely perverse to speak of a quasi or virtual Enlightenment in Spain
in the second half of the nineteenth century. Though Krause was clearly an
unoriginal and unadventurous adapter of the ideas of greater thinkers, and
Sanz del Río a mediocre imitator of Krause, the intellectual climate in
nineteenth-century Spain was such that Krausism was perceived as offering a
radical challenge to accepted values, and especially to the dominance of
conservative Catholicism, comparable in its dramatic impact to the intellectual
revolution which the Enlightenment had brought about in France and Germany, and, indeed, more profound in its effects on Spain than the tentative
Ilustración had been. As Juan López-Morillas has said,

> Las tentativas europeizantes que empiezan en España con el siglo
> XVIII . . . se habían contentado con abogar por la climatación de . . . ideas
> políticas, doctrinas económicas, prácticas sociales, maneras literarias,
> estilos de arte, sin advertir que tales principios y usos eran excrecencias
> orgánicas de una determinada postura ante la vida que . . . era desconocida
> en España. . . . No eran las formas aisladas de la cultura europea lo que [los
> krausistas] aspiraban a trasladar aquende los Pirineos. Era la interpretación
> racional del mundo de la que se alimentaban aquellas formas.[30]

> *(Those who had attempted to open Spain to Europe, from the eighteenth*
> *century on, had confined themselves to advocating the transplantation of*
> *political ideas, economic doctrines, social conventions, literary fashions and*
> *artistic styles, without realising that these principles and practices were the*
> *organic outgrowth of a certain attitude towards life, which was unknown in*
> *Spain. It was not, however, individual manifestations of culture that the*
> *Krausists hoped to transport across the Pyrenees: it was the source from*
> *which these manifestations sprang, namely, the rational interpretation of the*
> *world.)*

However debatable the application of the term 'Enlightenment' to the
phenomenon of Krausism, we are nonetheless on firmer ground if we use the

word more specifically to describe Galdós's understanding of the novelist's role in society. Though there is no evidence which would link Galdós unequivocally with didactic novelists of the French or German Enlightenment, it is nevertheless possible to think of his conception of the novelist's task as the rebirth in a Spanish context of a characteristically Enlightenment way of approaching the writing of fiction. Since this is a complex and important matter, it will be treated in a separate chapter.

Notes to Chapter 1

1. Juan Antonio Llorente, *Histoire critique de l'Inquisition d'Espagne* (tr. under author's direction), 2nd ed., 4 vols., (Paris, 1818), vol. 4, p. 103. Quoted in Jean Sarrailh, *La España ilustrada de la segunda mitad del siglo XVIII*, (Mexico–Madrid–Buenos Aires, 1979), p. 247. First French ed. 1954.
2. Quoted in Sarrailh, *op. cit.*, p. 364.
3. Sarrailh, *op. cit.*, p. 162.
4. Alberto Lista, *Ensayos literarios y críticos* (Madrid, 1844), p. vii.
5. *Discursos leídos ante la Real Academia Española en la recepción pública de don Cándido Nocedal* (Madrid, 1860), p. 7.
6. Vol. 1 (Madrid, 1861), p. li.
7. Vol. 22 (July–August 1879), p. 122.
8. Francisco Blanco García, *La literatura española en el siglo XIX*, Parte 1a, vol. 2 (Madrid, 1891), p. 14.
9. As part of a multi-volume history of literature written between 1801 and 1819 (translated into Spanish in 1829).
10. Inevitably, however, given the small number of Spaniards who knew German, the first works on German philosophy reached Spain through French translation. Even the Spanish version of Mommsen's history of Rome was done from a French translation. This information, and most of the information on Krausism in this chapter, comes from Juan López-Morillas, *El krausismo español*, 2nd ed., (Mexico–Madrid–Buenos Aires, 1980). First ed. Mexico, 1956.
11. Quoted in López-Morillas, *op. cit.*, p. 60.
12. López-Morillas, *op. cit.*, p. 32, n. 2.
13. Raymond Carr, *Spain 1808–1939* (Oxford, 1966), p. 284.
14. *op. cit.*, p. 290.
15. Antonio Ruiz Salvador, *El Ateneo Científico, Literario y Artístico de Madrid (1835–1885)* (London, Támesis, 1971), pp. 103–4.
16. Quoted by Demetrio Estébanez Calderón in his '*Doña Perfecta*, de B. P. Galdós, como novela de tesis', *Boletín de la Biblioteca de Menéndez Pelayo*, 55 (1979), p. 108.
17. Fernando de Castro, *Memoria testamentaria*, ed. José Luis Abellán (Madrid, 1975), pp. 18–32, 54–65.
18. Castro, *op. cit.*, p. 94.
19. William H. Shoemaker, ed., *Los artículos de Galdós en 'La Nación'* (Madrid, 1972), p. 428.
20. See also H. Chonon Berkowitz, *Pérez Galdós, Spanish Liberal Crusader* (Madison, 1948), pp. 74–6.
21. Julián Sanz del Río, *Textos escogidos*, ed. by Eloy Terrón (Barcelona, 1968), p. 186.
22. *op. cit.*, p. 277.
23. These sentiments stand within a moralistic tradition of some antiquity, deriving as they do from medieval preaching, via Erasmus and Spanish religious writers of the sixteenth century such as Luis de Granada and Antonio de Guevara. Galdós's immediate source was probably the *Sueños* of Francisco de Quevedo (1636), which has connections with the tradition of visionary literature represented principally by Virgil and Dante. In other words, despite the reputation

which Galdós acquired in his own lifetime for political radicalism, and the impetus which he was to give to innovation in prose fiction in the 1880s, his thought contains large elements of traditionalism and conservatism, which, as we shall see, have a marked influence on his literary theory, and on his conception of his task as a novelist.

24. Stephen Miller recognises that between the early 1870s and the mid-1880s, Galdós 'sustituye su creencia ingenua en el progreso español por una apreciación más compleja de la historia patria'. He sees this gain in political realism as arising chiefly from the overthrow of the Republic by General Pavía in January 1874, and the Restoration of the Bourbons in the following year. In my view, however, Galdós's disillusionment with the pre-Revolutionary optimism of the Progressives more probably dates from the assassination of Prim in 1870. Miller overlooks the fact that Galdós was sharply critical of what he regarded as the naivety and irresponsibility of the Republican government, which was, indeed, one of the principal factors in his disillusionment. Furthermore, it is not quite fair to say that Galdós believed that nothing had changed, since his *La Prensa* articles of the 1880s show that he regarded the Restoration, with all its faults, as an improvement on the turbulence of the period between 1868 and 1874. (See Stephen Miller, *El mundo de Galdós* [Santander, 1983], pp. 21–22.)

25. Benito Pérez Galdós, *Los artículos políticos en la 'Revista de España', 1871–1872*, ed. Brian J. Dendle and Joseph Schraibman (Lexington, Kentucky, 1982), p. 24.

26. Carr, *op. cit.*, p. 357.

27. Cf. Miller, *op. cit.*, p. 21.

28. Benito Pérez Galdós, *Ensayos de crítica literaria*, ed. Laureano Bonet (Barcelona, 1972), p. 116.

29. Luis Antón del Olmet & Arturo García Carraffa, *Galdós* (Madrid, 1912), p. 93.

30. López-Morillas, *op. cit.*, pp. 29–30.

2

The Responsibility of the Writer

Literature and social change

The Revolution of 1868 was not only important in the political sphere, but also crucial to the emergence of the modern novel in Spain, as Leopoldo Alas was to point out in his essay 'El libre examen y nuestra literatura presente' ('Free Enquiry and contemporary literature') (1881).[1] Indeed, the effect of the Revolution on the Spanish novel was comparable to the impact of the French Revolution on the European novel in general. As Erich Auerbach has pointed out, 'modern tragic realism based on the contemporary' derives essentially from the period after the French Revolution, and both he and Georg Lukács, in their studies of Balzac and Stendhal, have given us brilliant analyses of the ways in which these writers depict the complex social movements and relationships which arose in the wake of the Revolution. As Auerbach says, speaking of Stendhal's *Le Rouge et le noir*,

> Now the dangers are known, and life is governed by the fear that the catastrophe of 1793 might be repeated. As these people [*i.e., the de la Môle household*] are conscious that they no longer themselves believe in the thing they represent . . . they choose to talk of nothing but the weather, music and court gossip. In addition, they are obliged to accept as allies snobbish and corrupt people from among the newly-rich bourgeoisie, who, with the unashamed baseness of their ambitions and with their fear for their ill-gotten wealth, completely vitiate the atmosphere of society.[2]

As we shall see in our detailed discussion of individual Galdós novels in the later chapters, the corruption of society and the fragility of contemporary institutions are powerfully portrayed in ways that make his sober and unromantic view of reality seem comparable to that which Auerbach ascribes to Stendhal. Stendhal and Balzac, however, were writing a generation after the French Revolution, and, in addition, experienced not only the repression which followed upon the Restoration of the Bourbons but also the upheaval of 1830. Consequently, they look on their society with the disillusionment born of hindsight, recording either the decline from the heroic standard of the Napoleonic period or the tragic erosion of aristocratic culture. Although Galdós would, in due course, be rapidly disillusioned by the events of 1868–73, the beginning of his career as a novelist coincided with the fall of Isabella and its initially promising aftermath. There is, therefore, in his early writing on the novel, a sense of excitement at the prospects opened up by rapid historical change.

This feeling of an urgent task to be tackled is the keynote of Galdós's 'Observations on the contemporary novel in Spain ('Observaciones sobre la novela contemporánea en España'). The essay appeared in the *Revista de España* in July 1870, i.e., after the pacification of the disturbances of the summer and autumn of 1869, but before the murder of Prim. It is not surprising that at that date Galdós should emphasise how the liberation of middle-class energy and initiative by the Revolution had provided the novelist with material of great interest and variety:

> La clase media . . . es hoy la base del orden social; ella asume por su iniciativa y por su inteligencia la soberanía de las naciones, y en ella está el hombre del siglo XIX con sus virtudes y sus vicios, su noble e insaciable aspiración, su afán de reformas, su actividad pasmosa. . . . tiene . . . en el momento actual . . . grandes condiciones de originalidad, de colorido, de forma.[3]

> *(Today the middle class is the foundation of the social order. By its initiative and intelligence, it is beginning to exercise political power over nations. It epitomises nineteenth-century man with his virtues and vices, his noble and insatiable ambition, his thirst for reform, and his astonishing activity. At the present time, it offers great scope for originality, colour and form.)*

Galdós's conviction that the time is ripe to attempt the regeneration of prose fiction derives not only from the achievement of political freedom by the Revolution, but also from his Krausist-inspired assumptions about the proper relation of literature to history, and about the educational responsibility of writers. To be sure, neither Krause nor Sanz del Río had given very explicit treatment to the place of literature in their system of thought, but Krause's general ideas have implications for the arts which were to be developed by Francisco Giner de los Ríos, who, in an essay entitled 'Considerations on the development of modern literature'[4] published in 1862, provided what was to become the classic formulation of Krausist literary theory. Though as we have seen Krause cannot strictly be considered an Enlightenment figure, he retains the characteristic Enlightenment belief that because reason is a basic human faculty common to all, worthwhile products of the human mind are distinguished by universality of appeal. However, Krause amalgamates with this the Romantics' recognition of the variety and range of human excellence, producing his characteristically eclectic conception of rich variety within universal harmony. Giner makes use of this idea, blending with it the general Krausist notion of human progress through education, cultural development, and the search for moral perfection and also his own personal discovery of Hegel, Schiller and Herder. Particularly useful to Giner is Herder's belief in the diversity of national genius or character, because it enables him to pay due attention to the writer's individual creative talent while still regarding particular literary works as the authentic expression both of universal values and of a national culture.

This was the source of Giner's rejection of most of French literature, for in adopting a standardised classicism the French had, he argued, turned their backs on their own national traditions, and shorn their literature of everything concrete or distinctive. Particularly reprehensible was their neglect of their own medieval literature, for the middle ages were, in Giner's view, the period when the diversity of national identities became established. Furthermore, despite Giner's indebtedness to the German Romantics, he regarded the French Romantics as guilty of the same error as the neo-classicists against whom they claimed to be reacting, for in indulging in a false medievalism, they had failed to understand the true nature of the relationship of literature to history.[5] 'History', for Giner, is not mere antiquarianism or an escape from the present, but the story of humanity's progress towards rational perfection. Literature only fulfils its proper function if it enables people to understand the various stages of this process:

No es otra cosa la Literatura que el primero y más firme camino para entender la historia realizada: Mentor universal, nos reproduce lo pasado, nos explica lo presente, y nos ilustra y alecciona para las oscuras elaboraciones de lo por venir.[6]

(Literature is no more or less than the most important and the soundest way of understanding history as it actually happened. It is our universal mentor, which re-creates the past, explains the present, and enlightens and instructs us on the still shadowy developments of the future.)

Literature which attempts to recreate the past, therefore, must do so with sober and serious intent, avoiding escapism and sentimentality. It follows that writers who strive to depict their own contemporary society have a serious responsibility to show it as it really is, so as to enable people to perceive how far they have advanced along the path towards rational perfection. Implicit, then, in Giner's literary theory is the notion that literature should be both didactic and true to life. Such an idea was scarcely original in 1862, but it is nevertheless of some interest to examine why in formulating it Giner found it necessary to define his terms in such a way as to make clear the difference between his theory and other competing ones which made similar claims but were in reality based on quite different ideological assumptions.

The novel and decorum

The difficulty of definition was compounded by the fact that in some respects
Giner appeared to be preaching to the converted, and this was because
classical ideas of literary decorum remained influential in Spain long after they
had become unfashionable elsewhere. This was partly due to the conservatism
of the official academic curriculum. One of the most dogmatic classicist
manuals produced in the nineteenth century, Gómez Hermosilla's *Arte de
hablar en prosa y verso*, was designated by an order of 19 December 1825 as
the official text for use in Humanities classes. Urbano González Serrano could
still complain in 1883 that classical precepts continued to dominate the
educational system.[7] Even as late as 1891, Blanco García declared that Coll y
Vehí's *Elementos de literatura* (1856) 'has still not lost its usefulness for
secondary education'.[8]

It is, of course, not at all easy to determine precisely how much influence
official education had, as distinct from the impact of literary developments in
the rest of Europe. However, given that all men of letters would have received
a broadly similar education, it is likely that a substratum of ideas was laid down
during their student days, which persisted into later life, whether they embraced Romanticism or Realism, or preferred to function within a more
consciously neo-classical framework. This is why, despite the deep ideological
rifts between groups of writers, there was a tacit agreement to observe certain
standards of decorum and elegance of diction, ultimately derived from the
academic habit of considering the classics as models of excellence. One result
was a certain old-fashioned fastidiousness about crudity or explicitness in
sexual matters, which is not to be explained solely by censorship or ecclesiasti-
cal strictures. By far the most important aspect of the classical literary
tradition, however, accepted even by those writers who would have considered
themselves as functioning outside the classical rules, is Horace's dictum that
poets strive to give both pleasure and profit: 'aut prodesse volunt, aut delectare
poetae'. Direct echoes of this may be found in the writings of many critics of
diverse views. When Antonio Gil y Zárate, for example, attempts to lay down
rules for the novel in his *Manual de literatura* (1842), he takes as his
starting-point the notion that the motto of the novel should be to delight and
instruct.[9]

In the first half of the century, most critics would have been careful to
interpret Horace's statement in a way which respected the primacy of the
aesthetic value in a work of art, avoiding direct didacticism. Alberto Lista, for
example, wrote in 1839 that the primary function of art was to give pleasure by
the contemplation of beauty; respect for morality arises as a consequence of
this pursuit, not as a precondition.[10] From the 1850s on, however, the
neo-Catholic revival and the rise of Krausism divided writers and intellectuals
into two groups. Conservative Catholic writers were now more disposed to
detach the notion of 'utility' from its classical roots and to subordinate
literature, especially the novel, to the general crusade in favour of morality and

the established order. In 1853, for example, in an open letter to Vicente Barrantes, Fernán Caballero (Cecilia Böhl de Faber, 1796–1877), declared that her aim was 'to instil wholesome ideas into the young people of today, giving a new direction to the novel of passion by guiding it into the simple path of duty'.[11]

Fernán was not alone in feeling that the novel raised special problems for the socially-responsible writer, not the least important of which was the fact that unlike other literary genres, the novel lacked a generally accepted poetics. Whereas the literary polemics of the 1830s and 1840s had centred on poetry and drama, the novel tended to be assimilated, in discussions of literary theory, to one or other of the traditional forms for which prescriptions were already available in the neo-classical manuals. Coll y Vehí's *Elementos de literatura* (1856) is a typical example of this tendency: more than half the work is devoted to oratory, the novel rating a total of five pages out of 432, and that in the section on epic poetry. Even Giner, when he wrote his 'Considerations on the development of modern literature' in 1862, did not foresee that the serious novel was to be the genre of the future. Though at the level of theory he postulated a literature which would maintain a close relationship with history, he did not see any immediate prospect of the novel genre giving rise to such a literature, for in the prevailing climate of confusion and transition, he argued, writers had become more introspective, hence the dominance of lyric poetry. Since the only novels being written were sentimental popular romances springing directly from this mood of lyricism, Giner thought it more likely that the serious literature of the future would emerge either from drama, which he regarded as the highest form of 'harmonic poetry', or from epic, which he called 'objective poetry'.

All serious writers, therefore, whatever their ideological complexion. shared a certain attitude of suspicion towards the popular novel on the grounds either of its supposed immorality or, at best, of its triviality. Conservative Catholic writers, however, carried this hostility to even greater lengths than their liberal counterparts. Implicit in Fernán's statement is the idea that the novel is *intrinsically* morally suspect until it is forced to tread the path of duty, and this view was shared by most of Fernán's conservative contemporaries. It followed that since the novel was characteristically pernicious, it could only achieve moral edification if it went against its own nature. In other words, the aim of 'utility' was to be attained, not by reflecting the world as it was, but by single-mindedly asserting transcendental or 'other-worldly' values, and cultivating, if necessary at the price of a certain strain and stridency, an idealistic and optimistic tone. Thus Antonio de Trueba begins the preface to his *Cuentos de color de rosa* (Rose-coloured Stories) (1859) by declaring,

> Estos cuentos te dedico, esposa mía, porque son lo más honrado que ha salido de mi pluma, y porque tu alma angelical y enamorada me ha hecho sentir mucho de lo hermoso y puro y santo que he pretendido trasladar a ellos.

Llámoles *Cuentos de color de rosa*, porque son el reverso de la medalla de esa literatura pesimista que se complace en presentar el mundo como un infinito desierto en que no brota una flor, y la vida como una perpetua noche en que no brilla una estrella.[12]

(I dedicate these stories to you, dear wife, because they are the noblest thing that has flowed from my pen, and because your angelic and loving soul has made me experience in abundance the beautiful, pure and holy things with which I have tried to imbue them.

I call them Rose-coloured Stories *because they are the opposite of that pessimistic literature which takes pleasure in presenting the world as a limitless desert where no flower grows, and life as an unending night where no star shines.)*

Liberal writers, it is true, would in due course display a comparable willingness to press the novel into service in the furtherance of their reforming ideals, with consequent selectivity in the presentation of reality, particularly after the Revolution of 1868, when ideological conflicts took on a redoubled intensity. Galdós's *Doña Perfecta* appeared in 1876, to be followed a year later by *Gloria*, which drew from the traditionalist José María de Pereda a riposte in the shape of *De tal palo, tal astilla* (1880). There is nevertheless an important difference in fundamental motivation and outlook between liberal writers like Galdós and their conservative contemporaries. However vehemently or one-sidedly liberals may defend freedom and tolerance, they are concerned with the here and now rather than the hereafter, though they often, of course, believe in the hereafter as individuals. Besides, since what they object to in their conservative adversaries is the subordination of life to naively simplified moral and theological schemes, they will not usually go quite so far towards reducing the representation of the world to those aspects which support their thesis.

A more significant difference, however, is that liberals influenced by Krausist literary theory regarded the novel as essentially good rather than intrinsically evil. This was because in Giner's theory ethics and aesthetics are inextricably bound up with each other. The traditional Platonic identification of beauty, goodness and truth lay at the heart of Krause's aesthetics, and determines Giner's conception of literary responsibility. Since truth cannot be conceived of separately from beauty and goodness, it follows that although the writer must strive to represent reality authentically, not all aspects of reality are suitable for depiction. Furthermore, despite his indebtedness to the universalising rationalism of the Enlightenment, and his castigation of French Romanticism, Giner retains a characteristic Romantic belief in the imagination, which, in his somewhat eclectic system, becomes the partner of reason, both being universal organising principles which enable people to make sense of their fragmentary experience. The work of the artist, therefore, is not slavishly to copy reality, but to 'aspire to reconstruct the forms [of reality], concentrated and purified by the synthetic power of the creative imagination'.[13] A further consequence of the identification of beauty, truth and goodness is that the artist's pursuit of aesthetic value is necessarily ethical as well, whether he has a consciously didactic intention or not: 'The artist, in pursuing exclusively aesthetic aims, implicitly acts in an ethical way, since every free act falls within the domain of morality'.[14]

Consequently, the word *didáctico* is for Giner free from those connotations of vehemence and oversimplification which its English cognate tends to carry in modern critical parlance. True, Giner was well aware that committed literature often displayed these characteristic defects, but when he wished to criticise them, he used the word *tendencioso*, derived from contemporary critical discussion in Germany of *tendenziöse Literatur*. This is the term which he was to use when he reviewed the first volume of Galdós's *La familia de León Roch* in 1878. For Giner, the crucial question was one of proportion. The best novels are those which strike a harmonious balance between the representation of the external world and the subjective intuition of general principles or values. The trouble with *León Roch*, he claims, is that everything has been sacrificed to the thesis which the author wishes to prove.[15]

Towards a novel of manners

I have described Giner's literary theory at some length because his 'Considerations on the development of modern literature' was the principal source of the ideas which Galdós expressed in his 'Observations on the contemporary novel in Spain' (1870) and 'Ramón de la Cruz and his age' (1871). The fact that the 'Observations' first took shape as a review of Ventura Ruiz Aguilera's two collections of short stories, *Proverbios ejemplares* (1864) and *Proverbios cómicos* (first published 1865, second edition, 1870), has led Stephen Miller to argue persuasively that Galdós's theory of the novel was derived from Aguilera.[16] It is true that in his prefaces both to the *Proverbios ejemplares* and to his earlier collection of poetry, *Ecos nacionales* (1849) Aguilera puts forward views on authenticity of representation, and on the need for literature to progress *pari passu* with general historical movements, which are very similar to those expounded by both Galdós and Giner. Such notions, however, were commonplace enough in nineteenth-century Spain. What Galdós derives from Giner is a distinctive synthesis, not found in Aguilera, whereby both writers conceive of historicity and truth to life as deriving primarily from the writer's educational concerns, and totally reject what they regard as the deleterious influence of debased French Romanticism, on the grounds of its alleged moral and social irresponsibility. Though Aguilera expressed mild regret at the pervasiveness of French cultural influence, there is no equivalent in his writing to the cultural nationalism and implacable Francophobia displayed by both Giner and Galdós.[17] If one compares Giner's references to the 'false warmth of an artificial and violent culture', to France as a 'vacillating and directionless [nation], the fickle devotee of all that is abnormal', and to the troubadours' 'puerile eroticism, at once metaphysical and sensual'[18] with Galdós's remarks about the 'grotesque and ridiculous habits', and 'the scurrility and effeminacy' (OC 6, 1468) introduced into eighteenth-century Spanish social life by the French, there can be little doubt that Galdós's principal mentor in matters of literary theory, at least in the early years of his career, was Giner, and it was in the light of Giner's ideas that he evaluated Aguilera's work in his 'Observaciones'.[19]

Derivative as Galdós's ideas may be, however, the 'Observaciones' have their own originality, for Galdós was the first to apply Krausist literary theory systematically to the novel. Galdós takes up Aguilera's concern with authenticity in the representation of Spanish social types and absorbs it into a more structured conception of the novel as a work of moral and intellectual utility, not necessarily crudely didactic, but displaying a serious concern for contemporary problems rather than taking refuge in romanticised visions of the past. It is precisely on these grounds that he repudiates the popular novel of sensation and melodrama, 'a plague originating in France, which has spread with the astonishing rapidity of all contagious diseases', and which panders to the taste of 'an extremely frivolous public . . . who only go to books in search of a brief pleasure or a passing distraction'. The true mission of the novel is not to concern itself with 'pale villains of sinister glance, angelic seamstresses, whores with haloes, fallen duchesses, romantic hunchbacks, adultery, extremes of love and hate',[20] but with the middle class, which is the class that determines the whole tone and pace of Spanish life at the present time:

> La novela moderna de costumbres ha de ser la expresión de cuanto bueno y malo existe en el fondo de esa clase, de la incesante agitación que la elabora, de ese empeño que manifiesta por encontrar ciertos ideales y resolver ciertos problemas que preocupan a todos, y conocer el origen y el remedio de ciertos males que turban las familias. La grande aspiración del arte literario en nuestro tiempo es dar forma a todo esto.[21]

> (*The modern novel of manners will express all the good and all the evil which exist at the centre of the middle class, the ceaseless turbulence which is giving that class shape, its desire to find certain ideals, to resolve certain problems which preoccupy everybody, and to discover the origin and the remedy for certain evils which disturb family relationships. The great aspiration of literary art in our time is to give all this a form.*)

True, Galdós is careful to say that the novelist is not called upon to offer solutions to the grave problems he depicts, but in choosing to call the type of novel he is advocating 'a novel of manners' ('una novela de costumbres'), he implies that it must offer not only an image of society, but also a running critical commentary on society's vices and moral problems. For all his concern in the 'Observaciones' with the truthful depiction of life, it is the ethical dimension of social reality that Galdós regards as paramount. Thus he argues that though the political and economic progress of contemporary Spain are something to be thankful for, these things still have their negative side.

Upward social mobility can lead to ambition; material progress can foster greed and selfishness; families can be broken up by moral turpitude, by loss of religious constraints, or by fanatical piety. It is the job of the novelist to reflect 'this deep turbulence, this incessant conflict between principle and experience which makes up the astonishing drama of contemporary life'.[22]

What the 'Observaciones' do not make explicit, however, is what kinds of literary representation will be most effective in achieving this blend of truth to life and moral seriousness. To the extent that Galdós and Giner insist that the novel must remain anchored in history and concern itself with contemporary issues, their theory may be said to be realist. Nowhere in the 'Observaciones', however, does Galdós use the term *realista*, and this is because the definition of the word was at that date a somewhat controversial matter in Spain. The terms in which the controversy was conducted tell us a great deal about the assumptions which writers brought to the task of representing reality, which include not only the notion of social and moral responsibility which we have studied in this chapter, but the attitude of writers towards their national literary heritage, and ultimately their understanding of the nature of reality itself. It is to this issue that we must now turn.

Notes to Chapter 2

1. This essay may be consulted in full in Alas's *Solos de Clarín* (Madrid, Alianza Editorial, 1971), pp. 65–78. An excerpt from the essay is included in Leopoldo Alas, *Teoría y crítica de la novela española*, ed. Sergio Beser (Barcelona, Laia, 1972), pp. 42–46.
2. *Mimesis*, tr. Willard Trask (Garden City, New York, 1957), p. 404. First English ed., Princeton University Press, 1953. First German ed., Berne, 1946.
3. Benito Pérez Galdós, *Ensayos de crítica literaria*, ed. Laureano Bonet (Barcelona, 1972), pp. 122–3.
4. 'Consideraciones sobre el desarrollo de la literatura moderna'. Subsequently reprinted in his collected *Estudios literarios* (Madrid 1866), and in the expanded version *Estudios de literatura y arte* (1876). Included in Juan López-Morillas ed., *Krausismo: Estética y literatura* (Barcelona, Labor, 1973), pp. 111–61. The introduction to this volume gives an excellent short account of Krausist literary theory. I have relied considerably on this and also on the same author's *El krausismo español*, 2nd. ed., (Mexico–Madrid–Buenos Aires, 1980). First ed. Mexico, 1956.
5. According to López-Morillas, however, Giner appears to have closed his eyes to the fact that medievalist escapism is also characteristic of *German* Romanticism. See *El krausismo español*, p. 120.
6. *Estudios literarios* (1866), p. 92. Also in López-Morillas, ed., *Krausismo: Estética* (1973), p. 114.
7. *Cuestiones contemporáneas* (Madrid, 1883), p. 175.
8. *La literatura española en el siglo XIX*, Parte 1a, vol. 2 (Madrid, 1891), p. 585.
9. 'Instruir y deleitar debe ser su lema'. (*Manual de literatura. Primera parte: Principios generales de Poética y Retórica*, 7th ed. [Madrid, 1856], p. 183. First ed. Madrid, 1842.)
10. See Ricardo Navas-Ruiz ed., *El romanticismo español: Documentos* (Salamanca, Anaya, 1971), p. 216.
11. 'Inocular buenas ideas en la juventud contemporánea . . . dando un giro nuevo a la apasionada novela, trayéndola a la sencilla senda del deber'. (Quoted in Donald L. Shaw, 'The anti-Romantic reaction in Spain', *Modern Language Review*, 63 [1968], p. 608.)
12. Second ed. (Madrid, 1862), p. 5.

13. López-Morillas, ed., *Krausismo: Estética*, p. 133.
14. 'El artista, al atender exclusivamente al verdadero fin estético, obra por implícita necesidad éticamente, pues toda acción libre cae bajo el dominio de la moral' (*ibid.*, p. 155.)
15. Francisco Giner de los Ríos, *Ensayos* (Madrid, 1969), pp. 67–8.
16. *El mundo de Galdós* (Santander, 1983), pp. 52–9.
17. Though Galdós copies Giner's anti-French stance, this is in his case something of a pose, since on his own admission (Ined 10, 39; OC 6, 1656) he had begun avidly to devour Balzac's works in 1867. Giner's Gallophobia in turn was in part derived from Sanz del Río, whose attitude appears to have been largely a personal quirk. On his way to meet Ahrens in Brussels in 1843, Sanz del Río had visited Victor Cousin in Paris, and his fastidious and puritanical temperament had been repelled by what he regarded as the superficiality of Cousin's eclectic philosophy, an impression which he then extended into a global condemnation of all French thought and culture. Writing to José de la Revilla in 1844, Sanz declared that France's sole contribution to Spanish cultural life was 'false learning, and, above all, immorality and petulant egotism'. (Quoted by López-Morillas in *El krausismo español* [1980], p. 24.)
18. López-Morillas, ed., *Krausismo: Estética*, pp. 120, 122.
19. Further evidence that Giner was the source both of Galdós's early literary theory and of his Francophobia is provided by the fact that Galdós chose in 1871 to devote a long essay to Ramón de la Cruz, whom Giner had mentioned in passing in his 1862 'Considerations' as the one eighteenth-century Spanish writer to resist the prevailing French influence. Cruz was practically unknown to Galdós's readers, to the extent that he had to supply biographical details from an eighteenth-century source which would appear never to have been reprinted after its first publication (José Antonio Alvarez y Baena, *Hijos de Madrid ilustres en santidad, dignidades, armas, ciencias y artes*, 4 vols. [Madrid, 1789–91]). The only plausible reason for writing at such length on such an obscure figure is that it gave Galdós the opportunity to extend the nationalist critique of French culture which he had derived from Giner.
20. ' . . . un público frívolo en demasía . . . personas, que únicamente buscan en el libro una distracción fugaz o un pasajero deleite. . . . peste nacida en Francia, y que se ha difundido con la pasmosa rapidez de todos los males contagiosos. El público ha dicho: "Quiero traidores pálidos y de mirada siniestra, modistas angelicales, duquesas averiadas, jorobados románticos, adulterios, extremos de amor y odio", y le han dado todo esto' (*Ensayos* [1972], pp. 115, 118.)
21. *op.cit.*, pp. 122–3.
22. ' . . . esta turbación honda, esta lucha incesante de principios y hechos que constituye el maravilloso drama de la vida actual' (*op. cit.*, p. 124).

3

Towards a Spanish Realism

Galdós's view of Aguilera

Despite the limitations I outlined at the end of the previous chapter, Galdós's 'Observaciones' have struck many critics at first glance as so lucid and coherent that they have understandably taken them as a realist manifesto, which sets out a programme for what Galdós actually achieved in his major novels of the 1880s. H. C. Berkowitz lent his authority to this notion as long ago as 1948, when he described *La familia de León Roch* (1878) as 'the inevitable next step in Galdós's plan'.[1] Referri..g to Galdós's next novel, *La desheredada* (1881), Berkowitz adds,

> After that he had intended to enter upon what he liked to call his second or third manner. In this new phase he would begin to apply in earnest his conviction about the essence of the modern novel of manners. He would abandon the realm of speculation, abstraction, and idealism and would concentrate on the direct observation of the role played by the middle class in contemporary society.

Though Berkowitz's view has been accepted uncritically by other students of Galdós,[2] it is inherently implausible that any writer would have a detailed *a priori* view of the various stages through which his literary career would develop. The structure of the present study, indeed, has been dictated by the fact that Galdós's literary development went through various phases, each marked by hesitation and tentative experimentation.

Berkowitz's most significant error, however, was to overlook the purpose for which the 'Observaciones' were originally published, and this led him and many subsequent critics to overlook the complexities of Galdós's early 'realism', and the extent to which it was shaped by historical and cultural circumstances. The 'Observaciones' were not a purely theoretical set of principles, but were initially written as a review of two collections of short stories by Ventura Ruiz Aguilera, the *Proverbios ejemplares* (1864) and the *Proverbios cómicos* (1870). Rather than 'short stories', it would be more accurate to describe these pieces as belonging to the genre known as the *cuadro de costumbres*, i.e., short, often satirical sketches of contemporary foibles, picturesque local traditions, or national types. Though the *cuadro* can give a vivid and authentic picture of an aspect of everyday life, it is primarily a moralistic genre, in which the area of reality represented is narrowly circumscribed by the overall purpose of making a generalisation about human behaviour or national customs: Aguilera's use of the word *Proverbios*, indeed, bears this out.[3] Given Galdós's assumptions about the moral utility of literature, which we examined in the last chapter, it is not surprising that he regarded Aguilera's stories, with their blend of moral seriousness and vivid authenticity, as providing an attractive contrast to the vapid escapism of the popular novel. Indeed, he went so far as to assert in the 'Observaciones' that Aguilera's *Proverbios* are a hopeful sign of the future regeneration of the novel, because of their blend of naturalness and humour:

> Allí estamos todos nosotros con nuestras flaquezas y nuestras virtudes retratados con fidelidad, y puestos en movimiento en una serie de sucesos que no son ni más ni menos que estos que nos están pasando ordinariamente uno y otro día en el curso de nuestra agitada vida . . . Los vicios y virtudes fundamentales que engendran los caracteres y determinan los sucesos son también estos de por acá. Nada de abstracciones, nada de teorías.[4]

> *(We are all there, with our weaknesses and virtues, faithfully depicted, and set in motion in a series of events which are no more or no less than those which commonly happen to us every day in the course of our overexcited lives. The basic vices and virtues which give rise to the temperaments [of the characters] and determine the events are also everyday ones. There are no abstractions and no theories.)*

Undoubtedly, Aguilera does, in certain respects, break new ground in fiction-writing, for the moral issues illustrated in the *Proverbios* arise from the kind of everyday problems, often financial, which were to provide the plots for many of Galdós's own novels. Nevertheless, it would be a mistake to exaggerate these superficially 'modern' aspects of Aguilera's stories, for his style frequently displays archaic, crude and sentimental features which Galdós apparently had no difficulty in accepting. Galdós's statement, for example, that Aguilera's stories do not contain digressions[5] is flatly contradicted by the evidence of the texts, where the narrative is frequently interrupted by long moralising passages. Galdós's assertion that Aguilera's plots are always logical and free from theatrical effects seems ingenuous when one realises how frequently the stories end with a stiff-jointed tying together of strands in the interests of strengthening the didactic impact. The Arenal sisters in *Al freír será el reír* correspond exactly to the literary stereotype of the virtuous poor seamstress about whom Galdós had waxed sarcastic in an earlier part of the

'Observaciones',[6] but when he comments on that story a few pages later, he only remarks that the sisters form part of a 'beautiful and artistically-composed group'.[7] Nor does Galdós apparently find in the least cloying the crudely sentimental devices which Aguilera uses on occasion to press home a moral point. At the end of *Amor de padre*, for example, the rays of the setting sun make a poor blacksmith, tending the graves of his dead infants, look like an archangel, while the 'insolent beauty' of a rich spoiled girl, indifferent to the memory of her departed father, reminds the narrator of Lucifer 'trampled by the victorious heel of the Virgin Mary'.[8]

Galdós's implicit acceptance of these features of Aguilera's style suggests that, at least at that date, his understanding of literary representation did not exclude explicit didacticism, or even unctuous sentimentality, features which would indeed appear in due course in some of his novels of the 1870s. It was not merely that the presence of such characteristics in Aguilera's prose was compensated for by the vividness and authenticity of his depiction of everyday life, but rather that Aguilera's idealistic tone implied a conviction that the 'reality' to be presented in the novel was not confined to the material sphere, but embraced moral and spiritual insights and values. Aguilera himself made this point quite explicit in his introduction to the *Proverbios ejemplares*:

> El perfume, el alma de la novela, o de otra flor cualquiera del pensamiento, es lo ideal depositado en lo real, el espíritu envuelto en la forma, la vida animando a la materia, y dominándola siempre, como la cabeza, santuario de la inteligencia, domina al resto del cuerpo.[9]

> (*The perfume, the soul of the novel, or of any other flower of the human mind, is the ideal inserted into the real, spirit clothed in form, life animating matter, and always dominating it, as the head, the sanctuary of the intelligence, dominates the rest of the body.*)

Aguilera is here articulating a view which was commonplace in Spain for most of the nineteenth century. Whatever reality is, it must entail the subordination of all manifestations of life to the human spirit and to its capacity for apprehending universal ideals. It follows that any view which equates reality with the merely physical is unworthy of thinking men. Indeed, in this very same preface, Aguilera equates 'realist' with 'coarse', when he speaks of 'a coarse, realist naturalism, verging on the obscene'.[10] Similarly adverse connotations of the word 'realist' were undoubtedly in Galdós's mind when he penned the following robust piece of raillery in 1866:

> Dennos novelas históricas y *sociales*; novelas intencionadas, profundas . . . Queremos ver descritas con mano segura las peripecias más atroces que imaginación alguna pueda concebir . . . si hay hospital, mejor; si hay tisis regeneradora, ¡magnífico!; si hay patíbulo, ¡soberbio! . . . Realidad, realidad (OC 6, 1556).

*(Give us historical and 'social' novels, profound novels with a moral
intention. We want to see the most atrocious adventures that the imagination
can conceive described with a steady hand. If there is a hospital, better still; if
a redeeming consumption, capital; if a gallows, splendid! Reality, reality [at
all costs].)*

Spain and European Realism

Galdós's understanding of literary representation was determined not only by
his conception of the social responsibility of the writer and his search for the
desirable balance between the real and the ideal, but also by cultural nationalism. To be sure, Galdós had come to know and admire Balzac's work by the
mid-1860s, and was almost certainly influenced by the example of the *Comédie
humaine* when he came to write his own novels. Galdós did not, however,
acknowledge any debt to Balzac until 1916, when he published his *Memorias de
un desmemoriado* (*Memoirs of a Forgetful Man*) in the journal *La Esfera*.
Apart from one glancing reference to Dickens, the 'Observaciones' are silent
about possible foreign influences, a silence which is all the more remarkable
when one considers the stage that the development of the novel in Europe had
reached. By 1870, Dickens and Balzac were dead, and Flaubert had produced
all his major work except *Bouvard et Pécuchet*. Indeed, realism as represented
by Balzac and Stendhal had already given way to naturalism. The Goncourt
brothers' *Germinie Lacerteux*, the preface to which was a provocative naturalist
manifesto, had appeared six years previously, and Zola had already produced
Thérèse Raquin and *Madeleine Férat*.

Galdós, however, writes his 'Observaciones' as if none of this had happened,
preferring to look for models within his own national culture. Thus he asserts
that the Spanish aptitude for accurate depiction of reality, as represented by
Cervantes and Velázquez, has been temporarily eclipsed by foreign importa-
tions.[11] The clear implication of the essay as a whole is that the regeneration of
the modern novel of manners entails returning to this interrupted national
tradition, a conviction which Galdós maintained consistently throughout his
writing career. As late as 1901, he could write that the furore which first
greeted Leopoldo Alas's *La Regenta*, published in 1884 when naturalism was a
burning issue in Spain, was out of place, because naturalism was merely 'the
repatriation of an old idea' (OC 6, 1448).

In seeking to present the regenerated Spanish novel as something continuous
with national literary tradition, Galdós was simply articulating widely-held
assumptions, for the 'Observaciones' stand fully within a current of cultural
nationalism which runs throughout the nineteenth century. Mesonero
Romanos, for example, writing in 1839, called on his countrymen to vindicate
their national character, which had been traduced by foreign writers, and to
uphold Spanish literary achievements such as the *Quixote* and the picaresque
novel.[12] The conservative neo-Catholic politician Cándido Nocedal, in his
reception discourse at the Royal Spanish Academy in 1860, described Cervan-

tes as only one of many predecessors of the modern Spanish novel, and cited a host of earlier works, including medieval collections of exempla, the *Conde Lucanor*, the *Cárcel de amor* and the picaresque novel. Juan Valera, surveying Spanish contributions to prose fiction, including *Amadis of Gaul* and the *Celestina* as well as the *Quixote*, declared in 1886–7 that 'if we look to the past, our superiority in the novel is unquestionable'.[13]

The talent for depicting life in well-written novels, then, is seen as something indigenous to the Spanish character and Spanish literary tradition.[14] Inevitably, therefore, the attitude of Spanish nineteenth-century writers towards the main current of European Realism is, to say the least, somewhat guarded, particularly since in Spain as elsewhere in Europe Realism was regarded as essentially a French movement. It was purely a historical accident that, as George Becker has expressed it, 'there was a series of French writers of genius who were attempting to write in a new way just at the time when substantial works were needed to define and consolidate the position of realism'.[15] From the Spanish point of view, however, this historical accident was unfortunate, for, as we have seen, France had long been the *bête noire* of patriotic Spaniards. It would, however, be unfair to dismiss this as mere bigoted parochialism. Precisely because the early theorists of French Realism were deliberately challenging established views of what literature should be (especially those inherited from Romanticism), they sometimes adopted a posture of extreme iconoclasm which, even in the country most closely associated with political and intellectual revolutions, did little to endear them to the *bien-pensant* majority among the reading public. It is worth recalling, in this connection, that Flaubert was prosecuted for obscenity in 1857 after the publication of *Madame Bovary*. As Harry Levin has pointed out, 'while art propagandized against the middle class, the middle class invoked morality as a weapon against art. Literature had come too close to life for comfort'.[16] The particular way in which the Realists sought to 'come close to life', however, often involved drawing on that sceptical and irreverent tradition in French culture which, as Albert Salvan has said, 'consists in jerking the reader back to sordid reality, by way of deliberate contrast with a literature cut off from real life by indulgence of fantasy'.[17] This tendency is particularly marked after realism begins to mutate into naturalism in the 1860s. In his *Essais de critique et d'histoire* (1865), Hippolyte Taine warns the squeamish reader against reading Balzac's *Comédie humaine*:

> If you are delicate, do not open his book; he will describe things to you as they are — that is, very ugly — crudely, without softening or embellishing anything . . . since he likes natural forces, and likes only them, he exhibits the grandiose deformities, the maladies, and the monstrosities which those forces produce when they are stepped up.[18]

In their famous preface to *Germinie Lacerteux*, the Goncourt brothers coupled their uncompromising assertion of the truth of the novel with a warning to the public that 'this book with its sad and violent distraction is bound to challenge [the public's] habits and upset its hygiene'.[19]

It is within this context that we must interpret the connotations which attached to the word *realismo* in nineteenth-century Spain. When Galdós reviewed Pereda's *Bocetos al temple* in *El Imparcial* in January 1877, he took great care to define *realismo* in such a way as to exclude works which showed an excessive predilection for the sordid and the ugly:

> Reina en los cuadros de Pereda una verdad prodigiosa que le coloca de lleno en la escuela llamada realista. Pero su realismo, ausente siempre por sistema de la reproducción de repugnantes fealdades morales y físicas, es como el realismo de Cervantes y de Quevedo, la real pintura de un aspecto particular de la naturaleza humana, tomando como base el eterno ideal de la justicia y de la belleza.[20]

> *(Pereda's* cuadros *are steeped in a compelling truth to life which places him fully within the realist school, but his realism systematically avoids the representation of disgusting moral and physical ugliness. Like that of Cervantes and Quevedo, Pereda's realism is the true depiction of a particular aspect of human nature, based on the eternal ideal of appropriateness and beauty.)*

Realismo, then, could be used in a morally neutral sense if suitably redefined, but as we saw earlier in this chapter it carried negative connotations when used without qualification. Even in the late 1870s, when Galdós's novels had made it possible to begin thinking of the concept in a new way, these adverse associations persisted. As late as 1880, José del Castillo y Soriano could declare that fortunately for humanity 'realism only holds sway in those abject places where crimes are hatched, and people live in constant conspiracy against the penal code'.[21] It would be erroneous, however, to suppose that Spaniards were more bigoted or pusillanimous in these matters than their European contemporaries. In Germany, Carl Bleibtreu, in a book published in 1886, accused writers who over-emphasised the animality of man of 'the same sin of untruthfulness as the unfeeling server-up of soothing-syrup'.[22] George J. Becker has amply documented the campaign of the National Vigilance Association in England in the late 1880s to suppress the sale of works by Flaubert, the Goncourts, Zola, Maupassant, Daudet, and Bourget.[23] Indeed, in some respects, Victorian Englishmen seem to have been even more fastidious in literary matters than Spaniards. The great publishing house of Macmillan refused to accept a translation of Valera's *Pepita Jiménez* because of the scene where Don Luis follows Pepita into her bedroom.[24]

Not only did Realism affront the sensibilities of the average *bien-pensant* reader, but it was widely perceived as involving a fundamental attack on religious belief. This was because the movement was closely identified with the new interest in scientific enquiry. In the *Avant-Propos* to the *Comédie humaine*, Balzac had equated social species with zoological species, drawing his inspiration from biologists like Buffon and Geoffroy de Saint-Hilaire. It was Balzac who introduced the term *milieu* into the discussion of literature, and

Taine seized on this aspect of Balzac's theory in order to re-interpret him as a precursor of Naturalism. Taine himself, in his *Histoire de la littérature anglaise* (1863–4), likened human beings to machines with cogs, and made the well-known statement that vice and virtue were products like vitriol and sugar. Claude Bernard's *Introduction à l'étude de la médecine expérimentale* (1865) was the inspiration for Zola's conception of the novel as an 'experiment'. Not for nothing did Bishop Dupanloup of Orléans regard the work of writers like Taine, Renan, and Littré as bringing about 'the overthrow of Christianity . . . and the whole moral and social order'.[25]

In the kind of intellectual climate illustrated by the foregoing statement, it is hardly surprising that critical judgements which purported to be purely literary were complicated by ideological factors, and this was no less true in Spain than elsewhere. As we saw earlier in this chapter, Galdós apparently had no difficulty in taking Aguilera's sentimentality and moralising in his stride, but when the same tendencies appear in the work of Fernán Caballero, he dismisses them as 'deplorable sanctimoniousness'.[26] Although in calmer moments a Krausist-influenced critic like Leopoldo Alas would probably have accepted Giner's distinction between didacticism and tendentiousness, in the polemical atmosphere of the 1870s, he could greet the publication of Galdós's *Gloria* with the words, 'the tendentious or philosophical novel is particularly opportune in our country at the present time'.[27] By contrast, in the somewhat more settled climate of the 1880s, the Catholic Emilia Pardo Bazán could take a more balanced view:

> Yo de mí sé decir que en arte me enamora la enseñanza indirecta que emana de la hermosura, pero aborrezco las píldoras de moral rebozadas en una capa de oro literario. Entre el impudor frío y afectado de los escritores ultranaturalistas y las homilías sentimentales de los autores que toman un púlpito en cada dedo y se van por esos trigos predicando, no escojo; me quedo sin ninguno.[28]

> (*For my part, I love the indirect teaching which emanates from beauty, but I abhor pills of morality covered with a layer of literary gilding. If I have to choose between the cold and affected crudity of ultra-naturalist writers and the sentimental homilies of those who have a pulpit for each finger and go about preaching, I prefer to do without either.*)

Pardo Bazán's statement suggests that writers and critics often had more in common with regard to their fundamental convictions about the nature of reality than their ideological quarrels allowed them to realise. The politico-religious controversies of the 1850s and later were primarily about the relationship between the citizen and the state. Insofar as the neo-Catholics' attacks on the Krausists had a doctrinal aspect, this was largely a side-effect of an essentially political position, i.e., that which identified the existing social order with the divine will. As we saw in the first chapter, however, the neo-Catholics were mistaken in regarding the Krausists as hostile to religion. What divided Krausists and traditionalists were issues like freedom of conscience and the relative importance to be accorded to external forms of worship and to inner spirituality, but both groups were at one in interpreting the world in religious rather than material terms. Both would have agreed that any view of reality which concentrated on what was empirically verifiable, and ignored the spiritual and transcendent, was partial and misleading. There were, it is true, differences in attitude towards the physical universe: for example, Giner, in an essay of 1871, explicitly repudiated the idea of the body as a prison, a notion then current in Catholic preaching.[29] However, both groups would have held that values, principles, and glimpses of ideal beauty and goodness were just as much part of reality as the observable phenomena of the material world, and that consequently spiritual awareness was a surer guide to truth than minute observation.

These assumptions had important consequences for the general understanding of literary realism. When in 1856 Fernán Caballero wrote that 'the mission of the novel is to enhance human nature, not in an exaggerated way, which would falsify it, but gently and undramatically, so as to reveal its true essence'[30] she used the Spanish word *real* to mean, not 'conformity to verifiable reality or common experience', but 'conformity to my understanding of ultimate truth, which derives from my religious beliefs'. The beliefs of a liberal writer sympathetic to Krausism, such as Aguilera, would obviously differ in many respects from those of a reactionary Catholic like Fernán, but in general terms both writers would have understood the relationship between belief and literary representation in a very similar way. Writers of opposed ideological tendencies differed in the priority which they accorded to the accurate depiction of everyday life, but in the last analysis, all adhered, in varying degrees, to the principle that external reality is the means whereby eternal values and ideals are mediated to us.

The world and the artistic imagination

At this stage in our argument, the question inevitably arises whether this understanding of the relation of literature to life merits the name 'realist' at all. Many critics would answer the question in the negative. Donald Shaw, for example, is crisply dismissive of Pardo Bazán's search for a judicious balance between the real and the ideal, which he describes as 'this rather facile *juste-milieu* sort of "realism"'.[31] In reply, however, it may be argued that the search for the *juste milieu* is part and parcel of the whole realistic attitude, in life as in literature. At the heart of any attempt to construct a truthful literary representation of the world is the difficulty of striking a balance between fidelity to the data of the material universe and of the common core of human experience, and, on the other hand, fidelity to the uniqueness of the writer's personal vision, whether this arises from ideological conviction or, more generally, from what Edmund Gosse called 'the human instinct for mystery and beauty'.[32] The truth of the matter is that as Damian Grant has aptly pointed out realism 'is not one tendency but two, the possible ultimate reconciliation of which should not obscure their practical contrareity. This opposition has in fact been only too luridly dramatized by literary polemic . . . [but] it is not simply a matter of some novels being "false" and others "true" . . . one obviously has to qualify this with the realization that different novelists may subscribe to different criteria of truth'.[33]

The two tendencies in question correspond roughly to two chronological phases in the development of the movement. Grant uses the phrase 'conscientious realism' to describe the mode which predominated during the early years, when the Realists sought to define their position in opposition to what they perceived as the Romantics' overindulgence of the imagination. Conscientious realism seeks 'to ballast its giddy imagination with the weight of truth, and submit its forms, conventions, and consecrated attitudes to the purifying ravishment of fact'.[34] Almost as soon as the realist novelist embarks on his task, however, he becomes aware of the creative work of his artistic imagination, and of the part played by his spiritual insights. As early as the 1850s, Flaubert, impatient with the writer's bondage to the world of fact, expressed the longing to write 'a book about nothing, a book with no reference to anything outside itself, which would stand on its own by the inner strength of its style'.[35] Later, Maupassant, in his preface to *Pierre et Jean* (1888), declared that 'truly great artists are those who manage to impose their private vision [*leur illusion particulière*] on the rest of humanity'. Grant calls this second phase 'conscious realism', in which truth 'is discovered and in a sense created in the very act of perception'.[36]

Grant is careful, however, to point out that conscious realism does not supplant conscientious realism, but establishes a harmonious relationship with it.[37] By about 1880, insistence on accurate depiction of the external world did not necessarily imply a materialistic philosophy, nor did respect for the claims of the imagination or of moral or religious idealism denote a desire to escape into the world of fantasy or sentiment. In the introduction to his *Le Roman russe* (1886), Eugène-Melchior de Vogüé produced a balanced view of realism which would have commanded wide assent, not only in Spain, but in the rest of Europe:

> [Realism] responds to one of our needs when it studies life with rigorous precision, when it uncovers even the tiniest roots of our actions in the fatalities that govern them; but it deceives our surest instinct when it voluntarily ignores the mystery which subsists beyond rational explanations, the possible quantity of the divine.[38]

Although the view of realism which emerged in Spain in the second half of the nineteenth century owed a great deal to the inbuilt cultural conservatism of the country, it was not, in practice, far removed from that expressed by de Vogüé. Far from inhibiting the talents of a writer such as Galdós, the late development of realism in Spain, and the fact that the theory of the novel contained so many traditional elements, proved, in the long run, to be an advantage. It ensured that Galdós would not become imprisoned in a narrow view of realism, but would remain receptive to all the insights available to him from Spanish literary tradition, from the earlier nineteenth-century debates on Realism in France and elsewhere, and from the development of the novel in his own time. Perhaps the best summary of the essential characteristics of Spanish realism as Galdós sees them is given in his introduction to the 1901 edition of Alas's *La Regenta*:

> Nuestro arte de la naturalidad, con su feliz concierto entre lo serio y lo cómico, responde mejor que el francés a la verdad humana . . . las crudezas descriptivas pierden toda repugnancia bajo la máscara burlesca empleada por Quevedo, y . . . los profundos estudios psicológicos pueden llegar a la mayor perfección con los granos de sal española que escritores como don Juan Valera saben poner hasta en las más hondas disertaciones sobre cosa mística y ascética.[39]

> (*Our art of naturalness, with its felicitous blend of the serious and the comic, corresponds more closely to the truth of human life than does the French approach. Crudities in description lose all their repulsiveness when concealed behind the burlesque mask used by Quevedo, and profound psychological studies can reach the highest degree of perfection with the grains of Spanish wit which writers like Juan Valera can incorporate even into the most profound disquisitions on mystical or ascetic subjects.*)

The mention of Quevedo here is particularly significant. As I pointed out in Chapter 1, Galdós's strictures on contemporary society in his *La Nación* articles in the 1860s owe a great deal to the moralistic perspective which Quevedo adopts in his *Sueños*. Quevedo's method of representing reality is based on the notion of *desengaño* (i.e., destruction of illusions), which involves piercing through the deceptive appearances of life in order to reveal the underlying truth, which can only be perceived by readers gifted with spiritual and moral insight.[40] It is, of course, undeniable that Galdós's brand of realism, especially as it evolved in the 1880s, is comparable in most respects to European realism at its most typical, and therefore very different from the quasi-allegorical style of the *Sueños*. Nevertheless, in keeping with his awareness of indigenous literary traditions, Galdós displays a much more insistent preoccupation than most of his European counterparts with the contrast between the authentic discernment of moral truth and conventional views of reality. The interplay between illusion and reality so characteristic of realism acquires, in Galdós's hands, a much sharper edge. It is not solely, as in Aguilera, a matter of showing the hypocrisy of the seeming-virtuous or the irresponsibility of those who live beyond their means, though both these themes exist in abundance in Galdós's novels. It involves, rather, a searching critique of those who identify 'reality' with the false appearances of Restoration social and political life, and consequently a radical calling in question of the entire moral and institutional framework of contemporary Spanish society.

Not surprisingly, therefore, Galdós was concerned from the very outset of his writing career with the complex relationship between, on the one hand, the world of phenomena, and, on the other, the world of ideas, states of mind, values and the working of the imagination. The source of this concern was two-fold. In the first place, as a working writer, he had to confront the immediate practical problem of the imagination as it affected the relationship between author, work and reader. Secondly, since he was influenced both by Quevedo's austere moralism and by the Krausist-enlightenment notion of the social and educational responsibility of the writer, he was particularly aware of the ways in which the wrong use of the imagination could interfere with a proper understanding of reality. Certain of his early fictional writings therefore reveal a deep preoccupation with the nature of the imagination, and it is to these that we must now turn.

Notes to Chapter 3

1. *Pérez Galdós, Spanish Liberal Crusader* (Madison, 1948), pp. 145–6.
2. Notably by José F. Montesinos, in his *Galdós*, 3 vols. (Madrid, Castalia, 1968–73), vol. 1, pp. 34–5, and by Laureano Bonet in his otherwise very sound introduction to his anthology of Galdós's critical essays, *Ensayos de crítica literaria* (Barcelona, 1972), p. 31. Interestingly, the notion that Galdós began his career with a clear programme of work already mapped out in his mind was already being suggested by Ramón D. Perés in 1892 (See *Ensayos*, ed. Bonet, p. 85, n. 12.)
3. For a detailed and interesting study of the nineteenth-century debate on the 'realism' of the *cuadro de costumbres*, see José Manuel González Herrán, *La obra de Pereda ante la crítica literaria de su tiempo* (Santander, 1983), especially pp. 26–31, 54–5.
4. *Ensayos*, ed. Bonet (1972), pp. 125, 127.
5. *op. cit.*, p. 125.
6. *op. cit.*, p. 118.
7. *op. cit.*, p. 129.
8. Aguilera, *Proverbios ejemplares* (Madrid, 1864), vol. 2, p. 296.
9. *op. cit.*, vol. 1, p. x.
10. *op. cit.*, vol. 1, p. vi.
11. *Ensayos*, ed. Bonet (1972), p. 118.
12. Ricardo Navas-Ruiz, ed., *El romanticismo español: Documentos* (Salamanca, Anaya, 1971), p. 267.
13. Juan Valera, *Obras completas*, vol. 2 (Madrid, Aguilar, 1949), p. 624.
14. This point is also made very cogently by Stephen Miller in his *El mundo de Galdós* (Santander, 1983). p. 67.
15. George J. Becker, ed., *Documents of Modern Literary Realism* (Princeton University Press, 1963), p. 8.
16. *The Gates of Horn* (New York, Oxford University Press, 1966), p. 73. First ed. 1963.
17. Albert Salvan, 'L'essence du réalisme français', *Comparative Literature*, 3 (1951), p. 219.
18. Trans. Becker, *op. cit.*, p. 107.
19. Trans. Becker, *op. cit.*, p. 118.
20. Quoted in González Herrán, *op. cit.*, p. 55.
21. José del Castillo y Soriano, 'García Gutiérrez', *Revista Contemporánea*, vol. 25 (1880), p. 443.

22. Trans. Becker, *op. cit.*, p.12.
23. *op. cit.*, pp. 350–382.
24. This information is contained in a letter to Galdós, dated 1 May 1883, from one Thomas H. Moore, which is now preserved in the Casa-Museo Pérez Galdós in Las Palmas.
25. Becker, *op. cit.*, p. 106.
26. *Ensayos*, ed. Bonet (1972), p. 122.
27. Leopoldo Alas, *Galdós* (Madrid, 1912), p. 42. The review may be consulted in full in Alas's *Solos de Clarín* (Madrid, Alianza Editorial, 1971), pp. 338–51. An excerpt is included in Leopoldo Alas, *Teoría y crítica de la novela española*, ed. Sergio Beser (Barcelona, Laia, 1972) pp. 91–5.
28. *Obras completas*, vol. 30 (Madrid, 1907), pp. 11–12.
29. 'Lejos de ser el cuerpo un obstáculo, una cárcel, un castigo, la raíz de todas las tentaciones infernales, según soñara el misticismo de todos tiempos, desde la India hasta nuestros días, constituye un órgano esencial y verdaderamente sagrado, que nos permite cumplir en nuestro límite una obra, aunque finita, semejante a la infinita de Dios' ('El arte y las artes', in *Ensayos* [Madrid, Alianza Editorial, 1969], p. 31).
30. Quoted in Sherman H. Eoff, 'The Spanish novel of "ideas": Critical opinion', *PMLA*, 55 (1940), pp. 531–58.
31. Donald L. Shaw, *A Literary History of Spain: The Nineteenth Century*, (London and New York, 1972), p. 153.
32. Becker, *op. cit.*, p. 393.
33. *Realism* (The Critical Idiom, no. 9), (London, Methuen, 1970), p. 19.
34. Grant, *op. cit.*, p. 14.
35. Quoted Grant, *op. cit.*, p. 17.
36. *op. cit.*, p. 9.
37. *op. cit.*, p. 59.
38. Trans. Becker, *op. cit.*, p. 322.
39. *Ensayos*, ed. Bonet (1972), p. 216.
40. For an excellent analysis of this issue, see Robert Pring-Mill, 'Some techniques of representation in the *Sueños* and the *Criticón*', *Bulletin of Hispanic Studies*, 45 (1968), pp. 270–284.

4

The Shaping Imagination

Nothing is more beautiful than reality, nor as strangely novelesque as what has actually happened (Galdós, article in La Ilustración de Madrid, *15 January 1872.)*

In *The Situation of the Novel*, Bernard Bergonzi remarks that early pioneering experiments in the craft of fiction, such as *Don Quixote* or *Tom Jones*, tend to contain a high proportion of literary criticism, or, more particularly, of reflection on the process of composition itself.[1] Galdós's early writings are no exception. Like any novelist, he was involved in a series of inescapable dualities: between subjectivity and objectivity, materialism and idealism, the self and the world. In addition, however, as an heir of the Krausist enlightenment, he was preoccupied with the relationship between, on the one hand, intuitive knowledge and the capacity of the mind to generalise, and, on the other, the empirical approach to experience. In this chapter, I want to analyse three short pieces of narrative which were all published in 1871–2. I shall not observe strict chronological order because I wish to devote more space to *La sombra*, and shall therefore deal with it last, though it was actually written earliest, in 1866.

'Un tribunal literario'

Let us consider first 'Un tribunal literario', published in 1872. This short story may be regarded as the expression in literary form of the objections to various types of popular fiction which Galdós had discussed theoretically in the 'Observaciones'. The narrator of the story is a budding novelist who is submitting his first composition to a panel of judges. We only have a fragment of the opening chapter of the young man's offering, but it is clearly a typical piece of sentimental love-intrigue. An impoverished law-student falls in love from a distance with a lady whom he can see from his garret window. To his eyes, she appears the epitome of beauty and grace, but, we are told, the idealising effect of distance is compounded by the fact that the student is short-sighted. He cannot see that his beloved's face is spotty, and that her nose is large and red. Her beautiful hair is a wig, and her figure is not so shapely on closer inspection.

At this point, the reading of the novel is interrupted when two of the judges who make up the panel intervene in tones of outrage, deploring the alleged crudity of the work. One critic in particular, a poetess, offers several suggestions for drawing the maximum amount of sentiment, intrigue and moral impact from the opening supplied by the young author. She would, for example, make the protagonist of his story 'very handsome, dark and interesting, a mediterranean type, sultry, a son of the desert' (OC 6, 461). Another critic, Don Marcos, asserts that such sugary nonsense is not for serious people, and that life should be presented in all its repulsive ugliness. He himself has written novels in which, as the narrator tells us, there are '28 hunchbacks, 80 one-eyed people, 60 ladies of easy virtue, two and a half dozen old lechers, and as many deceitful old women' (OC 6, 463). A third critic declares that since the modern world is devoid of poetry, the setting of the novel should be transferred back to the seventeenth century. He 'would open the scene with the clash of swords and cries of "'Sblood" and "'Sdeath"' (OC 6, 467).

We must, of course, avoid reading too much into what is, after all, merely a piece of humorous writing. The story is an early example of Galdós's talent for parody and ironic deflation, which was to become a key characteristic of his style of writing. Not only is the conventional theme of virtuous poverty unmercifully burlesqued, but the pompous literary judges eventually become involved in an undignified brawl. The deflationary urge is, however, held in check by humour, which prevents the parody from degenerating into the kind of inverted idealism practised by Don Marcos. We saw, indeed, at the end of the last chapter, that Galdós valued the picaresque and satirical tradition represented by Quevedo precisely because it enabled the crudities of life to be toned down by humour, 'perhaps the most characteristic expression of our race' (OC 6, 1448).

'La novela en el tranvía'

A rather more complex kind of parody is used in 'La novela en el tranvía' (1871). The narrator is making a journey by tram across Madrid, when he is joined by an acquaintance who begins to tell him a story about a certain countess he knows, who is unhappily married to a worthless husband. She is also the innocent victim of blackmail by a former butler. The narrator is at first bored by his friend's chatter, but gradually becomes interested in the details of this murky intrigue. However, having whetted the narrator's curiosity, his garrulous acquaintance reaches his stop and has to get down without finishing the story. A few moments later, the narrator's attention is caught by a fragment of a serial novel on a piece of newspaper which he has used to wrap up some books. This fragment bears a remarkable resemblance to the story he has just heard, containing as it does a scene in which a rascally butler is threatening a countess with exposure of her guilty secrets unless she will yield to him. She resists valiantly, and the fragment breaks off with Mudarra, the butler, sitting down to plot his revenge by forging a letter from the countess to her lover.

Scarcely has the narrator raised his eyes from the scrap of newspaper than to his horror he sees seated opposite him a man who answers to the physical description of Mudarra given in the serial novel fragment. When shortly after this the narrator falls asleep, he has a dream which continues the plot of the novel from the point where the newspaper extract ended. Rafael, the countess's lover, has been summoned to an assignation by means of a forged letter, and the Count finds them together, as Mudarra intended he should. With feigned bonhomie he invites Rafael to stay to tea, and insists that his terrified wife play some music on the piano. As she plays, she suddenly utters a piercing cry and the narrator wakes up.

By now the 'novel' has so taken possession of the narrator's mind that he is totally convinced of its reality. So obsessed is he, indeed, that he interprets several scraps of talk which he hears around him as having to do with the fate of the countess. Avid for more information about her tragic end, he keeps butting into other people's conversations, until his increasing agitation convinces those around him that he is mad. His irrational behaviour culminates in his giving chase to 'Mudarra' when he espies him from the tram window on the return journey. For several months, he remains in a state of temporary insanity, convinced of the truth of the story he has forged in his mind, and only gradually coming to realise how foolish his imaginings were.

The humour of this story conceals a serious point. 'La novela en el tranvía' is not just a satire on meretricious writing. It is really about the power of fiction to convince the imagination that it is 'reality', and, conversely, the power of the imagination to impose its own pattern of meaning on otherwise random events. Though it is clear that the narrator's behaviour is to some extent influenced by his reading of popular novels, he is no Don Quixote. He is, on the contrary, well aware that the fragment he has read is probably a translation of some 'absurd novel, such as [the *romans-feuilletons*] of Ponson du Terrail or Montépin' (OC 6, 489). It is really life itself which feeds his fantasies. Significantly, the starting-point is not his reading of the novel fragment, but the anecdote told to him as true by his friend. His belief in his version of the countess's story is to a large extent ostensibly corroborated by details he observes around him. As soon as he reads the fragment, he sees someone who looks exactly like Mudarra. When he awakes from his doze, he sees sitting opposite him a young man who bears a striking resemblance to the Rafael of his dream. This person is telling a friend about an incident exactly like the scene with which the narrator's dream ended. 'Rafael's' account confirms the narrator's suspicions that the husband's invitation to tea was merely a pretext to poison the guilty couple. Fortunately, 'Rafael' has recovered, but what of the countess? Was she poisoned or put to death in some other way? The narrator's curiosity is once again unsatisfied, for his two neighbours leave the tram before 'Rafael' has clarified the matter. As if this were not enough, he overhears two other people discussing a poisoning case, apparently a murder. When he is told somewhat curtly that the victim was a washerwoman, he assumes that the speakers are trying to conceal the truth from him.

If fiction can exercise this kind of effect on the mind, it is partly because truth and fiction overlap. The narrator has the evidence of his own ears to prove that there really is a countess who is being blackmailed by a former retainer, that a certain husband did force his terrified wife to play the piano while her lover almost succumbed to the effects of poison, and that an unfortunate woman has been murdered. Any of these elements, singly or in combination, would make a very interesting novel. Moreover, given that they are pieces of empirically observed reality, they are, *prima facie* at least, suitable for inclusion in a 'realist' novel, especially one inspired by the tenets of 'conscientious realism', to borrow Damian Grant's phrase. As Galdós was to write many years later, 'Wherever a man goes, he carries his own novel within him' (OC 5, 40). 'La novela en el tranvía', indeed, is almost a practical demonstration of Galdós's remark quoted in the epigraph to this chapter, that 'nothing is as strangely novelesque as what has actually happened'.[2]

An even more significant reason for the power of fiction, however, is the need of the human mind to make sense of experience by arranging random detail into intelligible categories. Though the details observed by the narrator may be, in a certain sense, 'true', they are meaningless in isolation, and therefore cry out to be interpreted in some way. Though the countess of the serial fragment and of the narrator's dream has no objective existence, her story acquires a certain coherence, albeit a specious one, as a result of the narrator's attempt to impose order on disjointed facts. In a very crude and rudimentary way, the narrator of 'La novela en el tranvía' may be said to be using his imagination 'creatively'.

It is precisely in recognising the scope of such imaginative activity that Galdós is forced to consider the limitations of Krausist literary theory, for although, as we saw in Chapter 2, Giner de los Ríos regarded the artistic imagination as an important organising principle, he saw it as essentially a revelatory rather than an inventive faculty. That is to say that the imagination, rather than creating fictitious alternative worlds, should serve to disclose the universal principles underlying the disjointed appearances of the material universe. Galdós, however, was made acutely aware, as soon as he confronted the practical problems of writing, of the inventive power of the imagination, both his own and that of his readers, and this made him strive to understand and truthfully depict its workings. Since his overall purpose was to foster true perception of reality, he had to show, vividly and sympathetically, the seductiveness of imaginative creations, while at the same time ensuring that the reader would always be able to distinguish truth from falsehood, and receive the message which he was trying to transmit. He had, in other words, to use his inventive faculty for revelatory purposes, inviting the reader to enter into a fictional world and experience its persuasive power, while encouraging him simultaneously to compare this fictional world not only with the real one but also with other fictional worlds existing in the minds of deluded characters. In short, Galdós appears to have realised at an early stage that however strong his desire to exploit literature for educational ends, his message could not be a simple one, for his task entailed the representation not only of life, but also of the imaginative processes whereby people try to reconstruct life in their minds in an effort to come to terms with it.

La sombra

Galdós's emergent awareness that the shaping and revelatory power of the imagination is inseparable from its inventive exuberance is further illustrated by *La sombra*, written, according to Galdós's own testimony, in 1866 or 1867, but not published until 1871. Critics have rightly emphasised that this short novel is an early example of Galdós's interest in the imagination, and especially in pathological mental states, which was to remain with him throughout his literary career.[3] Few commentators, however,[4] pay enough attention to one fact which seems to me crucial: that Anselmo is not only the protagonist of the story but its principal narrator. I say 'principal narrator' because there is a second, the unnamed interlocutor to whom Anselmo tells his tale and who records it in writing for us, incorporating some comments of his own on the way. Since there are no grounds for assuming that this figure is to be identified with Galdós,[5] I shall, for convenience, call him simply the narrator, to distinguish him from Anselmo.

Anselmo's gifts as a story-teller are emphasised very early in the novel. It is in story-telling that he finds his true personality: 'Narration was his habit, his temperament, his personality. When he told a story, he was himself, Dr Anselmo in his most genuine form, expressed in the most faithful way' (OC 4, 193). The other significant fact about Anselmo as story-teller is that he is narrating his account some time after the events have taken place. Though his feelings are obviously still involved, he is nevertheless capable of a certain detachment. At the end of the novel, for example, he agrees with the narrator's rational explanation of the fantastic tale which has been told.

Anselmo begins with an exaggerated and quite incredible description of the house, or 'palace', as he calls it, which he inherited from his father. If we were to believe him, the varied and sumptuous architecture, and the number and variety of the works of art collected there would make the house unique on the globe. The effect of this description is to induce in the narrator an attitude of amused disbelief, which quickly turns to boredom as Anselmo shows no sign of exhausting the vein of his inventiveness.

Extravagant as this description may be, however, it is not entirely devoid of some modicum of structuring, for it comes to rest on the detail of the painting of Paris and Helen, and this provides a smooth transition to the story of Anselmo's marriage. We learn that he was married late in life, that his wife was much younger than he, that the marriage was an arranged one, and that the couple had hardly known each other before the wedding. All the conventional literary ingredients for a drama of jealousy are there, but it is a drama which will be played out almost entirely in Anselmo's mind. One day, his wife expressed admiration for the beautiful figure of Paris in the painting, and it was shortly after this that Anselmo's hallucinations began: he saw, or thought he saw, that the figure of Paris had disappeared from the canvas.

We are not, however, told this immediately, for at this point Anselmo's narration suddenly takes on a nightmarishly melodramatic quality. Just as he is about to reveal what it was he saw (tantalisingly keeping both his listener and the reader in suspense by repeating "I saw . . . ', 'I saw . . . '), some apparatus he is using for one of his scientific experiments explodes, spreading flaming liquid over the room and setting fire to the cat, which runs about writhing in agony. Bizarre as the incident may appear, we should remember that from the narrator's point of view it belongs to life, not fantasy: the physical danger from the fire is real enough. Indeed, the bizarreness is the very point Galdós is making. The narrator, who has been listening to Anselmo's story with increasing scepticism, suddenly has a melodramatic and Hoffmannesque reality thrust into his experience.[6] Although the narrator remains sceptical after this event, Galdós has successfully alerted the reader to the existence of strange and unexpected things in life, and thereby encouraged him not to dismiss Anselmo's story out of hand.

Anselmo, when the fire has been put out, continues his narration as if nothing had happened. He tells how his suspicions of his wife's fidelity became more acute when he thought he heard a man's voice in her room. He burst in, searched the room frantically for evidence of his supposed rival's presence, and subjected the terrified Elena to verbal abuse, despite her protestations of innocence. It was on the evening after this that he noticed that the figure of Paris had disappeared from the canvas. That night, he heard voices coming from Elena's room, and when he rushed in, he was convinced that he saw and heard someone drop from the window to the garden below. He ran down to the garden, and saw a figure very like Paris taking refuge in a well, which Anselmo then filled with earth and stones. To his consternation, however, Paris came to see him next day, an incident which, needless to say, puts the greatest strain on the credulity of Anselmo's listener. After declaring that all Anselmo's efforts to destroy him were useless, because he was immortal, Paris went on to reveal something of his essential nature:

> Yo soy lo que usted teme, lo que usted piensa. Esta idea fija que tiene usted en el entendimiento soy yo. Esta pena íntima, esa desazón inexplicable soy yo. Pero existo desde el principio del mundo. Mi edad es la del género humano, y he recorrido todos los países del mundo donde los hombres han instituido una sociedad, una familia, una tribu (OC 4, 207).

> *(I am what you fear, what you think. I am that fixed obsession in your mind, that intimate suffering, that inexplicable malaise. But I have also existed since the beginning of the world. I am as old as the human race. I have traversed all the countries of the world where men have instituted a society, a family, a tribe.)*

This is only part of an extensive speech which is too long to quote in full, but it illustrates adequately the oblique and imprecise way in which Paris defines himself. Though the narrator describes him as the embodiment of Anselmo's obsession, this obsession is too complex to be encapsulated in a single word like 'jealousy', for in addition to fears about his wife's fidelity, Anselmo's state of mind is complicated by his unusually developed capacity to build a self-consistent imaginary world out of his suspicions. Moreover, Paris represents not only the temptations and anxieties which beset the married state, but also the public aspect of adultery, the prurient gossip arising from perverse use of the imagination whereby society puts its own construction on random details.[7] It is this that makes Anselmo's story seem less fantastic than at first glance, for his fears have a basis in reality. Though Paris is a hallucination, the image in Anselmo's mind bears a strong physical likeness to a young man who actually exists, one Alejandro, who is widely believed by society at large to be carrying on an affair with Elena. The question whether Elena mentally consented to the temptation to infidelity is never resolved either way, since to all intents and purposes we see the entire experience through Anselmo's eyes. It is nevertheless clear that we are dealing, not with a real adultery, but with an imagined one, imagined not only by Anselmo, but also by society, which, from the simple (and in itself morally neutral) fact that Alejandro frequently visits Anselmo's house, creates an atmosphere of scandal and vicarious excitement. The problem of the couple's reputation is no less real for being composed entirely of something which has no objective existence.[8]

The rest of Anselmo's story may be told briefly. The strain to which Elena had been subjected by Anselmo's erratic behaviour soon had adverse effects on her health, and she went into a decline which shortly brought about her death. This entailed the eclipse of Paris, since what he represented depended for its existence on the marriage bond.

By the time Anselmo reaches the end of his story, the attitude of the narrator has changed considerably. Up to the end of Chapter 2, the narrator maintains his posture of amused scepticism, frequently interrupting Anselmo to point out that his story is straying further and further away from verisimilitude. By the beginning of Chapter 3, he is sufficiently curious to want to find out what happened next, though he still has a poor opinion of Anselmo's sanity. As Anselmo's story advances into the realm of concrete social reality (his father-in-law and a friend both visit him on separate occasions to advise him about the threat to his reputation posed by Alejandro), the narrator becomes more and more deeply interested. He still, however, seeks a rational explanation for the co-existence in Anselmo's life of two areas of experience, hallucination and social reality, which overlap in such uncanny ways. Eventually he hits on an explanation:

> El orden lógico del cuento . . . es el siguiente: usted conoció que ese joven galanteaba a su esposa; usted pensó en aquello, se reconcentró, se aisló; la idea fija le fue dominando, y, por último, se volvió loco, porque otro nombre no merece tan horrendo delirio (OC 4, 227).

(The logical order of the story is the following. You found out that that
young man was paying court to your wife. You brooded over it, became
wrapped up in yourself, and cut yourself off from other people. The
obsession began to prey on you, and you eventually went mad, for there is no
other name we gan give to such a horrible mania.)

Yet despite this rationalistic approach, the very last words of the narrator
show that he has unconsciously been influenced by Anselmo's way of presenting his experience:[9]

Al bajar la escalera me acordé de que no le había preguntado una cosa
importante y que merecía ser aclarada, esto es, si la figura de Paris había
vuelto a presentarse en el lienzo, como parecía natural. Pensé subir a que
me sacara de dudas, satisfaciendo mi curiosidad; pero no había andado dos
escalones cuando me ocurrió que el caso no merecía la pena, porque a mí
no me importa mucho saberlo, ni al lector tampoco (*ibid.*).

(Going down the stairs, I suddenly remembered that I had not asked him
something very important, which ought to have been clarified, namely,
whether the figure of Paris had reappeared on the canvas, as seemed natural.
I was on the point of going back to clear up the matter and satisfy my
curiosity, but I had not taken more than a few steps when I thought that it
really was not worth the effort, because I am not interested in finding out, nor
is the reader.)

This casual detail shows how far the narrator has gone towards accepting as
possible something which is clearly fantastic. While the incident of the figure of
Paris stepping out of the painting is explicable as part of Anselmo's psychological projection of his anxieties, it is in literal terms the most far-fetched incident
in the whole story. Though the narrator hastily recalls himself to a commonsen-
se view of things, he does momentarily think of the incident in literal, not
allegorical terms.

We thus return to the point I made at the outset about Anselmo's gifts as a
story-teller. Despite his disbelief, the narrator is made aware from an early
stage of the possibility that Anselmo may be instinctively structuring the story
so as to give it a particular focus: 'Tal vez, sin saberlo el mismo doctor, había
hecho un regular apólogo . . . una pequeña obra de arte, propia para distraer y
aun enseñar' (OC 4, 197). (Perhaps the doctor, without realising it, had
constructed a well-ordered fable . . . a little work of art, which could entertain
and even instruct.) We have already had occasion to note Anselmo's instinct
for keeping his hearer in suspense, when he is about to reveal the disappearance of Paris from the canvas. As the narrator enters into the spirit of
Anselmo's story, he recognises that it has acquired a certain inner logic, similar
to that of a work of art, and that the *dénouement* will inevitably come soon.

The most remarkable indication, however, of Anselmo's creative powers is
his capacity for detachment. Though his perception of reality was distorted at

the time of the events, the almost clinical way in which he discusses the narrator's rationalised account of what happened suggests that he can evaluate his experience calmly from the distancing perspective afforded by the passage of time. In this respect, he is looking at his painful past with the eye of an artist. 'Doesn't this seem like an incredible yarn?' he asks the narrator at one of the most dramatic points of his tale (OC 4, 205). Not only does he agree with the narrator's rationalist explanation, but he admits that he deliberately reversed the actual sequence of the events in order to give a more accurate portrayal of the mental processes he lived through at the time. In other words,[10] Anselmo's story has to be presented in a way which runs completely counter to the demands of 'conscientious' realism if the inner psychological truth of his experience is to emerge. A more factual and apparently verisimilar presentation would, in effect, have obscured part of the truth.

In *La sombra* Galdós may be said to have dramatised his own practical problems in seeking to convey the complex interplay of truth and fiction, imagination and reality. The difficulty of finding a suitable literary vehicle for his artistic and educational purposes is very considerable. He has to portray, vividly and convincingly, the powerful human tendency towards fantasy while still enabling the reader to discern clearly how fantasy conflicts with the verifiable data of the external world. He also has to show how the imagination can simultaneously be a destructive source of self-torture and an inventive faculty which, by imposing a pattern on random experience, can create a new kind of truth. Galdós's solution to the formal problems posed by his theme is ingenious: he chooses as his main character someone who is not only the victim of a hyperactive imagination, but is also a consummate story-teller in his own right. *La sombra*, and to a large extent also 'La novela en el tranvía', may therefore be regarded as sophisticated pieces of 'conscious' realism, not least because of the ironic detachment whereby Galdós encourages the reader to stand at a distance from the narrator-characters, impartially observing their attempts to make sense of their strange experiences by shaping them into narrative according to certain principles of coherence.

Impartiality, however, does not entail indifference, for the reader is sufficiently involved in the experiences of Anselmo and the narrator of 'La novela en el tranvía' to be acutely aware of how difficult it is to decide on how much credence to give to intuitive knowledge on the one hand and empirical verification on the other. Both sources of knowledge can lead to an understanding of truth, and, conversely, both can lead into error. External appearances can be deceptive, and the shaping work of the imagination can lead it to the borders of insanity, as the experiences of the narrators in both stories show all too clearly. There is, however, an important difference between the two narrators, and it is that whereas the protagonist of 'La novela en el tranvía' is bewildered precisely because he is still undergoing his experience as he narrates it, Anselmo comes to his task with the benefit of whatever limited hindsight and detachment he has acquired through the passage of time, and can therefore exercise greater artistic control over his material.

It is as if Galdós were trying, in these early writings, to give himself an object-lesson in how to behave as an artist. Artistic detachment, however, is easier to maintain when the subject-matter is fanciful and remote from everyday experience. Realism, however, as J. P. Stern has reminded us, is 'programmatically connected with the world outside literature'.[11] The further the claim of literature to immediate contemporary relevance is pressed, the more likely it is that author (or reader) may succumb to the temptation to react emotionally towards a particular representation of reality as he would towards the reality itself if he actually experienced it. He may, in short, behave like the narrator of 'La novela en el tranvía' or like Anselmo when he was actually undergoing his traumatic experience of jealousy. This is precisely what happened to Galdós in the 1870s. Most of the novels he wrote during that decade focus on ideological conflicts in which Galdós as a citizen committed to fostering enlightenment was directly involved, and this leads him at times to present reality in a biased and selective way.[12] At the same time, the talent for a detached and multi-faceted depiction of life, which we have seen in the stories studied in this chapter, remains vigorous. The interest of the 1870s novels therefore lies in the tension between these conflicting relationships with reality, and we shall now look at this in detail.

Notes to Chapter 4

1. (Harmondsworth, Penguin Books, 1972), p. 222.
2. B. Pérez Galdós, *Crónica de la quincena*, ed. William H. Shoemaker (Princeton, 1948), p. 62.
3. See, e.g., Joaquín Casalduero, '*La sombra*', *Anales Galdosianos*, 1 (1966), pp. 36–8; Rodolfo Cardona, 'Introducción a *La sombra*', in Douglass M. Rogers, ed., *Benito Pérez Galdós* (Madrid, Taurus, 1973), pp. 247–55; R. Bosch, '*La sombra* y la psicopatología de Galdós', *Anales Galdosianos*, 6 (1971), pp. 21–42.
4. With the exception of Harriet S. Turner ('Rhetoric in *La sombra*: The author and his story', *Anales Galdosianos*, 6 [1971], pp. 5–19), and Sebastián de la Nuez ('*La sombra*, primera novela de Galdós', *Letras de Deusto*, 4 [1974], pp. 145–6).
5. *Pace* Turner. See *art. cit.*, p. 6 *et passim*.
6. Indeed, as Sebastián de la Nuez has persuasively argued, Hoffmann probably inspired many of the details of *La sombra* (*art. cit.*, pp. 138–9).
7. It has been well said by Harriet Turner that 'Paris reveals to don Anselmo his *social* origin and identity as a "sombra". He is an apparition fabricated by society's desires and vain suppositions' (*art. cit.*, p. 16).
8. 'Elena's adulterous desires and society's malicious speculations have also fabricated the image and hence they, too, participate in the phenomenon of insanity' (Turner, *art. cit.*, p. 17).
9. Turner also draws attention to this (*art. cit.*, p. 12).
10. As Cardona has aptly pointed out (*art. cit*, p. 254).
11. *On Realism* (London, 1973), p. 39.
12. In arguing that Galdós delayed writing the fully realistic novel adumbrated in the 'Observaciones' until 1881 (*La desheredada*) because he lacked experience or sufficient command of literary technique, Stephen Miller overlooks the direct political pressure on Galdós of the turbulent events of 1868–76, which included not only the Revolution, the abdication of Amadeo and the overthrow of the Republic but also the Carlist War and the attack on intellectual freedom represented by the Orovio education laws of 1875 (*El mundo de Galdós* [Santander, 1983], pp. 79–82).

5

The Novelist as Citizen: *Doña Perfecta*

> *The didactic assumes importance in narrative art whenever that art seeks a generalised connection with the real world (Scholes and Kellogg, The Nature of Narrative.)*

Realism and ideology

We saw in Chapter 2 that Galdós's understanding of the novelist's function in society, as expressed in the 'Observaciones', was in large measure a response to the political climate which followed immediately on the Revolution of 1868. His first full-length novel, *La Fontana de Oro* (1871), still unpublished when he wrote the 'Observaciones', had been written in 1867–8, under the influence of the controversies which immediately preceded the Revolution.[1] The events of the novel are set in the turbulent period of the 'Liberal Triennium' of 1820–23, during the reign of Ferdinand VII, but Galdós makes it clear in a foreword that he means the reader to draw parallels with the contemporary situation. This contemporary relevance, together with Galdós's personal commitment to liberal values, give rise to a certain partisanship in the presentation of characters and attitudes. *Coletilla*, the King's secret agent, is grotesquely caricatured in Chapter 2 as the representative of obscurantism and tyranny. His nose resembles the beak of a bird of prey; his mouth is a mere slit, his cheeks are so thin that they show the bones of the skull; his eyes are like those of a nocturnal bird, and his emaciated hands mere talons. The Porreño sisters are similarly caricatured, in a chapter significantly entitled 'The Three Ruins', as representatives of the absurd pomposity and religious bigotry of the minor aristocracy.

In keeping with his tendency to present issues in black-and-white terms, Galdós ended the novel with a violent and melodramatic denouement: Lázaro, the liberal hero, and his beloved Clara are surprised by *Coletilla*'s agents as they try to flee from Madrid, Lázaro is stabbed to death, and Clara dies of grief four days later. For many decades, the vehement quality of this ending was obscured by the existence of a purported 'first edition' of 1870 (the basis for modern editions), which had a happy ending, but recent research has shown convincingly that the title-page of this 'first edition' is a forgery, and that this is really a re-issue of an edition of 1892.[2]

Even in the editions which had the melodramatic ending, however, Galdós's tendency to simplify matters is modified by that capacity for aesthetic detachment and sensitivity to the complexity of reality of which we saw evidence in the last chapter. This emerges especially in the presentation of Paulita Porreño, the youngest of the three 'ruins'.[3] Paulita's characterisation is initially affected by the two-dimensional way in which Galdós portrays all three of the Porreño sisters as representatives of attitudes which he scorns. She has given herself over to devout practices since childhood, and has a deserved reputation for saintliness and asceticism. But when she meets the handsome and dashing Lázaro, she finds her mysticism crumbling. Her hopeless love for him is not only poignantly portrayed, but also reveals Galdós's instinctive talent for presenting human behaviour realistically as well as moralistically. In the conversation between Paulina and Lázaro in Chapter 42 the words and actions of the characters are natural and convincing because they arise, not from the representative aspects of their roles, but from their temperaments and from the circumstances in which they find themselves. Lázaro now appears, not as a paladin of liberalism, but as a somewhat obtuse young man who is blissfully unaware of the disturbing effect of his presence in awakening Paulita's latent sexuality, and who remains uncomprehending even when she tries to make her desperation explicit. She, for her part, comes close to acquiring tragic status because she has been given a glimpse of a richer and more authentic existence which she is fated never to enjoy: 'God has deceived me: he has made me see that the virtue of which I was so proud was only a sham, and that my seeming perfection was madness. . . . There can be no greater perfection than that offered by domestic life' (OC 4, 180).

Galdós's emerging capacity for realistic presentation is also revealed in the way in which Lázaro (in all editions of the novel) is shown progressing from idealism to gradual disillusionment. He discovers at an early stage that the world is not moulded according to his naive assumptions, when his first attempt to capture the sympathies of the habitués of the *Fontana de Oro* cafe is a resounding flop. Gradually he becomes aware that the noble ideal of freedom ostensibly espoused by the club has been corrupted by greed and hatred. Though his second speech is a success, its consequences appal him, for he suddenly realises that he has unwittingly been used by the King's agents to provoke an outburst of murderous violence.

That Galdós structured *La Fontana de Oro* around a sharp polarisation of good and evil in response to contemporary political events can be corroborated negatively, so to speak, by the fact that in the calmer climate of 1885, he replaced the original violent ending with a more sober and realistic one in which Lázaro is shown achieving happiness by marrying Clara, abandoning his political ambitions, and settling down to a quiet rural existence. Even in the revised edition, however, all the other elements of vehemence and melodrama remain, with the result that the novel illustrates very clearly the dilemma of the writer of morally serious, educative literature who seeks to give his readers a truthful view of issues in which he is personally involved. He may reject the rigid and simplified visions of reality proferred by conservative ideologies on the grounds that they do not do justice to life as it is actually lived, but in the last analysis his personal preferences may lead him into just the kind of simplification and partisanship which he professes to deplore. Realistic comprehensiveness, that 'undertaking to look all the relevant facts of a situation in the face', as Stern has expressed it,[4] is difficult to reconcile with a clear didactic stance, however respectable the values the author is trying to defend. Failure to opt single-mindedly for either a didactic or a realistic focus may lead to a fundamental duality of purpose at the heart of the literary work.

Such a duality is adumbrated by *La Fontana de Oro*, but it is even more clearly displayed in *Doña Perfecta* (1876). This novel was written shortly after the end of the Second Carlist War (1872–6), and has traditionally been interpreted as depicting the conflict between liberalism and reaction which gave rise to that war. This view has recently been reiterated by J. E. Varey, who declares that the novel 'can be described as "littérature engagée"'.[5] Nevertheless, a critical consensus has begun to emerge which would see the presentation of reality in *Doña Perfecta* as more complex than has hitherto been supposed. Varey himself concedes that the novel 'foreshadows in many respects the great novels of Galdós's mature period',[6] a notion which has been developed even further by other recent critics. Richard Cardwell, for example, while recognising that 'many of Galdós's techniques are crude and aesthetically insensitive' decisively rejects the suggestion that *Doña Perfecta* displays the partisan defence of a thesis, and declares that Galdós is seeking 'to eschew catechising and to attempt an unbiased presentation of reality'.[7] Cardwell illustrates his argument by various references to the employment of ironic techniques which, he claims, make it difficult for the reader to discern the author's precise sympathies.

One can only agree with the main thrust of Cardwell's interpretation, for there are, indeed, insuperable obstacles to a reading of the novel which would see it as consistently didactic or schematic. Varey draws attention to various symbols, such as the train which wakes the countryside with its whistle and, as he sees it, 'heralds the symbolic dawn'.[8] These symbols, however, are not sufficiently sustained to be effective for didactic purposes, for Galdós seems always to be aware of the reverse side of the piece of reality he is presenting. Thus, as Varey himself points out, the symbolic 'dawn of progress' is followed by the description of the travellers riding back through time, into the heart of Spain.[9] An even clearer example of this realistic avoidance of schematism occurs when Galdós describes the entry into Orbajosa of central government troops sent to forestall a Carlist rising in the area. At first, the liberal soldiers are said to represent vigour and energy by contrast with the decrepitude of the city: 'The city was all sadness, silence and age, the army joy, noise and youth'

(OC 4, 458). Only a few lines later, however, Galdós reminds the reader of the well-known capacity of soldiery for committing outrage against the civilian population:[10]

> Si un ejército es gloria y honor, una reunión de soldados puede ser calamidad insoportable . . . todo fue miedo y desconfianza en la episcopal ciudad, que, si bien pobre, no carecía de tesoros en gallinas, frutas, dinero y doncellez, los cuales corrían gran riesgo desde que entraron los consabidos alumnos de Marte (OC 4, 458).

> *(If an army is glory and honour, a gathering of soldiery can be an insufferable disaster. The episcopal city was full of fear and mistrust, for although poor, it was not devoid of certain treasures in the form of chickens, fruit, money and maidenheads, all of which were at great risk from the moment the aforementioned pupils of Mars arrived.)*

This instinct for realism displays itself above all in the presentation of the main characters. Though Galdós may have wished initially to cast them in symbolic or representative roles (the names Perfecta, Rey, Inocencio Tinieblas suggest this), he endowed them with a complex cluster of psychological, social and economic motives which make their behaviour appear more authentic. Though Doña Perfecta comes in time to appear as a monster of fanaticism and cruelty, she is not initially perceived as such by her nephew Pepe Rey, who for the first third of the novel is above all conscious of her kindness and affection. Though she soon begins to have doubts about Pepe's suitability as a husband for her daughter Rosario, she is nevertheless at first determined to go through with the match, precisely because of the firmness of her religious and moral convictions, which will later prove so destructive. The reason is that she has made an agreement with her brother, Pepe's father, that Pepe and Rosario will marry, and is determined to keep her word. It is only when Don Inocencio, the reactionary local priest, begins to fill her mind with lurid stories of Pepe's alleged wickedness and atheism that Doña Perfecta decides to prevent the marriage taking place. Even so, Don Inocencio later admits (Chapter 26) that he had to work very hard to overcome Doña Perfecta's scruples of conscience.

It is not unreasonable to cast Don Inocencio as the villain of this episode. Varey says that the potential for a harmonious relationship between Pepe, Doña Perfecta and Rosario is frustrated because 'the dark shadow of don Inocencio falls upon them, and discord is sown'.[11] It is, indeed, as a 'larga opacidad negra' (a long, black, opaque shape) that he is first seen by Pepe through the glass of the dining-room door. But it would be oversimplifying Don Inocencio's role to see him exclusively as the personification of religious fanaticism, for his behaviour springs in large measure from social and economic causes which have very little to do with religion. Don Inocencio has a widowed niece, María Remedios, who is utterly devoted to her son, Jacinto, and desperately anxious to help him to break free from the circle of poverty within which the family has always moved.[12] She has set her heart on Jacinto's marrying Rosario, and of course regards Pepe as an obstacle to this ambition.

It is probable that Don Inocencio would have undertaken his campaign of detraction against Pepe in any case, but the major motivating force is the pressure brought to bear on him by his niece.

María Remedios's ambition for her son turns into an obsession which leads her eventually to plot Pepe's downfall in a more direct and vigorous way. Though it is Doña Perfecta who, on the spur of the moment, orders the Carlist faction leader Caballuco to shoot Pepe, it is María Remedios who, with the connivance of Don Inocencio, persuades Caballuco to shadow Pepe's movements in the first place. Critics have rightly emphasised that Pepe is the victim not solely of religious fanaticism, but of María Remedios's scheming.[13] What is less often recognised, however, is the vividness and insight with which Galdós shows María Remedios's obsession as arising directly from an impoverished life:

> Una cosa es tener hijos y pasar amarguras por ellos, y otra cosa es cantar el *gori gori* en la Catedral y enseñar latín en el Instituto . . . ¡Pobrecito niño de mis entrañas! Tener tanto mérito y vivir condenado a un pasar mediano, a una condición humilde; porque no, señor tío, no se ensoberbezca usted . . . Por más que echemos humos, siempre será usted hijo del tío Tinieblas, el sacristán de San Bernardo . . . , y yo no seré nunca más que la hija de Ildefonso Tinieblas, su hermano de usted, el que vendía pucheros, y mi hijo será el nieto de los Tinieblas . . . , que tenemos un tenebrario en nuestra casa y nunca saldremos de la oscuridad, ni poseeremos un pedazo de terruño donde decir: 'Esto es mío', ni trasquilaremos una oveja propia, ni ordeñaremos jamás una cabra propia, ni meteré mis manos hasta el codo en un saco de trigo trillado y aventado en nuestras eras . . . ; todo esto a causa de su poco ánimo de usted, de su bobería y corazón amerengado (OC 4, 487–8).

> *(It is quite one thing to have children, with all the trouble that brings, and quite another to sing all those mournful chants in the Cathedral and teach Latin in the high school. My poor darling boy! To have so much ability, and to be condemned to a mediocre pittance, to a humble state in life. Because you needn't go getting a swelled head, uncle. We can give ourselves all the airs we like, but you will always be the son of Old Darke, the sexton of St. Bernard's, and I'll never be more than the daughter of your brother, Darke the ironmonger, and my son will be the Darkes' grandson. We've a regular patch of Darke in our house, and we'll never get out of it, never have a piece of land where we can say, 'That's mine', never shear a sheep of our own, nor milk a goat of our own. I'll never plunge my arms up to the elbow in a sack of corn threshed and winnowed on our threshing-floor. And it's all the fault of your spinelessness, stupidity and milk-and-water complacency.)*

This passage is a superb example of how perceptive Galdós could be about the real social and economic factors which influenced people's behaviour, even in the midst of a novel with so many didactic and schematic features. María Remedios is no longer merely a structural device for bringing about Pepe's murder, but becomes socially 'typical' in the sense in which Lukács uses the word. To be socially typical in Lukács's terms is very different from being a two-dimensional representative character such as *Coletilla*, who is little more than a whipping-boy for the reactionary obscurantism which Galdós wishes to castigate. María Remedios's typicality, on the other hand, arises from the way in which her motives, actions, and what she says in the above conversation with her uncle, encapsulate, with total naturalness and no sense of authorial manipulation, all the social and economic circumstances of her life. Perhaps the clearest symptom of the way in which Galdós's mind could suddenly grasp the deeper implications of an initially crude image is María Remedios's pun on the family name 'Tinieblas', which was presumably meant in the first instance to symbolise Don Inocencio's obscurantism. Here, by contrast, it expresses, in a very concrete way, María Remedios's realisation that as the widow of an impoverished artisan, she cannot escape from the circle of indigence in which she is imprisoned. By deepening the associations of the name, Galdós has contrived at a stroke to remind us of the rigidity of social barriers, the lack of economic prospects for Jacinto which confers a kind of perverse reasonableness on the otherwise unsuitable match between himself and Rosario, the lack of prospects especially for women in María Remedios's situation, and the backwardness of a society in which the only path towards social advancement is the Church. Furthermore, Galdós presents all these implications not only with insight but with sympathy as well. There is a special appeal in the warm, natural image of María Remedios plunging her arm into a sack of grain, for by contrast with so many of Galdós's fatuous social climbers, her desire for a better life is seen as wholesome and legitimate.

The temptation of intrigue

This scene, however, does not constitute more than a fleeting moment, and its implications are not developed in the novel as a whole. For the most part, María Remedios's role is to be part of the intrigue which brings about Pepe's death. Galdós does not always handle this intrigue with great finesse: 'poorly, and at times, grossly overplotted' is how Cardwell has aptly described it.[14] Nevertheless, Galdós's presentation of the chain of events is a good example of how his didactic interests are overlaid and modified by his grasp of the unpredictable and complicated nature of life. In a real sense, Pepe brings about his own downfall by various errors of judgement which ultimately prevent him from being a purely symbolic or idealised figure. Undoubtedly, some of the hostility which greets him in Orbajosa springs from rejection of the 'atheistic' values he represents, or is believed to represent. But he also provokes some of this enmity by his tactlessness and, on occasion, sheer bad manners.[15] True, Don Inocencio sedulously tries to nettle him at their first meeting, but Pepe's reaction goes far beyond the bounds of outspokenness and becomes positively provocative: 'In short, my dear Canon, the word has gone out to get rid of all the absurdities, lies, illusions, day-dreams, sloppiness and prejudice which obfuscate man's understanding' (OC 4, 423).

This somewhat mischievous side of Pepe's character eventually costs him his life. To clarify this, we need to trace carefully the events of the last half of the novel (Chapter 18 to the end), because the 'overplotting' to which Cardwell refers leads Galdós to cultivate an atmosphere of mystery which risks confusing the reader. What happens is as follows. When the government troops arrive, Pepe discovers that one of the officers is an old friend, Pinzón, and decides to enlist his help in circumventing Doña Perfecta's opposition to his marriage to Rosario. Pinzón is billeted in Pepe's room at Doña Perfecta's, while Pepe goes to stay at an inn in the town. Pinzón then begins to play on Doña Perfecta's natural fears of the soldiery by emphasising the ferocity of the commander, Batalla. He also tells Doña Perfecta that Batalla and Pepe are firm friends, and, by stressing that the two are often to be seen together, contrives to suggest that they are hatching something.

Pepe's object in remaining in close liaison with the army contingent is two-fold: he later refers to it as 'my half-serious, half-joking alliance with the army' (OC 4, 493). The serious purpose is to protect himself against the hostility of the town. The lighter one is to wreak, as he sees it, an innocent revenge on Doña Perfecta and her entourage by giving them a fright. But it is precisely at this point that his plan begins to go awry. The hints disingenuously dropped by Pinzón, doubtless egged on by Pepe, Pepe's flaunting of his connection with the army, and his veiled threats to Doña Perfecta to make Rosario his by fair means or foul, all convince Doña Perfecta that her house will be stormed by soldiers, and Rosario carried off by force. This produces the first of many undesirable results, for the ill-considered provocation of Doña Perfecta and her retainers brings about in Orbajosa an upsurge of Carlist activity which otherwise would not have happened. Though Varey is undoubtedly right to say that it is Doña Perfecta who directly stirs up the Carlist faction,[16] he glosses over Pepe's prior responsibility for this event. The newspaper report at the beginning of Chapter 21 makes it clear that though there is some rebel activity in nearby Villajuán, there is no danger of a rising in Orbajosa itself. Caballuco reveals later that he has promised the provincial governor that he will not lead his men out. Doña Perfecta, however, convinced that her house is about to be attacked, goads Caballuco into going back on his word.

It is true that Pepe admits in a letter to his father that at one time he felt justified in removing Rosario from her mother's house by force, because she was being kept there against her will, but there was never any question of doing so under cover of a military assault, and in any case he comes to realise the wisdom of proceeding with moderation. However, this laudable resolve is overtaken by another of the unforeseen consequences of his rashness. Disguised in Pinzón's greatcoat, Pepe has gone to Doña Perfecta's house and made Rosario his mistress, presumably hoping thereby to force Doña Perfecta, if not to welcome his marriage to her daughter, at least to acquiesce in it. Don Inocencio, however, suspects that Rosario has already yielded to Pepe, and shares Doña Perfecta's anxiety about a probable abduction. For these reasons he urges María Remedios to abandon all hope of Jacinto ever marrying Rosario. Out of acute chagrin and a desire for revenge, María Remedios tries to persuade Caballuco to intimidate Pepe into leaving the town. She and Caballuco follow Pepe one night when he is secretly going to give a message to Rosario. There is a scuffle between the two men in Doña Perfecta's garden, and Pepe is shot dead by Caballuco.

My object in tracing the plot in such detail is to show that for a large part of the novel Pepe is seen to have credible and ordinary human weaknesses which, despite the somewhat melodramatic ending, make him more convincing than a consistently didactic focus would do. Something comparable happens in the characterisation of Doña Perfecta. While for much of the time she is presented as a monster of tyranny, her opposition to the marriage of Pepe and Rosario arises from beliefs about the moral dangers of the match which, though wrong-headed, are deeply and sincerely held. As we have seen, Don Inocencio is able to work on Doña Perfecta's sensitive conscience by suggesting that Rosario's eternal salvation will be in jeopardy if she marries an 'atheist'.

At least in origin, then, Doña Perfecta's hostility to Pepe is not merely a personal quirk or a piece of gratuitous vindictiveness, but the consequence of her deepest convictions. Even more significantly, however, these convictions are not merely personal but social and institutional as well. One of Pepe's most serious mistakes is to ignore the fact that he is pitting himself, not just against a stubborn and authoritarian woman, but against the whole weight of collective belief and traditon.[17] The ancient patriarchal customs of the countryside may seem an aberration to the enlightened mind, but they represent a reality which is too solidly grounded to be swept away by a handful of soldiers. As Doña Perfecta explains to the somewhat slow-witted Maria Remedios,

> Mi sobrino no es mi sobrino: es la nación oficial, Remedios; es esa segunda nación, compuesta de los perdidos que gobiernan en Madrid, y que se ha hecho dueña de la fuerza material; de esa nación aparente, porque la real es la que calla, paga y sufre; de esa nación ficticia que firma al pie de los decretos, y pronuncia discursos, y hace una farsa de gobierno, y una farsa de autoridad, y una farsa de todo (OC 4, 481–2).

> (*My nephew is not my nephew: he is the official state, Remedios. He is that second nation, made up of the blackguards in the Madrid government, that has taken over the physical force of the country. [What they hold] is a travesty of a nation, for the real one is the one that says nothing, pays up and suffers. The other is a fictitious nation, which signs decrees, makes speeches, and carries on a pretence of government, a pretence of authority, and a pretence of everything.*)

Much as Galdós may strive to make Doña Perfecta appear odious to the reader, she is here articulating views similar to those which he himself expressed in other writings. Laudable as Pepe's liberal attitudes may be,

Galdós instinctively recognises that there is a sense in which Doña Perfecta and those around her embody the 'real' Spain more authentically.[18]

Taking a stand

These glimpses of complexity in the presentation of Doña Perfecta, Pepe, Don Inocencio and María Remedios make it impossible to regard *Doña Perfecta* as a consistently didactic novel. In the last analysis, however, these instances of realistic comprehensiveness are contradicted by Galdós's clear preference for the enlightenment values which Pepe represents. The portrait which Galdós gives at the beginning of the novel emphasises Pepe's moral excellence, intelligence and rationality:

> Su persona bien podía pasar por un hermoso y acabado símbolo, y si fuera estatua, el escultor habría grabado en el pedestal estas palabras: *inteligencia, fuerza* . . . en la conversación urbana sabía mostrar una elocuencia picante y discreta, emanada siempre del buen sentido y de la apreciación mesurada y justa de las cosas del mundo. No admitía falsedades ni mixtificaciones, ni esos retruécanos del pensamiento con que se divierten algunas inteligencias impregnadas de gongorismo (OC 4, 416).

> *(His person could appropriately be taken as a handsome and well-wrought symbol. If he were a statue, the sculptor would have engraved on the plinth the words 'intelligence, strength'. In polite conversation he could display a discreet and racy eloquence which was always the product of sound sense and a judicious and exact appreciation of the things of the world. He could not abide insincerity or any attempt to mislead, and had no time for the tortuous wit that amuses certain excessively baroque minds.)*

It is true that, later in the same paragraph, Galdós seems to admit that Pepe is less than perfect, when he says that 'he would sometimes use the weapon of sarcasm, and not always in moderation', but this is presented in such a way as to turn Pepe's outspokenness into a virtue: only the vulgar horde will be offended by it. The tone of the description as a whole is unmistakably that of symbolic idealisation of character, and there is no serious attempt on Galdós's part to undermine it by irony.

Galdós's approval of Pepe's attitudes is balanced by rejection of what Doña Perfecta represents. In tracing her detailed portrait in Chapter 31, he forgets the warm welcome she gave Pepe at the beginning of the novel, and her qualms of conscience when she is put under pressure by Don Inocencio. Instead, he emphasises her hardness and her capacity for hatred: 'No sabemos cómo hubiera sido doña Perfecta amando. Aborreciendo, tenía la inflamada vehemencia de un ángel tutelar de la discordia entre los hombres (OC 4, 495–6) (We do not know what a loving Doña Perfecta would have been like. In her hate, she had all the fiery vehemence of a guardian angel of human discord).

It is possible that this inconsistency in the characterisation of Doña Perfecta arises in part from the fact that the novel was first written to be published in instalments in the *Revista de España*. Leopoldo Alas reports that Galdós admitted to him in a letter that 'I began without knowing how I was going to develop the subject. I wrote it in fits and starts, that is to say, in bits, as it came out'.[19] However that may be, it is clear that Galdós's capacity for conveying the complexity of reality is ultimately limited by his tendency to take sides in current controversies, and to see issues of religious tolerance and freedom of conscience in stark black-and-white terms. This tendency remains strong even in the revised edition of the novel. As the late C. A. Jones pointed out, the original version, published serially in the *Revista de España* between March and May 1876, laid heavy emphasis on the cynicism and heartlessness of Doña Perfecta, and culminated in a ludicrously melodramatic ending which showed her and María Remedios getting their just deserts. After Pepe's death and Rosario's committal to a mental asylum, Doña Perfecta, seemingly unaffected by either of these tragedies, is about to marry Jacinto, twenty-two years her junior, thereby fulfilling María Remedios's long-standing ambition. But while the meat is being prepared for the Easter celebrations, Jacinto slips on a piece of offal in Doña Perfecta's kitchen, and dies impaled on a knife held by his mother.[20] One can only agree with those critics, such as Varey, who regard the ending of the revised edition (published as a volume later in 1876, and the basis for all subsequent editions) as more satisfactory.[21] The new ending simply records, in the form of letters to a friend from Doña Perfecta's absurd amateur-historian brother, Don Cayetano, that Pepe died, apparently by his own hand, and that Don Inocencio and Doña Perfecta have begun to decline into melancholia. As has been well said, there is a bitter irony in this ending, for 'by the intermediary of the historian, the lie supplants truth'.[22] Jones, however, surely went to unwarranted lengths in claiming that 'the broad-minded tolerance of Galdós's later work is glimpsed much more in the later version of this novel, which could be interpreted as a plea for moderation on the part of both the conservative and the progressive, despite the survival of the cryptic final chapter',[23] for this final chapter takes the form of a sententious moral to the effect that 'that is all we can say for the time being about those who seem good and are not' (OC 4, 501). The simplified moral perspective to which this statement testifies is reinforced by the fact that Galdós clearly wishes us to see Doña Perfecta's and Don Inocencio's ill-health as punishment for their responsibility for Pepe's death and Rosario's insanity. Moreover, in the revised edition, Galdós did nothing to alter the basically dramatic structure of the novel which, as Varey reminds us, would, in 1896, make it easy to adapt it to the stage.[24] The 'clash of opposing forces' which Varey rightly sees as the principle of the novel's organisation[25] is well illustrated by the chapter headings, which Galdós carried over from the serialised edition into the later versions: 'Discord Grows'; 'Discord Grows until it Turns into Open War'; 'Deadly Combat. Strategy'; 'Awake, Steel!'

When, therefore, critics such as Richard Cardwell tell us that *Doña Perfecta* is the work of a sophisticated ironist with an impartial approach to reality,[26] I remain, in the last analysis, unconvinced. Arnold Penuel is closer to the truth of the matter when he says that 'several of the ambiguities in *Doña Perfecta* are confusing rather than meaningful'.[27] Rather than ambiguity, one should perhaps speak of a dichotomy. Galdós, in my view, could not make up his mind whether to be an overtly committed writer, devoting himself single-mindedly to the defence of Krausist-enlightenment values by showing the results of this or that character's professed ideology, or to pursue his reformist aims more subtly by depicting in all their complexity the forces which actually determine human motivation and behaviour. He brings now one perspective to the fore, now the other, with consequent detriment to the coherence of the work. Having allowed the plot and the characters to develop to a certain point under their own momentum, thereby illustrating some of the economic, social and sexual motives which influence human relationships in rural Spain, he suddenly recalls himself to a simplified version of his educational duty, and strives to ensure that the reader's predominant impression will be of the dark and destructive potential of religious fanaticism.

This inconsistency of purpose is all the more noticeable because, as we saw in the previous chapter, Galdós displayed early the capacity for considerable skill and subtlety in the presentation of complex realities. But his artistic aptitude could conflict with his sensitivities as a citizen when the pressure of contemporary political polemics caused him to interpret his reformist and educational purpose in a narrow way. It was only by a process of trial and error extending over several years that Galdós came to realise that he could best pursue his educational and reformist aims as an artist rather than as a citizen. That is to say that the cultivation of a less overtly *engagé*, more comprehensive vision of reality was to prove a more effective means of making his readers understand the nature of the society in which they lived. In this process of trial and error, the writing of *La desheredada* in 1880–81 was to be a crucial stage, and it is to an examination of this novel that the next chapter will be devoted.

Notes to Chapter 5

1. As Juan López-Morillas has shown in his lucid study of this novel in his *Hacia el 98: Literatura, sociedad, ideología* (Barcelona, Ariel, 1972), pp. 45–77.
2. See Walter T. Pattison, '*La Fontana de Oro*: Its early history', *Anales Galdosianos*, 15 (1980), pp. 5–9. Pattison's article provides a useful corrective to the received view that Galdós replaced the happy ending with a violent one in 1871. For this earlier interpretation, see Florian Smieja, 'An alternative ending of *La Fontana de Oro*', *Modern Language Review*, 61 (1966), pp. 426–33; and Joaquín Gimeno Casalduero, 'Los dos desenlaces de *La Fontana de Oro*: Origen y significado', *Anejo de Anales Galdosianos* (Los Angeles, Del Amo Foundation, 1978), pp. 55–69.
3. See Juan López-Morillas, *Hacia el 98*, pp. 73–5; also Stephen Gilman, *Galdós and the Art of the European Novel, 1867–1887* (Princeton University Press, 1981), p. 48.

4. *On Realism* (London, 1973), p. 32.
5. *Pérez Galdós, 'Doña Perfecta'* (Critical Guides to Spanish Texts, no. 1, London, Grant & Cutler, 1971), p. 9. See also Stephen Miller, *El mundo de Galdós* (Santander, 1983), p. 103.
6. *loc. cit.*.
7. 'Galdós's *Doña Perfecta*: Art or argument?', *Anales Galdosianos*, 7 (1972), p. 44.
8. *op. cit.*, p. 10.
9. *op. cit.*, pp. 14–15.
10. Ricardo Gullón, in his over-optimistic reading of this episode, overlooks this critical stance on Galdós's part. See his *Técnicas de Galdós* (Madrid, Taurus, 1970), pp. 47–8.
11. *op. cit.*, p. 25.
12. Anthony Zahareas is one of the few critics to recognise that it is the 'social being' of the main characters 'that determines their consciousness about Spain, progress, the past, economic development, morality, etc.' (See his 'Galdós's *Doña Perfecta*: Fiction, history and ideology', *Anales Galdosianos*, 11 [1976], p. 41.) A similar point is made by Demetrio Estébanez Calderón in his '*Doña Perfecta*, de B. P. Galdós, como novela de tesis', *Boletín de la Biblioteca de Menéndez Pelayo*, 55 (1979), p. 126.
13. See, e.g., Varey, *op. cit.*, pp. 55–7; also Cardwell, *op. cit.*, pp. 36–7.
14. *op. cit.*, p. 35.
15. Stephen Gilman calls this his 'tragic flaw' (*op. cit.*, p. 388).
16. *op. cit.*, p. 63.
17. Ricardo Gullón calls him, with some justification, 'quixotic' (*op. cit.*, pp. 44–5).
18. Compare López-Morillas's remarks on *El audaz*, in *Hacia el 98*, p. 28.
19. Leopoldo Alas, *Galdós* (Madrid, 1912), p. 27.
20. C. A. Jones, 'Galdós's second thoughts on *Doña Perfecta*', *Modern Language Review*, 54 (1959), pp. 570–3.
21. *op. cit.*, pp. 68–9.
22. R. Gullón, *op. cit.*, p. 54.
23. *op. cit.*, p. 573.
24. *op. cit.*, p. 77. As is well known, Galdós's earliest literary efforts in the 1860s were in drama, though his first plays were never performed. In correspondence with Mesonero Romanos in 1877, he described the novelistic genre as 'sucesor del dramático, que muere' (quoted by José F. Montesinos in his *Galdós*, 3 vols. [Madrid, Castalia, 1968–73], vol. 1, p. 251.) Several years later, Galdós was to write, in a letter to Narcís Oller (8 December 1884), of 'el pícaro arte teatral, que hemos mamado en la leche y que se aposenta en la médula de nuestros huesos sin que lo podamos echar de nosotros'. But, he went on, 'es preciso que nos curemos de esto, y que extirpemos el infame virus' (W. H. Shoemaker, 'Una amistad literaria: La correspondencia epistolar entre Galdós y Narciso Oller', *Boletín de la Real Academia de Buenas Letras de Barcelona*, 30 [1963–4], p. 267).
25. *op. cit.*, p. 77.
26. *op. cit.*, pp. 32, 44. A similar assumption that Galdós's irony is conscious and sustained is made by Peter Standish in his 'Theatricality and humour: Galdós's technique in *Doña Perfecta*', *Bulletin of Hispanic Studies*, 54 (1977), pp. 223–31.
27. 'The problem of ambiguity in Galdós's *Doña Perfecta*', *Anales Galdosianos*, 11 (1976), p. 86.

6

A Nation of Dreamers: *La desheredada*

> *We are in every respect dreamers,*
> *incapable of descending from re-*
> *gions of the most sublime folly ('Ob-*
> *servaciones sobre la novela contem-*
> *poránea en España').*

> *These poor madmen are ourselves*
> *(*La desheredada, *Chapter 1).*

The limits of rationalism

The ideological conflicts which form the background to *Doña Perfecta* retained most of their force throughout the 1870s. Although there was no serious recrudescence of Carlism after the ending of the Second Carlist War in February 1876, the specifically religious aspects of these ideological controversies continued to provoke bitter and deep divisions. Religion had been a matter of intense public debate since the Constituent Cortes of 1869, when the position of the Church, and particularly its control of education, had been one of the major issues separating conservatives and liberals. After the Restoration, Cánovas, for all his good intentions, could do little to prevent the watering-down of the intellectual freedoms which the Revolution had won. In 1875, his Education Minister, Orovio, began supervision of courses and textbooks in the Central University to see if they accorded with Catholic teaching, a move which provoked the resignation of the leading Krausist professors. In the following year, a new Constitution was enacted which, though guaranteeing the private practice of religions other than Roman Catholicism, established Roman Catholicism as the religion of the state, and explicitly prohibited other forms of public worship. Even these restrictive provisions did not prevent Cánovas being condemned for his excessive liberalism by the Pope and the Archbishop of Toledo.[1]

Galdós's *Gloria*, published in two volumes in January and June 1877, springs directly from this context of religious controversy. *Gloria*, indeed, may be said to be more consistently didactic than *Doña Perfecta* or *La Fontana de Oro*, for whereas in these earlier novels the reader's interest is sustained by exciting plots involving political conspiracies, personal enmities, or civil war, *Gloria* is characterised by discursive *longueurs* in which characters debate this or that aspect of their religious beliefs. This discursiveness is only one of the many formal problems which Galdós created for himself in the writing of *Gloria*, for the novel is an unsatisfactory blend of ideological polemics, lyrical and elegaic elements culled from ill-digested reading of minor romantic works, and contrived melodramatic climaxes.[2] As Pereda was to remark in connection with *La familia de León Roch* (1878), 'if there is anything which falls outside the domain of art, and which by its very nature is soporific as well as dangerous, it is religious controversy'.[3]

Despite its shortcomings as a novel, however, *Gloria* is not without interest, because it provides confirmation of how Galdós's thinking about progress and enlightenment (as understood by the followers of Krausism), was developing in the 1870s, as he reflected on the reality not only of contemporary Spain, but of human nature in general. We have already seen in our examination of *La sombra* and 'La novela en el tranvía' that Galdós was well aware from an early stage in his career that human perception could be an unreliable guide to the understanding of reality, since empirical observation could be misled by deceptive appearances, and reason confused by the re-shaping work of the imagination. In the end, however, he asserts, at least implicitly, that the mind can be re-educated to a true view of things, either by reflection on experience (the case of the narrator of 'La novela en el tranvía') or by coming to terms with it through narration (Anselmo). We have also seen that in *Doña Perfecta* Pepe Rey's effectiveness as a standard-bearer of Krausist-enlightenment values is undermined by his passionate and impetuous behaviour. This, however, arises not solely from his own shortcomings but, more immediately, from the intolerable stress and provocation to which he is subjected by others, and does not entail calling in question the fundamental correctness of his beliefs.

By the time of writing *Gloria*, however, Galdós has become more pessimistic about the probability of the spread of rationality. It is true that the novel ends with a clarion call to the reader to strive for the harmonious union of different religions through love, but by then the search for the ideal religion of the future has driven the Jewish hero, Daniel Morton, insane. It is not solely reactionary Catholicism which is the enemy, but religious bigotry in general, 'a dread monster which defiles both history and philosophy with its horrible paws' (OC 4, 681). To be sure, Daniel wins Gloria's love not only by reason of his personal attractions but also because of his urbane and generous mind, but when he falls foul of the intransigence of institutional Catholicism, he displays a visceral loyalty to his Jewish identity no less uncompromising than Gloria's Catholic convictions.

This increasing readiness to question the optimistic assumptions which Galdós had expressed in the 'Observaciones' and other writings of the early 1870s also appears in his next novel, *Marianela*, written early in 1878, within a few months of completing *Gloria*. The Marianela of the title is a poor, physically-deformed girl who acts as guide to Pablo Penáguilas, a handsome young man who has been blind since childhood. Pablo comes to love Nela for her kindness and gentleness, but the situation changes radically when a successful operation restores his sight. He immediately falls in love with his beautiful cousin Florentina, who is the first person he sees when his bandages are removed. Nela, fearing that Pablo will reject her because of her physical ugliness, goes into hiding, and, though she is forestalled in an attempted suicide, dies broken-hearted soon afterwards.

Though *Marianela* is undoubtedly a minor novel, it makes an important philosophical point about the problematical nature of reality. Though Pablo has pretensions to 'enlightening' Nela by educating her out of her primitive animistic understanding of nature, his rational idealism leads him to interpret the world in an excessively naive way, and he remains out of touch with the facts of experience. Because he proceeds by deduction from quasi-Platonic universals, he cannot grasp that moral and spiritual qualities are not always accompanied by physical beauty. Though when he is blind he correctly perceives Nela's beauty of soul, when his sight is restored he does not recognise her until she touches his hand. Conversely, he is captivated by Florentina's physical beauty, and fails to realise the extent of her insensitivity and selfishness.[4]

Not only does the novel call in question rationalist idealism but it also raises doubts about the scientific, empirical route to knowledge. Teodoro Golfín, the oculist who restores Pablo's sight, thereby unintentionally precipitating Nela's death, confesses ruefully at the end of the novel that he can only treat eyes, not passions: 'we know nothing but superficial phenomena', he adds (OC 4, 754). Golfín, indeed, far from representing the liberating force of science, as Casalduero has suggested[5], is the principal instrument whereby Galdós challenges conventional rationalistic views of reality, and suggests that true understanding may be independent of the possession of physical vision: at the very beginning of the novel, Golfín has to rely on the blind Pablo to guide him safely through the mines of Socartes by night.

By 1878, in short, Galdós was prepared to make explicit his sense of the limitations both of rationalist idealism and of empiricism. Consequently, his last novel on the theme of religious discord, *La familia de León Roch*, written later that same year, has a somewhat different tone from *Doña Perfecta* or *Gloria*. León Roch is a Krausist intellectual, engaged in private scientific research, whose rational approach to life is not proof against his falling passionately in love with a fanatically pious Catholic. Contrary to his expectations, he is totally unable to persuade his wife María to adopt his own 'enlightened' views, finding that the 'exquisite clay' which he had hoped to mould has the consistency of flint. Though Galdós clearly sympathises more with León's general outlook than with that of María or her family, he takes an even more detached view of León than he does of Pepe Rey. León's predicament has as much to do with his own naivety and lack of understanding of other people as with his wife's intolerance. This emerges at the beginning of the novel, when he totally fails to appreciate that the erratic behaviour of Pepa Fúcar is due to the fact that she is head over heels in love with him. Francisco

Giner de los Ríos was surely right to regard León as indecisive and obtuse, though he overlooked the fact that it was probably Galdós's intention to present him as such.[6] Even if in the event Galdós ultimately took an ambiguous attitude towards León, partly sympathetic, partly ironic, the thrust of the novel as a whole is to demonstrate that rational self-discipline is an unsound basis for coping with human prejudice and passion.

In its presentation of the reality of human motivation, therefore, *León Roch* marks an important stage on the way to the more developed realism of the 1880s. In other respects, too, the novel may be regarded as transitional, for it does not focus exclusively on the religious conflict associated with León's marriage, but embraces the whole network of his family relationships. His in-laws, the Tellerías, are effete and debt-ridden aristocrats vainly struggling to keep up their accustomed life-style, and this takes us immediately into the sphere of social and economic reality, of the kind which will bulk even larger in the novels of the 1880s. Indeed, it is only because León's artisan father has, by dint of hard work and opportune investment, left him enough capital to be financially independent, that he is able to pursue his researches.

Galdós's interest in these connections between social role, ideology and economic infrastructure was to increase markedly in the years after 1878. Indeed, it is likely that even as he wrote *León Roch* he was already thinking of abandoning the exploration of religious discord. In this he was influenced partly by the opinions of critics and friends whose judgement he respected, such as Francisco Giner, who in December 1878 published in *El Pueblo Español* a very unfavourable review of the first volume of *León Roch*. Galdós wrote to Pereda on 4 March 1879 that in view of the poor reception of the first two volumes of *León Roch*, he had decided to start on a new work which had been simmering in his mind for some time.[7] Pereda's reply could only have confirmed him in this resolve, for in addition to his predictable anger at what he regarded as the unfair portrayal of Catholicism, Pereda now adduced a new and compelling argument about how Galdós's obsession with religious discord would affect his standing with the reading public:

> You have at last run your head smack against a stone wall. You have challenged the reading public of this country with six volumes of unorthodoxy, full of sustained controversy about something which is not of ultimate importance. The truth of the matter is that unbelievers are utterly indifferent to these things, but true believers will never forgive you for the unjustified and unjustifiable rancour with which you are fighting to uproot from their hearts what they most value, without offering them anything in return.[8]

Naturalism and 'La desheredada'

By a fortunate historical accident, new possibilities for the novel were already opening up. About six weeks after Pereda's letter was written, Manuel de la Revilla published in the *Revista de España* an article on Naturalism which, according to Pattison, was 'the first thorough and impartial analysis [of the concept] by a Spanish critic'.[9] A month later, the *Revista Europea* published an article on Zola's *L'Assommoir*. By the following year, the first Spanish translations of *L'Assommoir* and *Nana* had appeared,[10] and from then until the mid-1880s Naturalism was the subject of lively controversy in Spanish literary circles.

Naturalism was in essence an attempt to develop and systematise what had previously been the 'general tendency to mimetic Realism'.[11] This systematisation involved grafting on to Realism certain assumptions derived from philosophy and, more particularly, from the sciences. The most important of these assumptions originated in Darwin's *The Origin of Species* (1859), which was first translated into French in 1862. As Furst and Skrine have aptly pointed out, this book produced 'the most radical self-assessment in human history. Instead of being creatures of the Divine Will, [men] had to accept themselves as only slightly above the animal level, and life itself as a continuous struggle'.[12] Zola's thinking derived ultimately from Darwin's theories which, combined with notions of heredity derived from sources such as Prosper Lucas's *Traité philosophique et physiologique de l'hérédité naturelle*, produced a fundamentally pessimistic view of man as the victim of biological drives, a creature of heredity and environment. From Claude Bernard's *Introduction à l'étude de la médecine expérimentale* Zola culled the idea of the novel as an experiment in which the novelist places characters with a certain *tempérament* in a given setting, and impartially records the results.

The Naturalists' concentration on the ugly and sordid aspects of life was deplored in Spain, as it was in France and in Victorian England, and the scientific pretensions and deterministic philosophical framework of Naturalism were either imperfectly understood or sedulously ignored. Instead, most Spanish critics chose to regard Naturalism as Realism in a new guise, and discussion in Spain tended to be conducted from within the assumptions developed in the 1860s and 1870s regarding the desirable balance between the real and the ideal.[13] Nevertheless, a significant change in the intellectual climate had taken place since 1868. Whereas the reception of Realism prior to that date was largely hostile, there was a much greater willingness around 1880 to take seriously whatever might be valuable in Naturalism. Zola's claim, in the preface to *L'Assommoir* (1877), that his novel was 'la morale en action', and his description of Naturalists, in *Le Roman expérimental* (1880), as 'moralistes expérimentateurs' struck a sympathetic chord in all those writers and critics who, from differing ideological bases, were striving to make the novel the vehicle for the serious study of society.[14] It followed from this notion of serious study that the novelist should above all be an observer and analyst. As Emilia Pardo Bazán stated in the preface to her novel *Un viaje de novios* (1881),

> The novel has ceased being mere entertainment . . . and has been elevated to a serious study, which can be social, psychological, or historical, but always remains a study. It follows from this that the novelist needs observation and analysis no less than the adornments of the imagination.[15]

Galdós's *La desheredada* (1881) shows that like most of his contemporaries he adopted an eclectic attitude towards Naturalism,[16] accepting those aspects which he could most readily harmonise with his long-standing moralistic concerns, and rejecting excessive pessimism and philosophical rigidity. There is, therefore, no radical change from Galdós's previous practice, for the roots of his reaction to Naturalism lay in the Krausist enlightenment. This is reflected above all in his theory of character. Sanz del Río had written that 'harmonic rationalism recognises all the principal constituents of man and the world: reason and the senses; principles and the facts of experience; spirit and matter'.[17] Galdós's views as reflected in *La desheredada* are very similar: he gives due weight both to man's biological drives and to his spiritual and imaginative aspirations, believing that moral and mental health consists in the achievement of a balance between the two. What happens when this balance is disrupted is well illustrated by the contrasting characters of the protagonist, Isidora Rufete, and her brother Mariano, who represent 'two opposing kinds of moral disorder, for if she lived foolishly aspiring to higher things, he instinctively sought out what was coarse and low' (OC 4, 1077).

Galdós was wise enough to recognise that not everyone found it easy to establish the desirable balance, but he still believed that in the last analysis it was each individual's responsibility to strive towards it. This is why he ultimately shrinks from denying free will, even though at first glance there is much in *La desheredada* that could plausibly suggest a Naturalist emphasis.[18] The madness of Isidora's father and uncle is paralleled by her own delusions of grandeur, which, combined with her reading of sentimental novels, lead her to believe that she and Mariano are the illegitimate children of a high-born lady. Her spendthrift ways and her inability to face reality lead her gradually into poverty and prostitution. Mariano inhabits the squalid haunts of down-at-heel bullfighters and petty criminals, contracts epilepsy, and dies on the scaffold after an attempt on the King's life.

In the novel as a whole, however, there is little evidence of the characteristic Naturalist conception of the personality as a *tempérament*, a kind of blank cheque on which heredity and environment imprint a limited and predictable range of traits. Though Galdós's characters are to some extent predetermined by their innate qualities, the process whereby they acquire these qualities is not investigated. More significantly, though a person's inborn nature may incline him to make good or evil use of the opportunities offered by circumstances, there is nothing inevitable about the choices he makes. In other words, circumstances can make moral decisions more difficult, but the individual is not forced in any particular direction. This is borne out by Galdós's presentation of Mariano's moral development:

> La soledad en que vivía le despabiló antes de tiempo. Su precocidad para comparar y hacer cálculos no era común en los chicos amparados por padres o parientes cariñosos. Porque el abandono y el vivir entregado a sí propio favorecen el crecimiento moral en el niño. De la índole nativa

depende que este crecimiento sea en buen o mal sentido, y es evidente que los colosos del trabajo, así como los grandes criminales, han nutrido su espíritu en una niñez solitaria (OC 4, 1100).

(The solitude in which he lived had given him a premature astuteness. His precocious gift for comparing and calculating would not have been so common in children sheltered by loving parents or relatives. If a child is neglected and left to fend for himself, he will experience an [unusually rapid] moral development. His inborn nature determines whether this development takes a good or evil course: it is obvious that the spiritual formation of abnormally hard-working people, and of great criminals, has taken place in the context of a solitary childhood.)

As has been well said by one critic, 'Galdós is frequently at pains to emphasise the moral perfectibility of Mariano'.[19] Positive qualities as well as negative ones may develop from the same unpromising background. This is corroborated by Galdós's treatment of two characters who live in the same environment as Isidora and Mariano respectively, but who unlike the Rufetes remain untainted. Emilia Relimpio, though affected in her youth by the prevailing climate of vanity and social pretension, manages to outgrow these faults, and to find emotional fulfilment in marriage to an honourable and competent artisan, Juan José Castaño. Though many of the children growing up with Mariano in the poor southern suburbs of Madrid will probably turn into criminals, his friend *el Majito*, the son of a semi-invalid mother and a drunken and violent father, is a paragon of grace, vitality and charm (OC 4, 998).

It follows from Galdós's understanding of personality that the individual is capable of moral choice, and therefore responsible for his actions. Galdós goes to considerable lengths to ensure that this moral dimension is kept constantly before the reader's mind, even to the extent of injecting frequently a strong note of explicit censure. We are told, for example, about Mariano's 'low and disgusting parody of the dissipations of the upper class' (OC 4, 1084). We are invited to take a critical attitude towards Isidora's 'delirious ambition' (OC 4, 1030), the 'ill-concealed fatuousness' with which she speaks to her medical student friend, Augusto Miquis (OC 4, 993), and what Augusto later calls her 'highly imperfect moral state' (OC 4, 1154).

This insistent moralism is incompatible with a rigid determinism of heredity or physical environment: as we have seen, *el Majito* demonstrates that both these factors can be overcome. It is true that Isidora's delusions seem at first glance to be hereditary, but, as we shall see, the pattern of self-deception is too generalised in the novel to admit of a specific biological determinant in her case. The function of Tomás Rufete's madness is rather to cast an ironic light over Isidora's aspirations from the outset. Moreover, Galdós wishes to press home his moral criticisms at both the individual and national levels, and he therefore presents the Rufetes as a small part of a larger continuum of folly and self-indulgence which ultimately embraces the whole of society.

Social determinism

It is, however, in this area of social interaction that Galdós's greatest indebtedness to Naturalism is to be observed. There is in *La desheredada* a deterministic influence in the moral and social environment, though, as the case of Emilia Relimpio suggests, this determinism is not absolute. As Galdós would later make one of his characters say, in *Fortunata y Jacinta,* 'We are enmeshed in a mechanism, and we only move as we are moved by the wheel next to us' (OC 5, 491). Michael Gordon has dealt very perceptively with the ways in which Mariano is subjected to a 'long saga of moral subversion' by other characters, each of whom 'is responsible for depositing a few drops of their own moral poison in Mariano's weak and untutored mind'.[20] This responsibility extends even to Mariano's bluff and well-meaning employer, Juan Bou, who feeds Mariano with anarchist clichés, thereby unwittingly pushing him in the direction of the abortive assassination attempt which leads him to the scaffold.

One can only agree with Gordon's assertion that this diffusion of moral responsibility is one of the respects in which Galdós's novel stands apart from Zola's. Nevertheless, it is important to recognise that the context within which moral criticism operates in *La desheredada* is a vision of society which is quite new in Galdós's work, and which is almost certainly due to the influence of Naturalism. Society is now seen as an organic whole, a network of relationships of mutual dependence and mutual influence. Admittedly, the 'Observaciones' had centred on the idea that the novel should reflect the turbulence of a society in a state of flux, a concept which may owe something to Balzac's statement, in the 'Avant-propos' to the *Comédie humaine* (1842), that society moulds people differently, depending on the particular environment in which they act, creating 'as many different types as there are species of animal in zoology'.[21] Balzac, however, bulks less large in the 'Observaciones' than one might at first suppose, for in that essay Galdós thinks of society as essentially the sum total of the ethical problems which beset the individual. Besides, as we have seen, Galdós's practice up to 1881 was shaped predominantly by Spanish literary and cultural influences. It is as if the debate on Naturalism acted as a catalyst, enabling him to make use of whatever insights he could gain from Balzac and from European Realism in general. Zola himself had set the example by making more explicit Balzac's conception of man in society. In *Le Roman expérimental* (1880), he wrote that one of the most important functions of the novel was 'to show man living in the social *milieu* which he himself has created, which he modifies daily, and in the midst of which he experiences in turn a continual transformation'.[22]

There is a further respect in which Galdós's presentation of society in *La desheredada* is affected by Naturalism. Auerbach points out that for the Goncourts and Zola, 'realism had to embrace the whole reality of contemporary civilization, in which to be sure the bourgeoisie played a dominant role, but in which the masses were more conscious of their own function and power. The common people in all its ramifications had to be taken into the subject matter of serious realism'.[23] Though Galdós is more interested in the better-off artisans and the self-made professionals than in the labouring classes, the fact remains that there is a perceptible extension downwards of the frontiers of his world, as Alas was quick to recognise.[24] For the first time, Galdós pays detailed attention in this novel to the sphere of work: the functioning of Juan Bou's printing and engraving business; Miquis's training as a doctor and his success in establishing a good practice; Juan José Castaño's manufacture of orthopedic appliances; Mariano's operating a treadmill in a ropeworks for a wage of 18 *reales* a week.

Galdós's new understanding of society as a living organism is given most striking expression in the following description of the Puerta del Sol on a typical evening:

> La Puerta del Sol, latiendo como un corazón siempre alborozado, le comunicó [a Isidora] su vivir rápido y anheloso. Allí se cruzan las ansiedades; la sangre social entra y sale, llevando las sensaciones o sacando el impulso. Madrid a las ocho y media de la noche, es un encanto, abierto bazar, exposición de alegrías y amenidades sin cuento. Los teatros llaman con sus rótulos de gas, las tiendas atraen con el charlatanismo de sus escaparates, los cafés fascinan con su murmullo y su tibia atmósfera, en que nadan la dulce pereza y la chismografía. El vagar de esta hora tiene todos los atractivos del paseo y las seducciones del viaje de aventuras. La gente se recrea en la gente (OC 4, 1058).

> *(The Puerta del Sol, beating like a heart in a constant state of pleasurable excitement, communicated its rapid, panting life to Isidora. Various kinds of anxiety meet there. The social blood flows in and out, bringing sensations and releasing impulses. At half past eight in the evening, Madrid is a delight, an open bazaar, an exhibition of countless joys and pleasures. The gas signs of the theatres, the showiness of the shop-fronts, exercise a strong attraction. The murmur from the cafés, and the warm atmosphere, carry the fascination of pleasant idleness and gossip. Wandering about at that hour has all the attractions of an ordinary outing and the allurements of a journey in search of adventure. People simply enjoy each other.)*

It is significant that precisely at this point in the novel, Isidora, having had her claims to aristocratic parentage rejected by the Marquesa de Aransis, sees opening up before her a new vista of untasted pleasures and excitements. The surge and flux of city life, with its protean and unpredictable quality, dramatises this vision of new possibilities in a particularly effective way.[25]

La desheredada, then, displays Galdós's eclectic attitude towards Naturalism: he rejects biological determinism, but accepts that individual behaviour may be influenced by circumstances. Moreover, he is concerned with a wider range of life than in any previous novel. For the remainder of this chapter, I shall be concerned with two structural devices (literary reminiscences and Isidora's relationships with other characters) whereby Galdós keeps control of his more diverse material, while at the same time conveying his moral message clearly.

Given that in this novel Galdós is preoccupied with the imaginative side of the Spanish character and, more generally, with the tendency of all human beings to idealise reality, it is not surprising that the shadow of Don Quixote lies long over the work. Isidora's uncle is called Santiago Quijano-Quijada, and lives in La Mancha not far from El Toboso, unconsciously imitating the knight in his whole manner of life: he is unmarried, semi-retired, and spends most of his time reading novels (OC 4, 1060). To mention Don Quixote, however, is to be aware of differences as well as similarities. If we compare the world of heroic legend in which Don Quixote's imagination moves, and the childish sentimentality of the kind of romantic fiction which Isidora reads, we are made aware immediately that she is the product of a much more mediocre and prosaic world. Moreover, tilting at windmills may be merely foolish, but self-deception and self-indulgence are morally pernicious. The characters of *La desheredada* have recourse to 'literary' worlds of the imagination, not because they wish to restore the chivalric order, but because they seek to construct images of themselves which flatter their self-esteem and enable them to evade moral responsibility for their actions. The point is well illustrated by the following passage, which describes Isidora's frame of mind as she takes one of her frequent and short-lived decisions to support herself by her own work:

> El trabajo no la degradaba. ¡La honrada pobreza y la lucha con la adversidad cuán bellas son! Pensó, pues, que la costura, la fabricación de flores o encajes le cuadraban bien, y no pensó en ninguna otra clase de industrias, pues no se acordaba de haber leído que ninguna de aquellas heroínas se ocupara de menesteres bajos, de cosas malolientes o poco finas (OC 4, 1074).

> *(Work was not degrading. How beautiful are honest poverty and the struggle against adversity! She concluded, therefore, that sewing, or making flowers or lace suited her well, and she did not contemplate any other sort of work, because she could not remember having read that any of those heroines occupied herself in lowly tasks, or in coarse or smelly things.)*

The multiplication of instances of this sort of behaviour in the other characters is Galdós's principal method of suggesting that these weaknesses exist on a national scale.[26] Don José Relimpio has an almost hieratic conception of his accounting abilities, but never actually works to earn anything on which he can practise these skills. His son Melchor is full of grandiose schemes for making a quick fortune, but overlooks the simplest plan of all, which is 'to work at some skill, profession or craft, by which means he could earn some money, from one peseta upwards' (OC 4, 1021). It is, however, in the presentation of the relationship between Isidora and Joaquín Pez that Galdós most successfully combines the individual and national dimensions of human folly. The famous burlesque sermon which forms most of Chapter 12 of Part 1 establishes clearly that Joaquín and all his family are representative of the corruption of nineteenth-century Spain. Joaquín's younger brother, Adolfito, who at the age of fifteen has acquired a sinecure in the civil service, himself draws up an instruction to the customs authorities at Irún to allow through, duty free, a velocipede which he has ordered from London, an action which draws from Galdós the remark, 'What a flash of infantile genius, revealing in embryo a future Spanish statesman!' (OC 4, 1035). The Peces, indeed, pullulate throughout Spanish public life, from the highest positions in departments of state, down to the level of village schoolmaster. The head of the dynasty, Don Manuel Pez, is linked with every national manifestation of corruption and frivolity. He is a

> lumbrera de la Administración, fanal de las oficinas, astro de segunda magnitud en la política, padre de los expedientes, hijo de sus obras . . . la primera cabeza del orbe para acelerar o detener un asunto, la mejor mano para trazar el plan de un empréstito, la nariz más fina para olfatear un negocio . . . hombre, en fin, que vosotros y yo conocemos como los dedos de nuestra propia mano, porque más que hombre es una generación, y más que persona es una era, y más que personaje es una casta, una tribu, un medio Madrid, cifra y compendio de una media España (0C 4, 1033).

> *(A luminary of the Administration, a beacon of the office-world, a star of the second magnitude in politics, the source of much official paper, a self-made man . . . the best brain in the world for pushing forward or holding up a piece of business, the best hand for drawing up a plan for a government loan, the best nose for sniffing out a deal . . . a man, in short, whom you and I know like the fingers of our hand, because he is less a man than a whole generation, less a person than an epoch, not so much an individual as a caste or tribe, constituting half Madrid, which in turn sums up and epitomises half Spain.)*

For all their representative quality, however, the Peces lack the fuller social typicality displayed by María Remedios at certain moments in *Doña Perfecta*. The language of the above passage is more reminiscent of Enlightenment satire, especially as continued by the Romantic satirist Larra, whom Galdós greatly admired. Whenever any member of the Pez family appears, he behaves in a predictable and stiff-jointed way, because his sole function is to illustrate the social vices which Galdós wishes to castigate by means of humour and bitter irony. Nowhere, however, do the Peces' characters or the concrete situations in which they move embody social and economic determinants with the vividness and authenticity which we saw in our analysis of María Remedios's conversation with her uncle in Chapter 27 of *Doña Perfecta*. In other words, the increased social concreteness and density which Galdós derived from Naturalism operates, in *La desheredada*, within the limits imposed by the author's predominant concern with ethical principles and values. It is entirely in keeping with this concern that, in another part of the novel, the deprived children of the squalid suburb where Mariano is brought up should be presented rhetorically, as constituting a serious moral problem for the future: they are 'a seed-bed from which might perhaps spring useful citizens, but certainly idlers and criminals' (OC 4, 1001).

Reality and aspiration

As we have seen, the presentation of Isidora is affected to some extent by this satirical emphasis, and there is no doubt that she displays at an individual level some of the fatuousness which Galdós depicts as the characteristic national vice. As a result, some critics have seen her role as essentially no different from the representative one assigned to the Peces. Leopoldo Alas, for example, wrote that 'the generic aspect is still to the fore here. Isidora is still "a woman of the people" in such-and-such circumstances, rather than an individualised study of a female personality'.[27] Other, more recent, critics, have even gone so far as to see her as an allegory of Spain.[28] Such interpretations, however, overlook the way in which Isidora is made to appear as the victim of what I have called the determinism of social relations. Nothing in her past experience equips her to discern Joaquín's real nature, and when his apparent elegance and charm seem to confirm the expectations formed by the novelettes she reads, when, furthermore, Joaquín speaks of their relationship in clichés drawn from just such literature (e.g., OC 4, 1091–2), she has no defence against his readiness to exploit her for sensual gratification and financial gain. In certain respects, therefore, she outgrows the role Galdós appears initially to have assigned her, as the butt of his generalised moral criticism, and instead becomes an example of individual suffering.

Galdós's sympathy for Isidora, however, goes even further than this, for her delusions of grandeur arise not solely from her fatuity and self-deception, but also in part from a certain natural refinement of sensibility which makes her recoil from the harsh realities of life. As has been well said, 'Isidora's virtues are at one with, and inseparable from, her major failing — her inability to content herself with reality as she finds it'.[29] In this respect, Isidora has much in common with Flaubert's Emma Bovary and with Ana Ozores, the protagonist of Alas's *La Regenta* (1884–5). Each of the three novels reflects, to a different degree, an ambiguous reaction on the author's part to the dilemma of a sensitive heroine placed in situations which offend her sensibility. This ambiguity is clearly illustrated in the following outburst by Isidora:

¡Oh Dios!, ¡quién fuera cursi, quién fuera populacho! . . . Me pasaría la vida haciendo cigarros, lavando ropa, comiendo bodrio, durmiendo en un jergón asqueroso; me casaría con un cafre hediondo, tendría un chiquillo cada año, viviría como una bestia, toda imbécil, toda sucia . . . ; ¡pero sería feliz, como son felices los que no conocen el dinero! . . . ¿Qué es mejor: ser una piedra, que se está donde la ponen, o ser una criatura racional, que quiere ir a alguna parte? ¡No sé, no sé! (OC 4, 1124).

(Oh, I wish to God that I were common, I wish I were riff-raff! I would spend my life making cigarettes, washing clothes, feeding on swill, sleeping on a filthy mattress. I would marry some stinking brute, I would have a baby every year, I would live like an animal, moronic and dirty. But I would be happy, as only those who do not know what money is can be! Which is better, to be a stone, which stays where it is put, or to be a thinking being, who wants to get somewhere? I don't know, I really don't know!)

On the one hand, Galdós has not entirely dropped his tone of mocking irony (Isidora is perhaps too ready to assume that she is not 'common'), but on the other, he allows us to see that Isidora's dilemma is agonisingly real. Who can blame her for not wanting to 'pay for today's bread with tomorrow's eyesight' (OC 4, 1017), as the Relimpio sisters have to do, with their endless hours spent sewing by the feeble light of a smoky oil-lamp? Though Isidora later comes to envy the peace and cheerful contentment of the Castaño household, she cannot suppress a certain involuntary repugnance at the sights and smells associated with the making of orthopaedic appliances, which is the foundation of Juan José's and Emilia's prosperity: the house is 'honest, virtuous, a model of decency, industry and Christian living, but pervaded by a vague smell of uncured sheepskin, poorly-lit and full of the hum and clatter of activity' (OC 4, 1112). The plain fact is that, however attractive the ideal of virtuous poverty may be in theory, the reality is often an affront to a civilised sensibility. The encounter with the smelly and unkempt serving-maid in José Relimpio's house brings this home to Isidora very forcibly (OC 4, 1097).

It is at such points that Galdós decisively parts company with the Naturalists, for the Naturalist belief in social and biological determinism is incompatible with the Krausist notion of the perfectibility of human individuals and the superiority of the human spirit to the material world. The reason why Isidora manages to retain so much of Galdós's sympathy even when he is being critical of her vanity is that she refuses to regard the trivial and squalid realities of everyday life as normative. Gordon has traced very perceptively the various ways in which Isidora's sensitivity is compared favourably with the more coarse-grained attitudes of Mariano, Juan Bou, and her leech-selling aunt, Encarnación Guillén.[30] Perhaps the most striking example of this contrapuntal technique occurs in the scene where Isidora discovers to her horror that her brother spends the entire day in total darkness, working a treadmill in a rope-factory. Superficially, the scene has features in common with the Naturalist 'set-piece' descriptions of industrial conditions in the late nineteenth century. In fact, however, the emphasis falls almost entirely on Isidora's and her aunt's contrasting perceptions of the situation. As it twists and creaks, the taut, quivering rope becomes an image of Isidora's distress of mind. Encarnación, on the other hand, can only say matter-of-factly that it will do Mariano no harm to find out what it costs to earn one's bread. It is true that, elsewhere in the novel, Encarnación's earthy common sense provides a refreshing contrast to Isidora's self-indulgent day-dreaming, but it is clear from this scene that it is

Isidora who is capable of the wider and more humane range of feeling (OC 4, 982).

In addition to this capacity for feeling, Isidora comes to appear as someone imprisoned in a situation which she does not fully understand, and this brings her a step closer to acquiring tragic status. For most of the novel, she has no way of knowing that the documents on which she bases her claim to blood-relationship with the Aransis family are forged. Neither does she realise that even if she achieved her ambition, it would not necessarily make her any happier, for her supposed 'grandmother', the Marquesa de Aransis, is a stern and uncompromising lady whose harshness drove her erring daughter to an untimely death, and who for many years has eked out a solitary, remorse-filled existence. Consequently, when Isidora visits the Palacio de Aransis in the Marquesa's absence (in Chapter 10 of Part 1), her lack of experience and education cause her to set an exaggerated value on the beauty and refinement of what she sees. In fact, as Galdós has been at some pains to point out in the previous chapter, the house is mediocre, in disrepair and uncomfortable.

In the long run, however, Galdós shrinks from committing himself wholly to a tragic perspective. As a result, his overall view of Isidora contains an ambiguity deeper than that of *Madame Bovary* or *La Regenta*. Flaubert ultimately came down on the side of critical detachment, and Alas was to opt for a tragic emphasis. Galdós, however, hesitates between these two poles. Gordon sees this as a positive virtue:

> The apparent conflict between this tragic vein and the aforementioned didacticism, and the negative attitude to Isidora which it reflects, is not a question of the novel lacking unity or [of?] purpose or of Isidora having succeeded in transcending the limitations of Galdós's original intentions: rather it is a reflection of the Cervantine dualism underlying Galdós's whole approach to the conflict between illusion and reality.[31]

Persuasive as this view may be, however, I remain convinced that in the last analysis the reader is left not knowing whether to view Isidora as a tragic victim or a silly fool, because Galdós fails to choose decisively between satirising the social vice of pretentiousness (of which she is the main exemplar) and dramatising the psychological dilemmas which arise from the conflict between material and spiritual needs.[32]

It remains true that, taken separately, each of the two perspectives employed in the novel functions very effectively. As Alas rightly remarked, 'Galdós's talent has matured'.[33] As a social satire, *La desheredada* offers a compellingly lucid vision of how a particular vice runs through the whole fabric of society, influencing not only dress, life-styles and personal relationships, but also the political system, and ultimately the whole way in which people in a particular time and place perceive reality. As a piece of psychological realism, the novel opens up avenues of investigation, the importance of which Galdós had not hitherto realised: the influence of upbringing on character, the degree to which one's moral life is shaped by social pressures, and the conflicting demands of the workaday world and the realm of fantasy. In these respects, *La desheredada* points forward to the fully mature works of the mid-1880s. Galdós's failure, however, to integrate satisfactorily psychological and social realism is an index of how far the broadening influence of Naturalism was still constrained within the framework of his reformist, Krausist-enlightenment outlook. Not for nothing did Galdós dedicate the novel to schoolmasters, whom he described as the physicians of society (OC 4, 965).

The gain in artistic sophistication represented by *La desheredada* compared to, say, *Gloria* is nevertheless real and profound, and this lends some validity to the conventional view that this novel inaugurates a new phase in Galdós's writing. From another perspective, however, *La desheredada* may more appropriately be regarded as the last work of Galdós's apprenticeship. His next novel, *El amigo Manso* (1882) was to be his first major masterpiece, because for the first time he achieved a perfect match of subject and form, and a perfect integration of educational purpose with a densely-textured social and psychological realism. The achievement of this integration is in no small measure due to his willingness to subject Krausist-enlightenment ideology itself to critical scrutiny. The results of this process will be the concern of the next chapter.

Notes to Chapter 6

1. Raymond Carr, *Spain 1808–1939* (Oxford, 1966), pp. 350–52.
2. For a detailed study of the various literary sources on which Galdós probably drew in composing *Gloria*, see Walter T. Pattison, *Benito Pérez Galdós and the Creative Process* (Minneapolis, University of Minnesota Press, 1954), pp. 18–113.
3. Soledad Ortega, ed., *Cartas a Galdós* (Madrid, 1964), p. 76.
4. Peter Bly, 'Egotism and charity in *Marianela*', *Anales Galdosianos*, 7 (1972), p. 59.
5. *Vida y obra de Galdós* (Madrid, Gredos, 1961), pp. 61–3.
6. Francisco Giner de los Ríos, *Ensayos* (Madrid, Alianza Editorial, 1969), p. 69.
7. Carmen Bravo-Villasante, 'Veintiocho cartas de Galdós a Pereda', *Cuadernos Hispanoamericanos*, nos. 250–252 (Oct. 1970–Jan. 1971), p. 31.
8. Ortega, *op. cit.*, p.75.
9. Pattison, *El naturalismo español* (Madrid, 1965), p. 14.
10. *op. cit.*, p. 52.
11. Lilian R. Furst and Peter N. Skrine, *Naturalism*, The Critical Idiom, no. 18, (London, Methuen, 1971) p. 8.
12. *op. cit.*, p.16.
13. The writings of Revilla, Alas and Emilia Pardo Bazán typify this tendency very well. See Pattison, *Naturalismo*, pp. 34–6, 38–41, and 43–4.
14. It was precisely on these grounds that Federico Moja y Bolívar, writing in the *Revista Europea* in 1879, welcomed *L'Assommoir* (see Pattison, *Naturalismo*, p. 16), and Alas saw moral seriousness as a point of contact between Galdós and Zola (*Galdós* [Madrid, 1912], p. 101).
15. Quoted Pattison, *Naturalismo*, p. 39. Cf. Alas, *Teoría y crítica de la novela española*, ed. Sergio Beser (Barcelona, 1972), pp. 116–7.
16. Alas, *Galdós*, p. 99.
17. Sanz del Río, *Textos escogidos*, ed. Eloy Terrón (Barcelona, 1968) p. 85.

18. The novel was indeed perceived as Naturalist by many contemporary critics, including Pardo Bazán, Alas and Luis Alfonso. See Pattison, *Naturalismo*, pp. 39 and 90–97.
19. Michael Gordon, 'The medical background to Galdós's *La desheredada*', *Anales Galdosianos*, 7 (1972), p. 75.
20. *ibid.*
21. Honoré de Balzac, 'Avant-Propos' to *La Comédie humaine*, vol. 1 (Paris, Pléiade, 1962) p. 4.
22. Emile Zola, *Le Roman expérimental* (Paris, Charpentier, 1923), p. 19.
23. *Mimesis*, tr. Willard Trask (Garden City, New York, 1957) p. 438. First German edition Berne, 1946. First English translation Princeton University Press, 1953. Cf. Furst and Skrine, *Naturalism*, p. 12.
24. *Galdós*, p. 102.
25. As Stephen Gilman has rightly pointed out, 'the dichotomy of foreground and background, event and scene, which had prevailed in the "episodios" and had abbreviated the Madrid of *La familia de León Roch*, was gradually superseded by milieu' (*Galdós and the Art of the European Novel: 1867–1887* [Princeton University Press, 1981], p. 97.)
26. See Frank Durand, 'The reality of illusion: *La desheredada*', *Modern Language Notes*, 89 (1974), pp. 191–201.
27. *Galdós*, p. 129.
28. See Antonio Ruiz Salvador, 'La función del trasfondo histórico en *La desheredada*', *Anales Galdosianos*, 1 (1966), p. 56. Also Diane Urey, *Galdós and the Irony of Language* (Cambridge, 1982), p. 7.
29. Michael Gordon, '"Lo que le falta a un enfermo le sobra a otro": Galdós's conception of humanity in *La desheredada*', *Anales Galdosianos*, 12 (1977), p. 32.
30. *ibid.*, pp. 32–3.
31. *ibid.*, p. 32.
32. A similar inconsistency in the novel is noted by Gilman (*op. cit.*, pp. 125–6).
33. *Galdós*, p. 107.

7

Life as a Work of Art: *El amigo Manso*

Primum vivere, deinde philosophari.

It is written that the world shall be our mould, not our handiwork (El amigo Manso, Chapter 15).

The unreliable narrator

The composition of *El amigo Manso* appears to have caused Galdós some trouble, to judge from his remark in a letter to Francisco Giner that the novel was turning out 'a bit askew', because of the 'severe intrinsic difficulties' of the basic conception.[1] In the event, this diffidence was to make an important contribution to the artistic achievement of the work, for the strength of *El amigo Manso* arises in no small measure from Galdós's readiness to engage in a radical re-assessment of his previous artistic practice. Though his reformist intention remains essentially undimmed, his moral preoccupations are expressed with greater subtlety and finesse than in any previous work. This gain in artistic sophistication has been recognised by critics such as Gareth A. Davies, who remarks that 'didacticism . . . is so discreetly veiled that nowhere do we feel that [Manso] is a symbolical or allegorical figure'.[2]

Davies, however, takes what I believe to be a narrow view of the novel's scope, seeing it as primarily 'a comment on the over-hopeful optimism of the *Krausista* educationists'.[3] There is no doubt that Máximo Manso is identifiably a Krausist philosopher, notably in respect of the educational theory which he tries to put into practice in his relationship with his pupil, Manuel Peña, but in my view it would be a mistake to see his pedagogical ideas in isolation from the rest of his intellectual and psychological make-up. Krausism is, in Máximo's case, the foundation for a generalised rationalist idealism which determines not only his attitudes as a teacher, but also his political responses, his reaction to falling in love, his ethical standards and, above all, his attempt to shape his life in accordance with philosophical principles and ideal archetypes. The thrust of the novel is to call in question this outlook in its entirety, not simply in its specifically pedagogical aspect.

As we saw in Chapter 2, ethical and esthetic values were closely identified with each other in Krausist thought. The notion of moral perfectibility implies

giving shape and direction to an individual life in such a way as to make it a
thing of beauty. Francisco Giner de los Ríos made this identification explicit in
an essay of 1871:

> La vida toda nos aparece como una obra artística, desde que la concebimos
> y realizamos, no en el informe y confuso laberinto de contrarios accidentes
> entre los cuales, desorientado el hombre, pierde su centro y el dominio de
> sí propio y se deja arrastrar por el flujo y reflujo de las corrientes más
> opuestas, sino como el régimen libre, discreto, bien medido, firme y flexible
> a la vez de nuestra conducta en todas las relaciones.[4]

> *(The whole of life appears to us as a work of art, so long as we do not
> conceive and live it in the amorphous and confused labyrinth of conflicting
> contingencies, where man loses his sense of direction, his natural habitation,
> and his self-control, and is tossed hither and thither by the ebb and flow of
> opposing currents; [but it is a work of art] if we see it as the free, conscious
> and balanced governance, at once firm and flexible, of our conduct in all our
> relationships.)*

Máximo exemplifies this central Krausist attitude very clearly. From the very
outset of the novel, he declares that he has tried to give shape and direction to
his life by rational and ethical discipline, emphasising his sober and regular
habits, and his victories over 'immature passions which would have made me
unhappy' (OC 4, 1169). In the light of this attempt to give life a coherence
similar to that of a work of art, it is entirely appropriate that Galdós should
make Máximo narrate his own story — should, that is, involve him in the
process of artistic creation. Davies draws attention to the use of the first-person
narration in this novel, but the first critic to grasp its fundamental importance
was Robert H. Russell. As the title of his important study suggests, Russell
sees the novel as revealing 'Galdós with a mirror'. By this Russell means that,
by showing Máximo grappling with the problems of composition, especially the
autonomy of his 'characters', Galdós has dramatised the process whereby he
himself learned the difficult task of representing reality: '*El amigo Manso*
is . . . a kind of allegory of Galdós's own artistic pilgrimage'.[5] Russell's view is
borne out by the evidence of the text, for in the very first chapter, Galdós
presents himself in an oblique and almost self-mocking way. Máximo narrates
how the author came to him in search of a subject, intending to write on 'the
weighty subject of education'. However, lacking the means to do so immediately, and not wishing to remain idle, the author has decided to undertake
'a modest little work' (OC 4, 1165–6).

The gentle irony aimed here at the over-ambitious novelist is not, however,
simply a matter of Galdós ruefully deprecating his early crusading works, but is
primarily designed to direct the reader's attention to what the book is really
about. By emphasising that this novel is *not* about 'the weighty subject of
education', Galdós actively discourages us from interpreting the story narrowly
as a critique of Krausist educational theory. As we read *El amigo Manso*, we

soon discover that it is essentially a *bildungsroman*: it is really about the re-education of Manso in the school of life. As Russell shrewdly remarks, 'the person who receives the most upsetting and transforming education is Manso the teacher'.[6] The key to Galdós's success in conveying this message clearly is that Máximo's dual roles as educator and narrator are inextricably bound up with each other. His academic training not only causes him to think at a generalising, abstract level, and thus to misunderstand people and events, but also leads him constantly to dissect his experience in an obsessively analytic way, and it is out of this analysis that the novel is made. The words on the page are the record of the painful learning process through which Máximo passes, a process in which we as readers are made to share because as first-person narrator he is our only source of information.[7] Moreover, the re-education of Máximo ultimately involves reaching a more mature understanding of human nature and human experience, and it is in this sense that we may agree with Russell in seeing *El amigo Manso* as a kind of parable of Galdós's own apprenticeship in the art of representing reality.

It is, however, possible to develop Russell's insight further, for there is a sense in which Máximo is striving to produce not one artefact but two: the narrative of his life and the life itself. Galdós clearly wishes us to see analogies between Máximo's writing activity and his life, for in the very unconventional first chapter, where Máximo describes himself as suspended in a sort of limbo, before he is called into bodily life by the author, he makes Máximo stress with some vehemence that he only exists as a fictional entity:

> Yo no existo . . . Soy . . . una condensación artística, diabólica, hechura del pensamiento (*ximia Dei*), el cual, si coge entre sus dedos algo de estilo, se pone a imitar con él las obras que con la materia ha hecho Dios en el mundo físico (OC 4, 1165).

> *(I do not exist. I am an artistic distillation, a diabolical product of the human mind (the ape of God), which, if it gets hold of a modicum of style, begins by this means to imitate the work that God has done with matter in the physical universe.)*

It is, paradoxically, Máximo's insistence on his fictional nature that persuades us to take him seriously. As John Kronik has remarked, 'the cry of "Yo no existo" can be uttered only by a being existentially aware of himself'.[8] Even more significantly, however, the persuasiveness of the narration arises primarily from the fact that we are encouraged to consider Máximo's life and his narration on the same level, as works of art, for implicit in the opening chapter is the assertion 'My life is no more real than a fiction, but if you believe that the human mind can ape the creative work of God (i.e., that fictions have a certain kind of reality), then you can believe that my life was lived'. There is therefore no sense of strain when Máximo, after telling us how he was called into corporeal existence by the author with a spell involving a mixture of ink, pitch and sulphur, follows this up with matter-of-fact statements to the effect that he is a thirty-five year old non-smoking philosophy teacher who keeps fit by doing gymnastics.

It by no means follows, however, that we are bound to accept Máximo at his own evaluation. The whole point of the novel, indeed, is that he only achieves a clear understanding of his experience at the end. For most of the narrative, he is ignorant of certain facts which affect him personally, and his assumptions about human nature are mistaken. This makes him what Wayne C. Booth has called an unreliable narrator. That is to say that 'author and reader are secretly in collusion, behind the speaker's back, agreeing upon the standard by which he is found wanting'.[9] Sometimes the standard appealed to is the reader's common sense and general experience of life. Anyone who can say, as Máximo does in Chapter 2, 'I acquired a certain pedantic presumption, and a displeasing air of authority of which, thank God, I later cured myself completely' (OC 4, 1168) has patently not outgrown this failing. We smile knowingly when he interprets in a highly ingenuous way the embarrassment of his brother's governess, Irene, when he asks her once what she was reading late the previous night: he immediately supposes she has been reading one of his scholarly publications, and assumes that she does not want to admit it for fear of seeming a pedant (OC 4, 1204).

As it turns out, what Irene was most probably reading was a love-letter from Máximo's pupil and rival, Manuel. We cannot know this, of course, until we have read the novel at least once, and this suggests a second standard whereby we may measure Máximo's unreliability. There are, in fact, two distinct narrative perspectives in the novel. At one level, the narrative functions as a memoir: Máximo only tells the story of the events after they have happened, after, that is, he has drawn the lesson of his experience and realised that his story is worth telling. His incarnation in Chapter 1 is presented as a past event, on which he can look back after he has returned to 'these expanses of thought' (OC 4, 1165). Scattered throughout the novel are various phrases which help to sustain the logical supposition that it came into being as a memoir: 'I was 35 when this thing happened to me' (1166); 'To this day I do not know, though I am trying hard to get the bottom of the question, with the help of the spiritual serenity I now enjoy' (1196); 'How well I remember this!' (1209).

Such reminders, however, are comparatively rare, and serve mainly to direct attention to the crucial nature of certain events. For the most part, the story is told as if the details were being relayed to us at the moment when they occurred. The two temporal perspectives do not create an inconsistency of focus, but are perfectly integrated, enabling us to be aware simultaneously of the overall shape of Máximo's experience, and of his emotions and his limitations of vision as he responds to particular events. The key to this integration is Galdós's skilful use of unreliable first-person narration which, as we saw in the love-letter episode mentioned above, enables him to show Máximo recording incidents charged with a significance which he will only realise at the end, when they come flooding back into his memory to torture and humiliate him.[10] This technique also makes it possible for Galdós to place before the reader large general themes without resorting to the kind of discursiveness or melodrama which characterise some of his earlier novels, particularly *Gloria*. As Gareth Davies has rightly said, 'Galdós chose to present his issues at dramatic moments in the novel; moments where personal crises or antagonisms, wholly comprehensible in terms of the "character" novel, are combined with the presentation of ideological issues shown either in conflict, or in juxtaposition, for our clearer understanding of them'.[11]

Máximo in love

The most important instance of this process is Máximo's relationship with Irene, which is particularly relevant to the notion of life as a work of art, for just as Máximo tries to shape his own life in accordance with his idealist preconceptions, so he seeks to re-make Irene in his own image and likeness by forging in his mind a stereotype which bears little resemblance to the real woman. To his perception, she seems the 'ideal' woman in every sense, because he assumes that she shares his capacity for rational self-control:

> Noté que la imaginación tenía en ella lugar secundario. Su claro juicio sabía descartar las cosas triviales y de relumbrón, y no se pagaba de fantasmagorías como la mayor parte de las hembras . . . He aquí la mujer perfecta, la mujer positiva, la mujer razón, contrapuesta a la mujer frivolidad, a la mujer capricho (OC 4, 1196).

> *(I noted that imagination occupied a secondary place in her make-up. Her clear judgement knew how to put trivial and showy things aside, and she was not satisfied with idle fancies, like the majority of females. What we have here is the perfect woman, the practical woman, woman as reason, as opposed to woman as frivolity, woman as caprice.)*

At first glance, this seems as discursive as any of the discussions on religious tolerance in *Gloria*, but such utterances are now set within a context of psychological and social particularity which gives them a markedly more realist character. In the first place, this is a wholly authentic representation of how a person with Máximo's academic training in philosophy would speak. Even more significantly, however, Máximo's attitudes spring from the nexus of economic and social relationships on which his professional role and status depend. Though his family background is modest (his father was a village pharmacist), he has never known financial hardship. His mother sheltered him from the rough intrusions of the world when he was a student, and now that he is a comfortably-off bachelor professor in a state institution,[12] he can afford a housekeeper, who fulfils essentially the same role. The reason why he can idealise Irene's supposed dedication to reason and learning is that, enjoying as he does a relatively privileged position, he has little appreciation of the

economic pressures which drove her to become a teacher. It is highly significant that in the very same chapter from which the above passage comes, there is
a reference to the time when Irene, as a child, used to bring Máximo begging
notes from her sponging and grotesque aunt, Doña Cándida. Though Máximo
is well aware that Irene, as tutor to José María Manso's children, is far from
well-paid, and has to spend her evenings mending her own clothes, he
characteristically interprets these facts in terms of a conventional sentimental
image of decorous poverty (OC 4, 1195–6).

Máximo's unreliability as a narrator, therefore, is not merely a structural
convenience, but is closely bound up with his social conditioning. This is why,
as he has to admit later in the novel, there is a lack of connection between his
'pure reason' and his 'practical reason'. There is even an economic aspect to
the triangular love-intrigue involving Máximo, Manuel and Irene, for Irene is
so determined to escape the squalor of her aunt's house that she is resolved
either to marry Manuel or commit suicide:

> — Me mataría . . . ; tengo fuerzas para matarme y volverme a matar, si no
> quedaba bien muerta . . . Usted no me conoce. — Y ¡qué verdad! Pero ya
> empezaba a conocerla, sí (OC 4, 1275).

> (*'I would kill myself. I could bring myself to do it, and then to do it again, if
> I wasn't properly dead the first time. You don't know me.' How true that
> was! But I was certainly beginning to know her now.*)

Máximo's discovery of normal human needs and aspirations in Irene demonstrates the futility of his original attempt to reconstruct her personality in
accordance with his idealist assumptions. For Russell, this aspect of the novel
confirms that Galdós is trying, as it were, to give himself an object-lesson in
how to respect the autonomy of fictional characters:

> This stress on Manso's function as novelist is important, because as the
> story progresses, it becomes clear that the intellectual and sentimental
> process through which the philosopher Manso passes, is also, and perhaps
> more importantly, the process of the novelist Manso who learns a few
> things about his craft. . . . He is never aware of what is going to happen
> next, even though the story is in the form of a memoir, even though Manso
> believes he exercises a controlling power over the destiny of his
> characters.[13]

It is important nevertheless not to press this analogy too far, for although the
whole narrative and even the existence of the narrator are presented as
fictional, within this fictional world Máximo's existence and that of Irene are of
the same order. From *his* point of view, she is a flesh-and-blood woman, not a
fictional creation: his all-absorbing passion for her would not otherwise make
sense. The fact remains that the main point of the novel, as Russell has quite
rightly implied, is that Máximo's attempt to control and shape life as if it were

a work of art ultimately breaks down. It is not so much that his fictional creatures break free of his control, but that life refuses to subordinate itself to the expectations of either philosophers or didactic artists, and simply develops under the pressure of its own necessity. In the long run, the decisive effect of Máximo's loss of Irene is that he acquires a more mature and comprehensive moral vision than that provided earlier by his somewhat stiff-jointed rationalist philosophy. By reflecting on the reasons for Irene's preference for Manuel, he attains to greater understanding of the workings of human passion, and of the social, economic and psychological pressures which influence people's motivation and behaviour. His re-education is almost complete when, in the midst of the chagrin of his disillusionment, he finds that he can love Irene with an unconditional love freed from the constraints of his old watchful, analytical approach to human relations:

> Al representármela despojada de aquellas perfecciones con que la vistió mi pensamiento, me interesaba mucho más, la quería más, en una palabra, llegando a sentir por ella ferviente idolatría. ¡Contradicción extraña! Perfecta, la quise a la moda petrarquista, con fríos alientos sentimentales que habrían sido capaces de hacerme escribir sonetos. Imperfecta, la adoraba con nuevo y atropellado afecto, más fuerte que yo y que todas mis filosofías . . . Pero ya era tarde (OC 4, 1276).

> *(As I perceived her stripped of those perfections which my intellect had conferred on her, I found her much more interesting; in a word, I loved her much more, and soon came to feel for her a fervent adoration. What a strange contradiction! When I thought her perfect, I loved her in the Petrarchan mode, with cold sentimental promptings which might have made me write sonnets. Now that I knew her to be imperfect, I adored her with a new and violent passion, which was stronger than I, stronger than anything dreamt of in my philosophy. But it was too late.)*

Too late indeed: for if Máximo had known what he now knows, his life might have taken a different course. But he cannot have a second chance, so there is nothing left for him but to die.

Realism and myth

Just as the whole of *El amigo Manso* operates simultaneously on the levels of the general and the particular, the realistic and the abstract, so also Galdós provides a rational explanation for Máximo's death while underlining its wider thematic significance. The natural cause, though never precisely identified, is suggested by the psychological trauma he has undergone, and by the effort of keeping his emotions hidden. He is convinced that Irene guesses the true state of his feelings, and that in her eyes he has cut a sorry and ridiculous figure. This obsession provides a bridge between the levels of natural explanation and wider theme, for Máximo's subtle and analytical mind, which he formerly thought of as his greatest asset, is now a very efficient instrument of self-torture, driving him round and round in a never-ending cycle of self-dissection and regret. Consequently, the only way in which he can return to the serenity he once enjoyed is to emancipate his abstract, reasoning faculty from the pull of his emotions and the painful impact of his experience. As has been well said, 'his "death" is a manifestation of his superior cognitive powers and his open resumption of them'.[14]

We have already seen in Chapter 6 that the Krausist theory of personality was based on the idea of harmonious balance between intellect, appetite, feeling and imagination. But Galdós was well aware by 1878, when he wrote *Marianela* and *La familia de León Roch*, that in practice the Krausist emphasis on the discipline of reason could lead to an over-valuing of the intellect. Máximo Manso is a signal example of this tendency, in the way in which he adopts a censorious attitude towards the imagination and the passions, interpreting his educational responsibility towards Manuel largely in terms of uprooting what he sees as the young man's vices. Only gradually, as Máximo lives through his crucial experience, does he learn that the educator, the enlightener or the reformer must begin by accepting human nature as it is. There is a world of wisdom summed up in Máximo's recognition that 'humanity is as it has been made, or what it has made itself. Nothing can change it' (OC 4, 1284).[15]

If we apply this statement to Máximo himself, it becomes clearer that his story is not a commonplace one about a shy academic losing the woman he loves to someone more dynamic, but has a range of reference which can only adequately be expressed by Máximo's death. For in a real sense what is rejected is not simply Máximo's qualities or principles, but what he is. His discipline of rational self-control is not merely an aspect of his personality, it *is* his personality. He is appalled at finding himself in a sleazy cafe at four in the morning (Chapter 20), for if such things continue 'a time would come, God help me, when I would no longer recognise in myself anything of what made up my vigorous personality in happier days' (OC 4, 1213). This is not to say that Máximo is immune from the storms of passion, but that he erroneously believes that he can behave as if he were. Consequently, when he finds himself falling in love, it is natural for him to perceive this as the rebellion of instincts which ought to be kept under tight control: 'The over-riding influence of feeling was becoming stronger in me every day, to the extent that reason found itself disconcerted, like an authority losing its prestige in the face of popular insubordination' (OC 4, 1224).

Because rational self-discipline absorbs so much of Máximo's being, it follows that when rationalism alone is shown to be an inadequate basis for functioning in human society, he himself can no longer survive. Máximo, indeed, has always remained partly in the world of the spirit: 'Your shade wanders about your brother's drawing-room', Manuel tells him in the cafe scene in Chapter 20, 'but you remain in the lofty Cloud-cuckoo-land of thought' (OC 4, 1215). There is a sense in which Máximo's tragedy is that of a fictional being turned loose in the robust world of flesh-and-blood people. It is true that from one point of view the existences of all the characters in the novel are of the same order, as I pointed out earlier in connection with Máximo's love for Irene. It is also true that for most of the novel, with the exception of the unconventional first and last chapters, Máximo's life evolves within a particular social and historical context in a way typical of classic Realism. This realistic world, however, loses some of its substantiality when seen within the uncompromisingly fictional framework established by the first and last chapters. Only Máximo, however, is aware of this framework, and he therefore knows himself to be different from other people. Galdós's choice of the profession of philosophy for Máximo can now be seen as a formal necessity, for if Máximo had been an engineer like Pepe Rey, he would have been immersed more completely in human society, and would have lacked that capacity for viewing and experiencing life from a distance which is the essence of his identity. In order to function within the 'real' world of the novel, however, even as a philosopher, Máximo has to be invested with 'mortal flesh' by the author, and the affective elements he thus acquires are enough to destroy the hegemony of his intellect, and therefore his identity. As his love for Irene consumes him more and more, the call of the spirit-world, which is the only place where Máximo can regain his intellectual serenity, becomes stronger. In order to illustrate how Galdós could confer considerable poignancy on Máximo's human situation, while at the same time enabling the reader to keep the abstract dimensions of his role in view, it is worth quoting at some length from the last chapter:

> Era, a ratos, sombra desfigurada del señor Manso, como las que hace el sol a la caída de la tarde, estirando los cuerpos cual se estira una cuerda de goma.
> — ¿Pero qué tiene usted? — me dijo un día doña Javiera.
> — Nada, señora; yo no tengo nada. Por eso precisamente me voy. Entre dos vacíos, prefiero el otro.
> — Se queda usted como una vela.
> — Esto quiere decir que ha llegado la hora de mi desaparición de entre los vivos. He dado mi fruto y estoy de más. Todo lo que ha cumplido su ley desaparece . . .
> El mismo perverso amigo que me había llevado al mundo sacóme de él, repitiendo el conjuro de marras y las hechicerías diablescas de la redoma, la gota de tinta y el papel quemado, que habían precedido a mi encarnación.
> — Hombre de Dios — le dije — , ¿quiere usted acabar de una vez conmigo y recoger esta carne mortal en que, para divertirse, me ha metido? ¡Cosa más sin gracia . . . !
> Al deslizarme de entre sus dedos, envuelto en llamarada roja, el sosiego me dio a entender que había dejado de ser hombre (OC 4, 1289).

(Sometimes I was a distorted shadow of Mr Manso, like the shadows cast by the sun in the late evening, stretching out bodies like an elastic band.

'What's the matter with you, anyway?' said Doña Javiera one day.
'Nothing, ma'am, nothing. That is precisely why I am going. If I have to
choose between two voids, I prefer the other one.'
'You're the colour of wax these days.'
'That means that the time has come for me to disappear from the ranks of
the living. I have given my fruit and now I'm superfluous. Everything that
has fulfilled the law of its being dies . . . '
The same perverse friend who brought me into the world took me out of it,
repeating the old spell and the diabolical witchery of the flask, the drop of ink
and the burnt paper, which had preceded my incarnation.
'My dear chap,' I said, 'Would you mind finishing me off once for all, and
taking back this mortal flesh in which you have put me for your own
amusement? That was the most unfunny joke ever!'
As I slipped through his fingers, enveloped in a red flash, the ease I felt
made me realise that I had ceased to be a man.)

This last sentence points to the ultimate meaning of the novel. If Máximo's life is a failed work of art, it follows that the other work of art, i.e., the story of that life, lends itself to being read as a fable about human existence. The narrative of Máximo's re-education encapsulates important general truths about human experience, for it shows him trying to come to terms with the tension between intellect and instinct, spirit and matter, ideal and reality. In *El amigo Manso* the interaction of these forces acquires a quasi-mythic dimension. For example, though it is understandable that Irene's confession that she has another lover should come as a bitter blow to Máximo, the way in which it is described ('colossal crumbling, collapse of life, total destruction' [OC 4, 1250]) makes it appear as a cataclysm of cosmic proportions. This is entirely appropriate, for although, as I have already said, the novel concentrates for most of its length on the vivid depiction of Restoration society, we are reminded at certain strategic points that the drama we are witnessing is a microcosm of a larger one.

This is why the awakening of Máximo's feelings for Irene is presented as a radical undermining of his being: he fears these elemental forces of attraction, which threaten his rational self-discipline. Josette Blanquat has brilliantly summed up this fear as 'dread of the Beast's victory' ('la hantise du triomphe de la bête').[16] This is the keynote of the well-known *velada* scene (the charity benefit concert), rightly taken by most critics as the climax of the novel. It is undeniable that at one level, the scene functions as a satirical comment on the pretentiousness of Restoration society. Furthermore, the respective speeches of Manuel and Máximo, one flamboyant and specious, the other sober and reflective, illustrate the radical difference in their temperaments and in their attitudes to life. In the last analysis, however, the *velada* can only be fully understood within the context of the cosmic or mythic dimension of the novel. Just before the *velada*, Máximo is more strongly aware than at any time previously that his emotions are breaking free of the dominance of his reason, and that events involving Irene have moved beyond his knowledge and control.

These fears are confirmed, on the night before the *velada*, by a dream in which Máximo follows Irene to a house in the disreputable Calle de Fuencarral, and shortly after sees the arrival of his brother José María, whom he suspects of having dishonourable designs on Irene.

The power of the irrational becomes even more overwhelming after the *velada*. Máximo, on returning home, sinks into a deep depression. This is partly a natural result of fatigue, and the sudden relaxation of tension after the excitement of the evening, but is mainly due to vague fears of imminent calamity, which defy all his efforts to think clearly and rationally. In order to bring out the full implications of Máximo's state of mind, it is once again necessary to quote at length:

¡Oh negra tristeza! Fúnebre y pesado velo, ¿quién te echó sobre mí? ¿Por qué os elevasteis lentos y pavorosos sobre mi alma, pensamientos de muerte, como vapores que suben de la superficie de un lago caldeado? . . .

Tú, imaginación, fuiste la causa de mis tormentos en aquella noche aciaga. Tú, haciendo pajaritas con una idea y enredando toda la noche; tú, la mal criada, la mimosa, la intrusa, fuiste quien recalentó mi cerebro, quien puso mis nervios como las cuerdas del arpa que oí tocar en la velada. Y cuando creía tenerte sujeta para siempre, cortaste el grillete, y juntándote con el recelo, con el amor propio, otros pillos como tú, me manteasteis sin compasión, me lanzasteis al aire . . .

La verdad es que no tenían explicación racional mi desvelo y mis tristezas. Se equivoca el que atribuya mi desazón a las heridas del amor propio por el pasmoso éxito del discurso de Manuel Peña . . . La causa de mi hondísima pena era un presentimiento de desgracias que me dominaba, sobreponiéndose a toda la energía que mi espíritu posee contra la superstición; era un cálculo basado en datos muy vagos, pero seductores, y con lógica admirable llegaba a la más desconsoladora afirmación . . . En vano demostraba yo que los datos eran falsos; la imaginación me presentaba al instante otros nuevos, marcados con el sello de la evidencia. Al levantarme, me dije:

— Soy una especie de Leverrier de mi desdicha. Este célebre astrónomo descubrió al planeta Neptuno sin verlo, sólo por la fuerza del cálculo, porque las desviaciones de la órbita de Urano le anunciaban la existencia de un cuerpo celeste hasta entonces no visto por humanos ojos, y él, con su labor matemática, llegó a determinar la existencia de este lejano y misterioso viajero del espacio. Del mismo modo adivino yo que por mi cielo anda un cuerpo desconocido; no lo he visto, ni nadie me ha dado noticias de él; pero como el cálculo me dice que existe, ahora voy a poner en práctica todas mis matemáticas para descubrirlo. Y lo descubriré; me lo profetiza la irregular trayectoria de Urano, el planeta querido; irregularidades que no pueden ser producidas sino por atracciones físicas. Esta pena profunda que siento consiste en que llega hasta mí la influencia de aquel cuerpo lejano y desconocido. Mi razón declara su existencia. Falta que mis sentidos lo comprueben, y lo comprobarán o me tendré por loco (OC 4, 1237).

(Oh black despair! Who threw this heavy funeral pall over me? Why did these thoughts of death creep slow and fearful over my soul, like vapours rising from the surface of a steaming lake?

You, imagination, were the cause of my torments on that ominous night. It was you who toyed with a certain idea all night, tossing it around as one might throw paper birds about a room. It was you, unruly, wilful, and intrusive as you are, who overheated my brain and stretched my nerves as tense as the strings of the harp I heard being played during the velada. *And when I thought I had mastered you for good, you broke your shackles, and joining forces with suspicion and* amour propre, *other rogues like yourself, you mercilessly threw me in the air, as if I were being tossed in a blanket.*

The truth of the matter is that there was no rational explanation for my sleeplessness and depression. It would be a mistake to attribute my unease to wounded pride caused by the astonishing success of Manuel Peña's speech. The cause of my profound suffering was an overwhelming foreboding of misfortune, which proved stronger than all the defensive powers of my spirit against superstition. It was a deduction based on vague, but persuasive pieces of evidence, which led me, with admirable logic, to the most grievous conclusion. In vain did I prove the evidence false, for imagination instantly presented me with new facts, which bore the stamp of incontrovertible truth. On rising, I thought:

'I am a sort of Leverrier of my own misfortune. This celebrated astronomer discovered the planet Neptune without ever seeing it, by sheer calculation, because irregularities in the orbit of Uranus betrayed the existence of a celestial body never before seen by human eyes. He, with his mathematical activity, established the existence of that distant and mysterious voyager in space. In the same way, I sense that there is an unknown body in my heaven. I have never seen it, nobody has told me of it. But my calculations tell me it exists, and now I am going to employ all my mathematical skill to discover it. And I will discover it: this can be predicted from the irregular trajectory of Uranus, the beloved planet, irregularities which can only be produced by physical attraction. This profound pain I feel arises from the fact that the influence of that distant and unknown body is affecting me. My reason postulates its existence. It only remains for my senses to verify it. And they shall verify it, or I shall think myself mad.)

This passage is a powerful expression not only of how jealousy can gnaw at reason but also, in a more general way, of the limitations of our modern, empirical, post-Enlightenment rationalism. If we do not find the rhetoric of this passage exaggerated, it is because Galdós has successfully persuaded us of the magnitude of the issues involved. A key element in establishing this magnitude is the image of the 'perturbations of Uranus', which immediately opens up a perspective of vastness and cosmic rhythm. Máximo is just the kind of person who would choose an analogy from the world of science, but ironically he chooses one which mocks his attempts to subject life to rational analysis, for his 'mathematical skill' shrinks into puny insignificance before the cosmic forces he is attempting to understand and forestall. The phrase 'physical attraction', by standing both for planetary movements and sexual interest, reveals that love between man and woman is part of the larger rhythm of the universe. Far from being comforted by this reflection, Máximo must needs fight against it: hence the intense inner conflict described in the first two paragraphs. And since what he is fighting against is ultimately life itself, he cannot escape being destroyed in the process. Thus, within the thematic scheme of the passage, his irrational fears appropriately centre on premonitions of death. Moreover, what no translation can quite succeed in bringing out is the ritualistic quality of the rhythmical apostrophes to 'fúnebre y pesado velo . . . pensamientos de muerte . . . imaginación'. When Máximo later receives confirmation of the identity of Irene's lover (Manuel), these ritualistic utterances recur, this time in explicit association with the *Dies irae* (OC 4, 1260–1).

Máximo as artist

Even in death, however, Máximo's failure to produce a work of art of the kind he intended is not total. His life did not turn out as he meant it to, but at least we have his narrative. We owe its existence to that capacity for conceptualisation which was his tragic flaw, but without which he would not have been able to make sense of his experience. Moreover, despite Máximo's unreliability in certain respects, the novel as a whole is, in the last analysis, not 'a fictional world [in which] each perspective will be as credible as the next',[17] but a statement which we can accept as trustworthy, not least because Galdós has himself learned a lesson analogous to Máximo's, about accepting reality as it is. Precisely because the novel is the story of Máximo's re-education towards true perception, he becomes more reliable as his writing proceeds. Even before this, however, there are areas in which we implicitly accept that his view of things is sound. On Máximo's own admission, his puritanical criticisms of Manuel and Irene for their brilliant social life after their marriage are exaggerated (OC 4, 1288), but his unflattering assessment of characters like José María and Doña Cándida is amply confirmed by everything they do. Paradoxically, the very unreliability of Máximo's narration is crucial to this corroboration, for since the plot to deliver Irene into José María's hands is hatched before Máximo learns of it, José María and Doña Cándida are made to appear as scoundrels independently of his mediating judgement. This independent confirmation of Máximo's view confers considerable objectivity on those parts of the novel which are concerned with José María's political and social role. It is true that Máximo's comments often strike us as either high-minded or blasé, but when we have made due allowance for his temperament, we can see that his view of Restoration society is corroborated by the sycophancy with which it welcomes the corrupt José María on his return from Cuba, and enables him to prosper. When Manuel in turn is launched on his political career by this same society, we are left wondering whether, for all the personal pique which underlies some of Máximo's remarks about Manuel's ambition, there is not a grain of truth in them.[18]

Despite the limitations of his rationalistic outlook, then, our philosopher-narrator is in many respects a shrewd observer, with a professional commitment to truth and high ethical principles. All the other characters perceive him as someone who can be relied on to provide standards of wisdom, integrity and cultural excellence at moments of crisis: Doña Javiera, Manuel's mother, asks him to undertake the education of her son; José María asks him to recommend a governess for his children; Lica seeks his help when José María proves unfaithful; Irene turns to him for protection against José María, and also enlists his aid to ensure that Manuel will keep his promise to marry her. In other words, although the rule of reason alone is inadequate as a means of coping with the unruliness of life, it is ultimately indispensable as a normative and organising discipline. Though the unreflective majority takes 'el amigo Manso' for granted, people keep turning to him because his gifts are perceived, albeit in a vague and inchoate way, as necessary.

There is, then, a sense in which Máximo is vindicated even in the midst of defeat. If the novel ended with his death, our final impression would be of him being slowly torn apart by his hopeless love for Irene, his remorse and humiliation, and his obsessive attempts at self-justification. Instead, however, he is allowed to record his return to the limbo-like state from which he emerged at the beginning, where he achieves a serenity and peace which enable him to look back on his sufferings and mistakes with humorous detachment. Though hardly any of what he wrote or taught in his professional role remains, his judgement of the other characters is borne out by their subsequent history: Doña Cándida continues as rapacious as ever, Manuel becomes an opportunistic politician, Irene scarcely remembers Máximo, and José María never progresses beyond his usual shallowness and vanity.[19]

Most important of all, however, is the fact that although Máximo may have failed to make his life a work of art in the Krausist sense which he intended, he has, by unselfconscious service to others, achieved a deeper and rarer beauty. In the end, the novel asserts the value of truth, wisdom and moral integrity, not by providing theoretical or discursive definitions of these things, but by enabling us to recognise them in concrete behaviour such as Máximo's unfailing spirit of sacrifice, even the sacrifice of his life. As Josette Blanquat wisely remarks, Máximo 'fulfils himself by effacing himself', and she adds that his social role 'is confined to assuming, quietly and unpretentiously, a human condition which renounces consolation and which follows the great law of lonely self-sacrifice, amid the indifference of others'.[20]

El amigo Manso therefore marks a crucial stage in Galdós's evolution towards a full-bodied realism. The denser and more varied social context is no longer, as in Léon Roch and La desheredada, incidental to the main didactic thrust, but becomes the locus in which values are given concrete expression. Moreover, the expression of values is now a more complex and problematical business than the relatively simple advocacy of religious tolerance, thrift, modesty, or common sense which we found in earlier novels. Galdós does not, to be sure, abandon his belief that humanity is ultimately perfectible, but he is now more clearly aware that such progress as can be achieved is limited by human nature itself, because man's ability to shape his life is constantly threatened by the forces of unreason. This realisation has implications for Galdós's literary technique: because he now has less confidence in simple assertion and demonstration, he will henceforth rely more on oblique irony, juxtaposition, implication and analogy.[21] It is, indeed, as just such an ironic and problematic expression of truth that we should read *El amigo Manso*: not as the refutation of Krausist educational theory, nor even as a portrait of Restoration society, but rather as the record and the vehicle of one man's discovery of what it means to be human.

Notes to Chapter 7

1. Quoted in M. B. Cossío, 'Galdós y Giner: Una carta de Galdós', *Boletín de la Institución Libre de Enseñanza*, no. 719 (29 February 1920), pp. 60–62.
2. Gareth A. Davies, 'Galdós's *El amigo Manso*, an experiment in didactic method', *Bulletin of Hispanic Studies*, 39 (1962), p. 23.
3. *ibid.*
4. F. Giner de los Ríos, *Ensayos* (Madrid, Alianza Editorial, 1969), p. 22.
5. Robert H. Russell, '*El amigo Manso*: Galdós with a mirror', *Modern Language Notes*, 88 (1963), p. 168.
6. *art. cit.*, pp. 166–7.
7. As Harriet Turner has expressed it, 'the values we discover become themselves the very mode of the search; as a result, we emerge changed by our understanding of Manso's story in ways that reflect how *he* has emerged changed by the telling and by participation in the very novel he has invented and reflected to us' ('The shape of deception in *Doña Perfecta*', *Kentucky Romance Quarterly*, 31 [1984], p. 125).
8. John W. Kronik, '*El amigo Manso* and the game of fictive autonomy', *Anales Galdosianos*, 12 (1977), p. 75.
9. Wayne C. Booth, *The Rhetoric of Fiction* (Chicago University Press, 1961), p. 304.
10. Harriet Turner remarks that the shared knowledge between reader and author 'is conveyed (1) by facts which Manso either overlooks or misinterprets as he narrates them, notably Irene's small deceptions, and (2) by the manner of telling which often exposes Manso as unwittingly guilty of the same errors of judgment he has so astutely perceived in others' ('Strategies in narrative point of view: On meaning and morality in the Galdós novel', in B. Brancaforte, E. R. Mulvihill & R. G. Sánchez, eds., *Homenaje a Antonio Sánchez-Barbudo* [Madison, University of Wisconsin, 1981], pp. 64–5).
11. *art. cit.*, p. 24.
12. Máximo is often loosely described as a 'professor' by critics, but is in fact a *catedrático de instituto*, i.e., a teacher in a state-run secondary school. Holders of such posts often were and are scholarly people, as is Máximo himself. They could also transfer to university posts, and indeed, in Chapter 15, Máximo's brother José María proposes this. Irene, for her part, has been trained as an elementary teacher.
13. *art. cit.*, p. 163.
14. Kronik, *art. cit.*, p. 78.
15. '"Educación" . . . cuts across boundaries between fictional and real worlds, posing for the reader profound epistemological questions. Reader and character reflect and refract one another in the shared experience of learning how to mix mind and heart, a keen eye with abstract ideas, "la razón pura" and "la razón práctica"' (Turner, 'Strategies', p. 65).
16. Josette Blanquat, 'Le Naturalisme espagnol en 1882: *El amigo Manso* de Galdós', *Bulletin Hispanique*, 64 bis (1962) (Hommage à Marcel Bataillon), p. 321.
17. Diane Urey, *Galdós and the Irony of Language* (Cambridge University Press, 1982), p. 72.

18. Nothing could be more unfair than Carlos Blanco Aguinaga's judgement that Máximo is 'la encarnación del pensamiento más vulgar de una pequeña burguesía que, en su carrera de ascenso hacia metas socialmente aceptables, tiene que negar sus orígenes: es decir, tanto la carnicería en que nace Manolito Peña como la existencia mediocre de Máximo Manso' (*La historia y el texto literario: Tres novelas de Galdós* [Madrid, 1978], pp. 26–7). Such an assertion totally overlooks Máximo's highly critical attitude towards Manuel's and José María's 'carrera de ascenso'.

19. 'The initial declaration "yo no existo," fraught with paradox, doubles forward and back to expose the emptiness and unreality of the "real" world' (Turner, 'Strategies', p. 66).

20. *art. cit.*, pp. 320, 331.

21. As Maurice Z. Shroder has written, 'the sensibility that produces novels . . . asks questions instead of making contrary statements' ('The novel as genre', in Philip Stevick, ed., *The Theory of the Novel* [New York, 1967], p. 18).

8

The Novel as Anti-Fiction: *Tormento*

> *Style is mendacious. Truth looks on
> and is silent* (Tormento, Chapter
> 12).

As we saw in the last chapter, *El amigo Manso* is essentially about the human
need to impose some kind of ordering or patterning on the inchoate flux of
experience in order to make sense of it. When Máximo fails in his attempt to
shape his life *a priori* according to his philosophical assumptions, he needs to
write his story down if he is to understand what happened to him. Galdós
constantly draws attention to the limited and subjective nature of Máximo's
perception, even though in the end he endorses his values and moral priorities.
In this respect, therefore, though *El amigo Manso* attains a new level of depth
and complexity, it reiterates some of Galdós's long-standing concerns, for some
fifteen years before, in *La sombra*, he had exploited the problematical nature
of narrative in a comparable way. Even in the novels of the 1870s, where
Galdós is more deliberately defending particular ideological positions, the
notion of the conventionality of accepted frames of reference is unmistakably,
if implicitly, present. Political conservatism, pietistic religion, or family and
church authority are seen as 'things made', as distorted products of the human
mind, rather than part of reality in any wider or more objective sense.

'Fiction', then, interpreted as the art of creating mental constructs, is a
constant undercurrent in Galdós's novels up to *El amigo Manso*, whether he is
explicitly concerned with the act of writing or not. In *El amigo Manso* and
subsequent novels, Galdós turns more frequently to literature and the arts as a
source of images and narrative devices. *El doctor Centeno* (1883) is the story of
an unsuccessful romantic dramatist, Alejandro Miquis, who is struggling to
write a play in which he hopes to recreate the heroic age of Spain's greatness in
the seventeenth century, but whose impractical approach to life leads him to
neglect his own interests and his health, until he dies penniless and consump-
tive. As with Isidora in *La desheredada*, Alejandro's basic inability to come to
terms with reality is presented with a mixture of ironic detachment and
sympathy: his dilemma is aptly summed up at the end of the novel by José Ido
del Sagrario, who declares that 'it is a terrible thing to be a poetic man in this
age of prose' (OC 4, 1448). Ido announces to Alejandro's servant and
companion, Felipe Centeno, that he is thinking of becoming a writer of serial

novels, at which Felipe suggests that he should write about his deceased master's life. Ido, however, takes the view that unembellished reality is an unsuitable subject for a literary work: 'The poet must dip his pen in the ambrosia of beautiful lies, not in the stew of horrible reality' (4, 1452).

The fiction of morality

The possibility adumbrated at the end of *El doctor Centeno* comes to fruition in Galdós's next novel, *Tormento* (1884), which is constructed around the contrast between two alternative visions of the same reality. At the beginning of the novel, Felipe and Ido meet again, and Ido tells him that he has carried out his intention to become a hack-novelist. He is now, he says, writing a novel based on the lives of two real people, Amparo and Refugio Sánchez Emperador (whose story, when told from a different point of view, will form the substance of *Tormento*). As perceived by Ido's imagination, the two girls are models of virtuous poverty, earning their living by sewing, and resisting the blandishments of those who would corrupt them morally by offers of wealth (OC 4, 1457). Ido's sentimental view is later given a rude jolt by the public revelation of Amparo's past liaison with the unfrocked priest, Pedro Polo, but he characteristically assimilates this fact to his literary stereotypes. Amparo, he says, can only redeem herself by becoming a Sister of Charity, and devoting the rest of her life to caring for the sick. 'This,' he later explains to Felipe Centeno, 'as well as being poetic, is a means of regeneration. Just think how pretty she will be with her white coif' (OC 4, 1565).

If Ido were the only one to make this suggestion, we could easily dismiss it as shallow and trivial, but the idea has already been mentioned by another character possessed of a much more practical and unsentimental nature. In Chapter 5, Rosalía Bringas, in whose house Amparo has an indeterminate status midway between poor relation and unpaid servant, declares that Amparo should become a nun, and in succeeding chapters tries to interest her wealthy relative Agustín Caballero in supplying the dowry. On the face of it, Rosalía's suggestion seems sensible enough: in the Spain of 1867 (when the events of the novel are supposed to occur), girls as poor and friendless as Amparo were usually faced with a choice between successful marriage, prostitution and the convent.[1] The first seems initially unlikely and the second is unthinkable, so the third seems the only realistic choice. Ironically, however, Amparo's ultimate achievement of economic security has more in common with the morally unacceptable second alternative than with any other, and this has the effect of throwing the naivety of Rosalía's solution into relief. Furthermore, her suggestion appears in an even more ironic light when it is echoed by Ido's absurd notions about the plot of a possible novel based on Amparo's life, and this in turn undermines the reader's confidence in the social structure which sanctions Rosalía's solution.

With *Tormento*, then, Galdós has taken a further step towards a full-bodied social realism. In parodying Ido's novel, he is seeking not merely to underline the greater sophistication of his own work, but to suggest that sentimental fiction is one of the many conventional ways in which people falsify reality in accordance with their own preconceptions.[2] In *Tormento*, the popular novel is presented primarily as a socially-sanctioned frame of reference, and to that extent forms part of what a Marxist critic would call an 'ideology'. That is to say that the popular novel, like other frames of reference, such as religion, politics or conventional morality, provides a validating context within which relationships and motivations which are fundamentally economic may be rationalised as something else. The significance of *Tormento*, therefore, is that it is the first novel in which Galdós seriously calls in question the whole 'ideology' of bourgeois society.

This critique of bourgeois society co-exists in *Tormento* with Galdós's long-standing interest in individual ethical choices. Ethics, however, now acquires even deeper social roots than before, not least because the society which Galdós is subjecting to critical analysis is that to which the reader also belongs. Since Galdós's questioning of the accepted 'ideology' is radical and pervasive, it follows that many of the assumptions which he undermines will inevitably be those dear to his readers. He therefore takes considerable care to guide the reader's moral understanding by techniques of ironic juxtaposition. A good example is his treatment of Amparo's feelings of guilt about her past liaison with Pedro Polo. At one level, Amparo's moral bewilderment leads her to feel that she can partly exonerate herself, but for the most part she unquestioningly accepts the conventional wisdom of society:

> Lo de marras fue alucinación, desvarío, algo de inconsciente, irresponsable y estúpido, como lo que se hace en estado de sonambulismo o bajo la acción de un narcótico. Pero tales argumentos, amontonados hasta formar como una torre, no destruían el hecho, y el hecho venía brutal y terrible a encender la luz de su clara lógica en el vértice de aquel obelisco de distingos (OC 4, 1530).

> *(What happened in the past was a hallucination, a fit of madness, something unconsious, irresponsible and stupid, such as one might do when sleep-walking or under the influence of a drug. But such arguments, piled on top of each other so as to make a sort of tower, did not annul the fact in itself, and the fact arose, brutal and terrifying, to light the lamp of its clear logic on the tip of that obelisk of mental reservations.)*

It is understandable that the mere fact of a love-affair with a priest should be a source of moral anguish, and Galdós conveys Amparo's inner torment with great vividness and sympathy. Nevertheless, 'the fact in itself' clearly does not constitute grounds for a moral judgement, unless questions of motivation are also taken into account. As if to underline this, Galdós structures the climax of the novel around the public disgrace which ensues when Doña Marcelina Polo finds Amparo alone with Don Pedro in his rooms, and draws the wrong inference. Far from engaging in any licentious behaviour, Amparo was successfully resisting Polo's attempts to make her spend the night with him as the price of his silence about their affair.

That the general public's interpretation of the facts is so wide of the mark makes the reader less willing to accept at its face value Amparo's self-condemnatory view of her relationship with Polo. Moreover, the extent and nature of Amparo's guilt is called in question at an even more fundamental level, for although at certain moments she thinks of herself as the victim of Polo's predatory instincts, we are left in no doubt that there is more to the relationship than this. Though in her second interview with Polo in Chapter 28 she tries to push the responsibility for her situation on to him, she does not contradict him when, playfully lifting her on to his shoulder to demonstrate his strength, he says, 'You needn't turn prim all of a sudden, because it isn't the first time' (OC 4, 1536). Nor has she any answer to his claim that she once reciprocated and encouraged his passionate devotion:

> — ¿Para qué me miraste? . . . tu boca preciosa, ¿qué me dijo? ¿No lo recuerdas? Yo sí. . . . Las cosas que entonces oí no se oyen sin desquiciamiento del alma. Y ahora, ¿lo que tú desquiciaste quieres que yo lo vuelva a poner como estaba? (OC 4, 1537).

> ('Why did you look at me? . . . What did your lovely lips say? Don't you remember? I do. . . . A man can't listen to the things I heard then without being shaken to the core. And now it's my job, is it, to put back together what you turned inside out?')

The revelation of this aspect of the relationship makes Amparo's remorse seem misplaced, not because she is being too hard on herself, but because her feelings of guilt are directed to the wrong object. Her mind is so occupied by anguish over her transgression against the letter of the moral code that she does not perceive that her past relationship with Polo contained an element of honesty and mutual trust, and that in repudiating him she may well be turning her back on something very genuine.

The fiction of institutions

At an even deeper level, however, Amparo's attachment to conventional morality is a rationalisation of an economic motive, because of the competing claims on her affections of the poverty-stricken Polo and the wealthy returned colonist, Agustín Caballero. The presentation of Agustín has been interpreted as indicating Galdós's admiration for the entrepreneurial class, in whom he allegedly sees 'the only possible hope of a future regeneration of Spain'.[3] It is true that Galdós describes Agustín as bearing the physical marks of that 'colonising apostolate which, at the cost of the lives and health of so many noble workers, is shaping the powerful civilisations of the Hispanoamerican world' (OC 4, 1467). This remark, however, arises from Galdós's personal nostalgia for Spain's imperial past, which was very pronounced in the mid-1880s,[4] and in any case such comments are extremely rare in *Tormento*. What Galdós emphasises most about Agustín is that, having spent all his adult years accumulating wealth in a society characterised by greed, barbarism and moral anarchy, he now longs to enjoy the fruits of his labours in what he believes to be a more orderly and civilised environment. Though he is critical of certain aspects of Spanish life, it is because he is disappointed that many of the people he encounters do not measure up to the ideal of sobriety, modesty and moral rectitude which he has forged in his mind.

We can now see more clearly why Galdós's ironic criticism of Ido's sentimental version of Amparo's story has such wide social and economic implications, for it is precisely because of Agustín's desire to enjoy his *rentier* existence in peace that he constructs in his mind an ideal image of Amparo scarcely distinguishable from that projected in Ido's novel: 'Just looking at her told me all I needed to know about her. Suspicions of deceit, of double-dealing, of untruthfulness . . . Ah, no such thing could find a place in my heart when I saw her' (OC 4, 1479). This idealised image of Amparo will, of course, be poignantly shattered when Agustín finds out about her affair with Polo, and undoubtedly Galdós presents Agustín's reaction to the discovery with great understanding and sensitivity. But however much we may sympathise with Agustín, we must regard his reaction as predictable, because of the way in which his feelings about Amparo are bound up with his wholehearted commitment to existing religious, moral, and social institutions.

These institutions are clearly presented in the novel as resting on somewhat flimsy foundations. It can hardly be fortuitous that Galdós places the events of *Tormento* a few months before the Revolution of 1868, and the frequent references to growing unrest in the country imply a comment on the fragility of the values which Agustín and most of the other characters pursue. True, as we saw in Chapter 1, Galdós was well aware that the Revolution had changed very little, inasmuch as the general moral climate of Restoration society was essentially similar to that of Isabelline Spain (OC 4, 1465). Nevertheless, Galdós is less concerned in *Tormento* with the long-term consequences of the Revolution than with establishing that the values and institutions by which Agustín sets such store are not as natural or as permanent as he likes to suppose.

It follows that the doubt and irony which surround social and moral institutions in the novel affect our response to the relationship between Amparo and Agustín. True, the early stages of their friendship contain elements which would appeal to most readers: their shyness at the outset; the distress they experience when Amparo's secret becomes known; their sensible and down-to-earth approach to the organisation of their married life, which forms such an attractive contrast to the frivolity and pretentiousness of most of the other characters; Amparo's poverty, and her patience in the face of the humiliations daily inflicted on her by Rosalía Bringas. If, however, Galdós takes such pains to establish that the aspirations of the couple are natural and legitimate, it is because he wishes to emphasise that self-interest may underlie the most normal human relationships. While giving due weight to the appealing features listed above, he skilfully introduces touches of irony designed to prevent us from identifying fully and uncritically with the happiness of the couple. 'One could never see, by the light of a gas-lamp in the populous solitude of a drab street, a more innocent or insipid idyll' (OC 4, 1511). This remark is strategically placed just at the stage when Amparo and Agustín are beginning to experience the euphoria of new love, and is quickly followed by another devaluing image from the world of sentimental religious art: 'Caballero was so proud and so moved that he would not have changed places with the angels who play their harps on the steps of the Creator's throne'.

Ultimately, however, the most important of these ironic techniques is the way in which the development of the relationship is inextricably associated with the complex of conventional values which the author consistently calls in question. It is noticeable, in the following passage, how Agustín's quest for stable and predictable patterns of life expresses itself simultaneously in the public and private spheres. It is also worthy of note that, despite the frequent emphasis on Agustín's generosity with his money at various points in the novel, his thoughts group themselves decisively around the idea of his own comfort and convenience:

> Aquel buen hombre ... tenía, al entregarse al descanso, la pasión del orden, la manía de las comodidades, y de cuanto pudiera hacer placentera y acompasada la vida ... Había establecido en su casa un régimen por el cual todo se hacía a horas fijas. Las comidas se le habían de servir a punto, y hasta en cosas muy poco importantes ponía riguroso método ... Este prurito de orden y regularidad se manifestaba más aún en las cosas de más alto interés. Por lo mismo que había pasado lo mejor de su vida en medio del desorden, al llegar a la edad madura sentía vehemente anhelo de rodearse de paz, y de asegurarla arrimándose a las instituciones que la llevan consigo. Por esto aspiraba a la familia, al matrimonio, y quería que fuese su casa firmísimo asiento de las leyes morales (OC 4, 1512).

> *(When he came to devote himself to leisure, our good friend had a passion for order, a mania for comforts and for anything that could make life pleasant and smooth. He had established in his house a regime whereby everything was done at fixed hours. Meals had to be served punctually, and he was rigorously methodical even in very trivial matters. This desire for order and regularity was displayed even more clearly in higher concerns. Precisely because he had spent the better part of his life in the midst of disorder, he now felt, in his mature years, an ardent desire to surround himself with peace, and to ensure it by seeking the protection of institutions and ideas which bring peace. That was why he aspired to family life and marriage, and why he wanted his home to be the sure seat of moral law.)*

The fiction of religion

The public and institutional concerns which influence Agustín's thinking are less marked in Amparo's perception of their relationship, but the element of personal advantage still bulks very large. Though she does not brazenly and cynically exploit the affections of a wealthy man, and aspires only to a modest decency, her presentation is nevertheless characterised by ironic touches which make us question her image of herself. One of the most important examples of this occurs in the first scene between herself and Polo in Chapter 13. Amparo has resolved, four months previous to the events of *Tormento*, not to see Polo again, but relents when she receives a letter suggesting he is on the point of death. When she arrives at his lodgings, she breaks down almost immediately:

> Vuelta la espalda al enfermo, estaba inmóvil y en pie, como una de esas bonitas imágenes que, vestidas de terciopelo, barnizada la cara y con un pañuelo en la mano, representan con su llanto eterno la salvación por el arrepentimiento (OC 4, 1493).

> *(She stood motionless with her back to the sick man, like one of those pretty statues clothed in velvet, with varnished faces and a handkerchief in one hand, which represent, with their eternal weeping, salvation by repentance.)*

Though we have no warrant for supposing that Amparo is deliberately modelling herself on an artistic representation, it remains true that the comparison underlines the stereotyped and artificial nature of her behaviour: the use of the word 'varnished', with its overtones of 'superficiality' or 'veneer', is particularly significant here. This is only one of several occasions in the novel when she either sees herself, or presents herself to others, as the innocent victim of another's lust, devoting her life to 'repentance'.

Just as Amparo has a conventional view of herself, so also she sees the two men in her life respectively as terrifying persecutor and generous benefactor. Precisely because money governs her relationship with Agustín from the beginning, her dominant feeling towards him is gratitude. Affection is bound up with self-interest in *both* partners: Agustín sees Amparo as guaranteeing his comfort, peace and security; she in turn perceives him as providing a sound economic future. This is borne out by the way in which the beginnings of the couple's relationship are presented in Chapters 9–12. Just before the end of Chapter 9, Amparo has received the first tenuous intimation of Agustín's devotion. A few days later, early in Chapter 10, Don Francisco Bringas refuses Amparo her usual weekly gratuity, an incident witnessed by Agustín. About two hours later, Agustín's servant Felipe Centeno arrives with an envelope for Amparo which proves to contain a substantial sum of money. Her first instinct is to return the gift, but to give herself time to think she engages Felipe in conversation. Felipe expatiates at length on his master's wealth, and on the sumptuous décor and fittings of his new house. The description comes to rest on the detail of a certain music box, in the form of a cage with mechanical birds. Though Amparo is amused by Felipe's chatter, her eyes, at this point, suddenly fill with tears. Why this should happen is not explained, but in any case the reasons are unimportant, for the main effect of Amparo's tears, and the break in Felipe's narration, is to underline the detail of the mechanical birds, which may be taken to sum up all the images of luxury and material wealth in the description of the house. The chirping of these same mechanical birds will later provide an ironic counterpoint to Amparo's attempted suicide, when she believes her secret has been revealed by Doña Marcelina Polo: 'Por un instante, la monomanía del suicidio se suavizó, permitiéndole contemplar la bonita habitación. ¡Qué sillería, qué espejos, qué alfombra! . . . Morirse allí era una delicia . . . relativa' (OC 4, 1555) (For a moment, her obsession with suicide abated, allowing her to take in the beautiful room. What fine chairs, what elegant mirrors, what a beautiful carpet! To die there was a delight . . . relatively speaking).

The first phase of the relationship between Amparo and Agustín (up to her attempted suicide in Chapter 34), is, then, neatly bracketed, as it were, by these images of opulence. Furthermore, it is money that first puts their relationship on a firm footing. On the first occasion when they meet after Agustín's initial gift is delivered by Felipe, Amparo's words are all of gratitude, and from this point on, Agustín, assuming rather than asking her consent, takes charge of her financial affairs and provides her with a regular income, so that she can prepare for marriage in a decorous manner. Though the genuineness of Agustín's generosity and Amparo's thankfulness is never in doubt, money nevertheless comes to imprison them in their situation. Ignorant of Amparo's guilty secret, and mistaking her hesitation for modesty, Agustín heaps further gifts upon her, and this makes it both more difficult for her to be frank with him and more likely that he will feel betrayed when the secret inevitably comes out. Amparo, for her part, finds it increasingly difficult to exercise independent moral judgement as Agustín assumes a benevolent but firm control over her material affairs, and the anguish of her conscience is intensified by her failure to speak out, which she feels becomes more criminal as her financial dependence is strengthened. At a strategic moment, Galdós chooses to emphasise that the combination of moral scruple and self-interest which makes up Amparo's dilemma is really the key to her character: 'Oh selfishness, the root of life, how you hurt when the hand of duty tries to pluck you out! [She] was neither perverse enough to commit fraud, nor self-denying enough to avoid it' (OC 4, 1518).

The search for authenticity

It is against this background that we must understand the role of Pedro Polo. It is significant that both the encounters between Amparo and Polo are immediately preceded by explicit insistence on the theme of money: the first meeting comes just after the receipt of Agustín's first gift, the second after Amparo's visit to her luxuriously-appointed future home. The object of this juxtaposition is not merely to highlight Polo's poverty or the threat which he poses to Amparo's matrimonial prospects, but to suggest a deeper contrast with Agustín, and, by implication, with the values he represents.

One difference between Polo and Agustín which strikes the reader immediately is the ex-priest's external demeanour. Where the older man is correct and sedate in everything he does, Polo is vehement, prone to bouts of maudlin self-pity, frequently coarse in speech and violent in action. This contrast is the external expression of the respective success or failure of each in fulfilling his assigned role within bourgeois society. Whereas Agustín is quite comfortable in the character of a retired entrepreneur, legitimately enjoying the fruits of years of hard work, Polo has repudiated his assigned role, and is still in search of another. Now that he has withdrawn from the priesthood, there is no niche into which he will fit, nor are there any guidelines he can follow. Consequently, he has to rebuild his life and integrate his personality anew by trying to be true to his own intuitions.

Galdós skilfully exploits Polo's search for an authentic personality so as to express an alternative set of values to those pursued by Amparo and Agustín. In the midst of all his coarseness and self-pity, Polo retains a certain kind of uncompromising honesty. It is precisely this, indeed, which has caused the disintegration of his previous identity as a priest, and has led directly to his present disorientation and inertia. He now realises that his priesthood did not spring from a true vocation, but constituted what he calls, with characteristic abrasiveness, 'el gran error de mi vida, que es haberme metido donde no me llamaban y haber engañado a la sociedad y a Dios, poniéndome una máscara para hacer el bu a la gente' (OC 4, 1499) (the great mistake of my life, which was to wade into where I had no call to be, and to deceive society and God, putting on a mask to scare the daylights out of people).

Polo's rebellion against pretence extends to all the institutions and conventions of the society in which he lives.[5] His uncompromising independence of outlook, however, does not make him proof against slipping into sentimental clichés, superficially akin to those used by other characters. For example, when Amparo gives him a small packet of cigars, he is almost moved to tears, and thinks of her as a benevolent fairy or nymph (OC 4, 1498). There is, however, an important difference between Polo and the other characters, for his fabrication of mental fictions displays a certain child-like simplicity which is of a different order from their use of literary or artistic clichés as a cloak for egoism. Consequently, when in Chapter 17 we find him deliberately plunging into reverie in order to escape from his present condition, we should be slow to dismiss him as an idle pipe-dreamer. It is true that his visions are nebulous in some respects, but too much precision would be implausible. In the main, Galdós structures the day-dreams carefully so that their salient features can emerge with great clarity and force. The most important result of this procedure is that we may observe a progression in the three alternative roles

Polo dreams of (as an intrepid warrior, a prosperous farmer, and a citizen of a modern industrial state), from remoteness and vagueness towards greater concreteness and feasibility. Furthermore, even the most apparently far-fetched image of all, that of the *conquistador*, has some basis in reality, for Galdós stresses that Polo might, in a more heroic age, have found an outlet for his energies: 'He was born to tame savages, to command soldiers of fortune, perhaps even to conquer an empire like his fellow-Extremeñan Cortés' (OC 4, 1495). From Polo's vision of military glory we return via more mundane occupations to the political realities of contemporary Spain. The end of the reverie is worth quoting at some length to show how Galdós, by making a smooth transition from the visionary to the everyday, contrives to suggest that there is nothing intrinsically absurd about Polo's secret aspirations:

> Sentado luego con joviales amigos alrededor de una mesilla, echaba tragos de espumosa cerveza; cogía un periódico tan grande como una sábana . . . ¿En qué lengua estaba escrita? Debía de ser en inglés. Fuera inglés o no, él lo entendía perfectamente, leyendo esto: 'Gran revolución en España; caída de la Monarquía; abolición del estado eclesiástico; libertad de cultos . . . '
> — El periódico, el periódico — gritó la espectral Celedonia poniéndole delante un papel húmedo con olor muy acre de tinta de imprimir.
> — ¡Qué casualidad! — exclamó él . . .
> Empezó . . . a leer su periódico con mucha atención. Desgraciadamente para él, la Prensa, amordazada por la previa censura, no podía ya dar al público noticias alarmantes, ni hablar de las partidas de Aragón, acaudilladas por Prim, ni hacer presagios de próximos trastornos. Pero aquel periódico sabía poner entre líneas todo el ardor revolucionario que al país abrasaba, y Polo sabía leerlo y se encantaba con la idea de un cataclismo que volviera la cosa del revés. Si él pudiese arrimar el hombro a obra tan grande, ¡con qué gusto lo haría! (OC 4, 1503).

> *(After this, [he saw himself] sitting with a group of jovial friends around a table, quaffing draughts of frothy beer. He picked up a paper as big as a bedsheet. What language was it in? Probably English. Whether English or not, he understood it perfectly, and this is what he read: 'Major revolution in Spain; fall of the Monarchy; abolition of the clerical estate; freedom of worship'.*
> *'The paper, the paper,' cried the ghostly Celedonia, thrusting at him a still-damp newspaper which smelt pungently of printer's ink.*
> *'What a strange coincidence!' he exclaimed.*
> *He began to read his newspaper very attentively. Unhappily for him, the press, muzzled by the censorship, could no longer give the public disquieting news, nor mention the risings in Aragon, led by Prim, nor predict imminent upheavals. But that particular newspaper managed to express between the lines all the revolutionary ardour which was then inflaming the country. Polo knew how to interpret it and was delighted at the prospect of a cataclysm which would turn everything upside down. If he could throw his weight behind such a worthy task, how pleased he would be to do it!)*

The fiction of motives

What this reverie episode ultimately does, then, is to underline once more the fragility and relativity of existing institutions and categories of value. This makes Polo's desire to emigrate, and his hopes of finding elsewhere a more natural and egalitarian society, seem valid by contrast, even if in practice they are unlikely to be realised. Naive and idealised as his vision of life in the colonies may be, we judge it not as a practical project but as an expression of priorities and ideals. This is particularly so because his vision of a creative and authentic life overseas contrasts markedly with Agustín's more conventional view that the colonies exist solely to be exploited materially by Europeans.

We are now perhaps in a better position to interpret Amparo's behaviour in her two interviews with Polo. As regards their first encounter, it is by no means certain that she would have gone to see him at all had she not, shortly before, received the first intimation of Agustín's intention to marry her, and his initial gift of money. Although her conscience tells her that she should help a sick and abandoned person who has some claim on her loyalty, her real motivation arises from the threat which she believes Polo poses to her matrimonial prospects (OC 4, 1500).[6]

Amparo's equivocation confers on the episode which follows in Chapters 13–16 a rich texture of implications which it is all too easy for the reader to overlook. It is true that she rejects Polo partly because her rather puritanical and fastidious temperament recoils from his coarse manners and undisciplined life-style. Indeed, were Polo a more obviously attractive character, Amparo's preference for Agustín would imply a more deliberate choice of wealth for its own sake, and this would put her egoism in sharper relief than Galdós appears to intend. What is certain, however, is that Amparo is better placed than anyone to know that there is another side to this rather contradictory man. In their first meeting, she herself reminds Polo of how he paid for her father's funeral and even sold his own clothes so that she and Refugio could eat; in the second, she witnesses his tenderness towards the ailing Celedonia. It is not, however, Amparo's personal revulsion against Polo which is primarily emphasised in the first interview, but the contrast between his visionary breadth of spirit and her ungenerous and conventional outlook. When he expresses his need for a freer atmosphere than that of Spain, she stubbornly keeps repeating that she intends to dedicate her life to repentance. But if repentance really were the guiding principle of her life, she would not later agree to become Agustín's mistress. The truth of the matter is that repentance is a convenient religious cliché behind which self-interest can hide, and the same is true of the way in which she thinks of her assisting Polo as an 'act of charity'.

There is a special irony in this latter excuse, for Amparo shows clearly in this scene that she has a natural talent for domestic management. It is, indeed, primarily as mistress of a household that Amparo is perceived by both Agustín and Polo, but the emphasis in each man's thinking is characteristically different. Whereas for Agustín she is the person best qualified to implement his

ideas of domestic order and regularity, Polo sees her as someone who has the
gift of shedding light and life around her wherever she goes:

> Cierto día entró inopidamente en [la casa] alguien que parecía celestial
> emisario, y aquel recinto muerto y lóbrego tomó vida, luz. Pronto se vio
> aparecer sobre todo esa sonrisa de las cosas que anuncia la acción de una
> mano inteligente y gobernosa, y quien con más júbilo se alzaba del polvo
> para gozar de aquella dulce caricia era el doliente, aterido, desgarrado y
> maltrecho don Pedro Polo (OC 4, 1496–7).

> *(On a certain day, someone who seemed a messenger from heaven unexpec-
> tedly came to the house, and that dead and gloomy place took on life and
> light. Soon everything began to show that smiling aspect which reveals the
> action of an intelligent and efficient hand, and it was the sick, numbed,
> tattered and bruised Pedro Polo who most joyfully arose from the dust to
> receive that tender caress.)*

Not for nothing does Polo visibly revive in this episode, progressing in a matter
of minutes from indolence and depression to greater cheerfulness and vitality.
It is Amparo's presence which works this miracle, but she is too wrapped up in
her own concerns to see how necessary she is to Polo's well-being, or to realise
that if she were to join him in his quest for a more purposeful and authentic
existence, there would be a greater prospect of this quest succeeding. One of
the least far-fetched parts of Polo's reverie in Chapter 17 is that in which he
imagines himself married to Amparo. Far from being centred on his own
comfort, Polo's thoughts are full of images of fertility, love and joy, suggesting
a more natural and vital kind of opulence than the purely material riches
associated with Agustín:

> Se recreaba oyendo cómo resonaban sus propias carcajadas dentro de
> aquella sala rústica, con anchísimo hogar de leña ardiendo, poblado el
> techo de chorizos y morcillas, y viendo entrar y salir muy afanada a una
> guapísima y fresca señora . . . No se confundían, no, aquellas facciones con
> las de otra. ¡Y qué manera de conservarse, mejorando en vez de perder! A
> cada pimpollo que daba de sí, aumentando con dichosa fecundidad la
> familia humana, parecía que el Cielo agradecido le concedía un aumento de
> belleza. Era una diosa, la señora Cibeles, madraza eterna y eternamente
> bella . . . Porque nuestro visionario se veía rodeado de tan bullicioso
> enjambre de criaturas, que a veces no le dejaban tiempo para consagrarse a
> sus ocupaciones y se pasaba el día enredando con ellas (OC 4, 1502).

> *(He listened with delight to his own laughter resounding through that rustic
> room, with its blazing wood fire and its roof-beams festooned with sausages
> and black puddings. He delighted, too, in watching an attractive and
> apple-cheeked lady bustling in and out. Impossible to confuse her features
> with anyone else's. And how well preserved she was! Her looks seemed to
> improve with the years, rather than fade. Each time she brought forth a*

bonny babe, increasing the human family with her happy fruitfulness, it seemed as if Heaven, in thankfulness, granted her an increase in beauty. She was a goddess, dame Cybele, the eternal matron, eternally beautiful. For our visionary saw himself surrounded by such a boisterous brood of children, that they sometimes left him no time for his work, and he would spend the whole day playing with them.)

This glimpse of rich, creative life makes Polo's future activity as a missionary in the Philippines seem altogether sterile. One of the most tragic ironies in the novel is that Don Pedro only achieves his wish to go abroad at the price of stifling the real self he has been struggling to discover. It is true that there are many practical arguments in favour of his adopting Fr. Nones's suggestion that he apply for readmission to the priesthood and go abroad, but as Robert Ricard has shrewdly remarked, there is a real danger that in that environment, without Nones to keep him on a tight rein, he will finally collapse into moral degradation.[7] Even more significant is the fact that Polo himself[8] is lucid enough to realise that his acceptance of Nones's plan entails a kind of spiritual suicide: 'The beast lives,' he writes to Amparo, 'the sensitive being dies. But what matter — oh excruciating irony! — if principle has been salvaged?' (OC 4, 1524).

The main reason why Polo, against his better judgement, acquiesces in Nones's plan is that Amparo refuses to share his vision of an alternative future. Amparo, of course, does not realise the full implications of her refusal. Her blindness on this point both mitigates the callousness of her decision and underlines the conventional nature of her moral thinking and her economic priorities. Nevertheless, there is still something appalling about the ease with which she can fall back on sentimental images drawn from the world of fiction in order to assuage her guilty feelings about continuing to conceal her secret from Agustín:

> Veía un hombre bárbaro navegando en veloz canoa con otros salvajes por un río de lejanas e inexploradas tierras, como las que traía en sus estampas el libro de *La vuelta al mundo*. Era un misionero que había ido a cristianizar cafres en aquellas tierras que están a la otra parte del mundo, redondo como una naranja, allá donde es de noche cuando aquí es de día (OC 4, 1526).

> *(She saw a barbarian sailing with other savages in a swift canoe on a river in distant and unexplored lands, like those which figured in the illustrations to the book* Around the World [in Eighty Days?].[9] *He was a missionary who had gone to Christianise Hottentots in those places which are on the other side of the world, round as an orange, where it is night when here it is day.)*

This is as good an example as any of Galdós's radical critique of bourgeois 'ideology'. Trivial and immature thinking such as Amparo displays here is fostered by, among other things, the industrialisation which makes available to the public at large illustrated editions of popular novels such as those of Jules Verne. 'To Christianise Hottentots' ('cristianizar cafres') is a contemptuous echo of views such as that which Doña Marcelina expresses on the eve of her brother's departure to the Philippines: 'You will have plenty of opportunities to become virtuous and meritorious, because there are lots to savages to convert out there' (OC 4, 1542). 'Round as an orange' recalls the naive ideas of foreign geography which Amparo displayed in a conversation with Agustín in Chapter 8, and, by extension, reflects the shallowness of conventional education. The last phrase in the passage is a direct reminiscence of a remark by Polo which brings the relativity and falseness of received values back into sharp focus: 'Institutions . . . seem like grains of sand when we . . . transport ourselves to where it is now night' (1499).

This nexus of implications lends a particular dramatic intensity to the second interview between Amparo and Polo in Chapters 28 and 29. In addition, there is by then a new quality in Amparo's demeanour. Though bewilderment, fear and moral confusion are still the dominant influences on her behaviour, the element of calculation and purposefulness comes to acquire more prominence as her economic dependence on Agustín is confirmed.[10] Not only does she realise that her interests are best served by a cool-headed and diplomatic approach, but she has a new awareness of the power which Polo's hunger for affection gives her: 'You will defeat the monster,' she tells herself, 'for you are the only person on earth who can do it. That wild beast, whom no-one can chain, will yield to your skilful hand' (OC 4, 1534). Whereas in the first interview Amparo had unconsciously modelled herself on an iconographical stereotype, she is now, much more deliberately, exploiting new-found acting and manipulative skills:

> — Bien veo lo que tú quieres: casarte y ser poderosa, y que el mismo día de la boda yo me pegue un tiro para que todo quede en secreto.
> — No, no quiero eso.
> Amparo sintió que se afinaban más sus agudezas y aquel saber de comedianta que había adquirido. Comprendió que un lenguaje ligeramente cariñoso sería muy propio del caso.
> — No, no quiero que te mates. Eso me daría mucha pena . . . Pero sí quiero que te vayas lejos, como pensabas y te aconsejó el padre Nones. No puede haber nada entre nosotros, ni siquiera amistad. Alejándote, el tiempo te irá curando poco a poco; sentirás arrepentimiento sincero, y Dios te perdonará, nos perdonará a los dos.
> Profundamente conmovido, el bárbaro miraba al suelo. Creyendo en probabilidades de triunfo, la cuitada reforzó su argumento . . . , llegó hasta ponerle la mano en el hombro, cosa que no hubiera hecho poco antes.
> — Hazlo por mí, por Dios, por tu alma — le dijo con dulce acento (OC 4, 1538).

> (*'I can see very well what you want. You want to get married and be rich, and you'd like me to shoot myself on the very day of the wedding, so that everything remains hidden.'*

'No, I don't want that.'

Amparo felt her acumen sharpening, along with that actress-skill she had suddenly acquired. She realised that a slightly affectionate tone would be appropriate to the occasion.

'No, I don't want you to kill yourself. That would grieve me very much. But I do want you to go away, as you had intended and as Fr. Nones advised you. There can be nothing more between us, not even friendship. If you go away, time will cure you little by little. You will feel sincere repentance, and God will forgive you, forgive us both.'

Deeply moved, the ruffian stared at the ground. Convinced that victory was near, the faint-hearted girl pressed her argument, even bringing herself to put a hand on his shoulder, something she would not have done even a few minutes before.

'Do it for my sake, for God's, for your soul's,' she said in dulcet tones.)

Amparo's treatment of Polo, and his final acceptance of it, enable him, with all his human limitations, to acquire a quasi-tragic status. It is, moreover this episode which gives the most specifically moral twist to the basic theme of the novel, the artificiality of bourgeois society. While Agustín loves a false image of Amparo, and cannot come to terms with reality when it is revealed, Polo is the only person to accept Amparo as she really is. Even though he knows what her true priorities are, and how much she detests him, he makes a supreme act of renunciation for her sake. Ironically, it is precisely Amparo's insistence on extracting a guarantee that Polo will not pursue her after her marriage that leads to the public revelation of her secret: she lingers in Polo's lodgings a little too long, and is discovered there by Doña Marcelina. We have already seen that Amparo is innocent of the specific misdemeanour which the public believes her to have committed, but by depriving Polo of the chance of ever finding himself again, and by opting for the values of the society which is erroneously condemning her, Amparo is guilty of an even graver sin, against which there are no laws, and for which she will suffer no loss of reputation.

Only by ignoring the implications of Amparo's relationship with Polo can we claim, as Ricardo Gullón does, that 'Amparo loves generously . . . In her conduct there is nothing ignoble'.[11] Furthermore, if we underestimate the extent of her egoism, we are likely to misinterpret the ending of the novel. It is true that Amparo finally does confess to Agustín that she had an affair with Polo, and that Agustín ultimately appears to repudiate all the social institutions he had formerly admired. Sherman H. Eoff, however, is going to unwarranted lengths in claiming that 'Caballero and Amparo together represent the victory of the individual over convention',[12] for his interpretation overlooks two important pieces of evidence. Firstly, Amparo's willingness to accept the stigma of living openly with Agustín as his mistress contrasts strikingly with her earlier efforts to avoid public disgrace at all costs, and is due to the material ambition which has throughout the novel determined both her feelings for him and her fear of exposure.[13] Secondly, Agustín's rebellion against convention is only apparent, for instead of rising above man-made laws and marrying Amparo, he accepts the commonly sanctioned view that having lost her reputation she is fit only to be his mistress. Unlike Polo, who rejects established morality as part of the search for more authentic values, Agustín is still primarily attentive to his own pleasure: 'When a fellow gets to forty-five, must he look old age in the face and not live a bit before it catches up with him?' (OC 4, 1567).

The truth of fiction

Any account of *Tormento* must come back in the end to José Ido, and his sentimentalised version of Amparo's story, but our feelings about him are likely to be somewhat different after we have read Galdós's narrative. Puerile as the starving hack-writer's fantasies may be, they are scarcely more insidious or meretricious than the egoism and moral blindness of most of the other characters. Besides, by the end of the novel we are as much aware of similarities as of differences between the two accounts. Like the popular novels written by the Idos of this world, *Tormento*, as has been rightly pointed out, ministers to the reader's demand for excitement, intrigue and suspense.[14] This not only ensures that the reader's interest is maintained but also forms part of Galdós's overall moral strategy. Superficially, *Tormento* is so like a conventional novel with a happy ending that we need to keep reminding ourselves that it is nothing of the kind. In other words, to read this novel is to be led continually to the brink of making the hasty and facile judgements that serve us for everyday purposes and then to draw back in deference to the deeper and maturer vision suggested by the implications of the book as a whole. It is to be made aware of how uncritically we accept the highly questionable assumptions on which bourgeois society rests.

Tormento both breaks new ground by reason of the trenchancy of its social criticism and consolidates tendencies present in Galdós's earlier work, especially *El amigo Manso*. Both these novels show that for Galdós realism is essentially an ethical matter, for both are concerned with depicting accurately that contrast between true judgement and blindness which society so urgently needs to discern in the interest of its own moral well-being. Even more important, however, is the way in which both these works encourage us to blur, or perhaps even to invert, the normal relationship between what we conventionally understand by the terms 'fiction' and 'reality'. In *El amigo Manso*, the character who most vehemently insists on his own fictional status is ultimately left in possession of the only realities that matter, while those who claim to have their feet firmly planted on the earth amply deserve Máximo's dismissive label of 'sleepwalkers' (OC 4, 1291). *Tormento* functions in a similar way, for if we defer to the wisdom of the work in the way I have suggested, we are taking an imaginative leap into a fictional world which is in a sense more coherent and truthful than our 'real' world of direction-less contingency. As in *El amigo Manso*, the concrete presentation of life is vivid and detailed, but in the end the only true realities are large abstractions like love, honesty and sacrifice. Conversely, those who pursue tangible values like money, status, or institutional stability are caught in a web of their own making, and are living in a kind of fantasy-world. The fictions of 'real' people appear false when set beside the reality of fiction. It is in this sense that one may speak of *Tormento* as anti-fiction, for, as we have seen, José Ido is not the only character to think in terms of stereotyped images: even the stolid Don Francisco Bringas says that Amparo's good fortune in winning the hand of the rich Agustín could be made into a novel entitled *El premio de la virtud* (*Virtue Rewarded*), and Amparo's ostensible dedication to repentance is expressed on different occasions in terms of popular iconography and drama. In short, both *El amigo Manso* and *Tormento* vividly illustrate the truth of Harry Levin's lapidary statement that 'fiction approximates truth, not by concealing art, but by exposing artifice'.[15]

In *Tormento*, the 'artifice' being exposed is not purely literary, but embraces the whole tissue of relationships, conventions and institutions on which bourgeois society rests. For this reason, we may say that it is a perfect fusion of both the Enlightenment and Realist approaches to fiction. The whole thrust of the novel presupposes that literature can be used for cognitive ends, and, in the last analysis, it upholds ideas, ideals, and values, especially the value of critical analysis and correct understanding. It does so, however, not directly or discursively, but by dramatising ideas in concrete situations which encapsulate the whole range of social forces which determine how people behave.

Notes to Chapter 8

1. This point is made forcefully by Stephen Miller in his *El mundo de Galdós* (Santander, 1983), pp. 110–111.
2. Cf. Germán Gullón, 'Tres narradores en busca de un lector', *Anales Galdosianos*, 5 (1970), pp. 78–9.
3. José F. Montesinos, *Galdós*, 3 vols. (Madrid, 1968–73), vol. 2, p. 110.
4. Galdós was capable at times of expressing intensely patriotic, not to say nationalistic feelings, especially in the context of the Berlin West Africa Conference (which took place from 15 November 1884 until 26 February 1885), and the raising of the German flag on the Caroline Islands (traditionally claimed by Spain, though no effective attempt at settlement was made until 1885) on the night of 25 August 1885. Admittedly these events occurred after the completion of *Tormento* in January 1884, but Galdós's vehement reaction expresses a long-standing resentment of German expansionism, which he felt was an unfair attack on the rights and interests of older colonising nations such as Spain and Portugal (see especially Ined 6, 59–60). A year before completing *Tormento*, in January 1883, he had written an article on the visit of the German Crown Prince to Madrid in which, in the midst of his attempted impartiality, one can clearly discern his fear that German ambitions would provoke a European war (Ined 6, 9–10). A similar nationalistic attitude underlies Galdós's epistolary debate with Oller, extending approximately from late 1884 to the middle of 1886, over the latter's use of Catalan in his novels. Not only does Galdós consistently describe his own language as *español* rather than *castellano*, but he refers to it as 'la lengua de los dioses'. Furthermore, Galdós complains that the interests of Spain as a whole have been unfairly sacrificed to Catalan protectionism (See W. H. Shoemaker, 'Una amistad literaria: La correspondencia epistolar entre Galdós y Narciso Oller', *Boletín de la Real Academia de Buenas Letras de Barcelona*, 30 [1963–4], pp. 273–4).
5. A point which Alas, dismissing Polo as a 'jaundiced bear', appears to have overlooked (*Galdós* [Madrid, 1912], p. 132).

6. William R. Risley takes a similar view. See his '"Narrative overture" in Galdós's early *Novelas españolas contemporáneas*', *Kentucky Romance Quarterly*, 31 (1984), p. 142.
7. *Aspects de Galdós* (Paris, 1963), p. 56.
8. *Pace* Alas, who sees him as clay in Nones's hands (*Galdós*, p. 133).
9. Amparo could not, of course, have read Verne's novel, which was not published until 1873, but an illustrated Spanish translation had been available to readers of *Tormento* since 1880.
10. 'No se puede evitar el llegar a la conclusión . . . de que bajo la apariencia de debilidad con la que se proyecta hacia el mundo exterior, se trasluce en muchos sentidos una voluntad de hierro y hasta de osadía, por parte de la anti-heroína folletinesca' (Alicia Andreu, *Galdós y la literatura popular* [Madrid, SGEL, 1982], p. 144).
11. Ricardo Gullón, *Galdós, novelista moderno* (Madrid, Taurus, 1960), p. 75.
12. *The Novels of Pérez Galdós* (Washington University Studies, St. Louis, 1954), p. 118.
13. Though I agree with Alicia Andreu that Amparo's final situation is intended as an indirect critical comment both on Rosalía's rapacity and society's hypocrisy, I have reservations about her claim that 'la distorsión final del cuento de Cenicienta, en la cual la hermosa muchacha termina siendo amante y no esposa, es el castigo — atenuado si se quiere — de Amparo por querer salirse de su condición socio-económica, a través del matrimonio con un indiano rico' (*op. cit.*, p. 149). It is true that Galdós disapproves of Amparo's ambition, but he does so primarily on the grounds of her moral insensitivity, and he would have done so in any case, even if he had chosen to end the novel with the wedding of Amparo and Agustín. Had Professor Andreu paid more attention to Amparo's relationship with Polo, she might have concluded, as I do, that Amparo's real punishment consists, not in having to settle for 'kept woman' status, but in remaining unaware of her moral obtuseness.
14. See Frank Durand, 'Two problems in Galdós's *Tormento*', *Modern Language Notes*, 79 (1964), pp. 520–21.
15. *The Gates of Horn: A Study of Five French Realists* (New York, 1966), p. 51. First ed. 1963.

9

Worlds Apart: *Fortunata y Jacinta*

> '*Yes, my dear, we must put our hand on the heart of the common people to feel its robust heartbeat, but sometimes what we feel is not a heartbeat but a kick' (Juanito Santa Cruz in* Fortunata y Jacinta, *Part 1, Chapter 5.)*

> *Moral: what had to happen, in the inexorable succession of human needs, came to pass (*Fortunata y Jacinta, *Part 3, Chapter 4.)*

The cash nexus

As we saw in the last chapter, *Tormento* is, among other things, a vivid illustration of how the entire tissue of relationships and conventions operative in bourgeois society is determined by money. *Fortunata y Jacinta*, published in four volumes in 1887, focusses Galdós's concern with social and economic matters more specifically on the divisions between social classes, displaying, for the first time, a clear understanding of the moral and psychological effects of these divisions. Accordingly, the social context is very much denser than in any previous work. In Chapter 2 of Part 1, Galdós establishes this context by tracing the history of two interrelated families, Santa Cruz and Arnáiz. Since both these families are engaged in the drapery trade, the chapter is, in effect, an account of the rise of the Madrid commercial bourgeoisie in the first half of the nineteenth century.

Galdós fills out this story in so much detail that many readers have found this section of the novel prolix and irrelevant. Leopoldo Alas, in an open letter to Galdós published in *El Globo* soon after the work first appeared, could only manage a fairly half-hearted defence of Galdós's procedure: 'In the story of the relationships, a sort of dark jungle of lineages, some cuts could have been made, though not many . . . because the illusion of reality and the quality of the social study made all this work, or nearly all, necessary'.[1] J. P. Stern has attempted a more effective defence by claiming that the novel exemplifies 'the charm of institutions . . . outside [which] realistic fiction cannot breathe. The explicit demonstration of *how* the system works yields the implicit affirmation *that* it works'.[2] One can only agree with Stern that social institutions are part of the central subject-matter of this novel, rather than forming a mere backdrop, but, as we shall see, the evidence of the novel does not support his optimistic contention that Galdós's purpose was essentially to celebrate 'the charm of institutions'. The main point of the present chapter, indeed, is that Galdós wishes the reader to see that the system does *not* work, or only works to a very limited extent. The real justification for the leisurely description of the rise of the Madrid commercial bourgeoisie in Chapter 2 of Part 1 is that it is the outlook and character of this class which determine the subsequent tragic course of events. As with previous novels, Galdós, in writing *Fortunata y Jacinta*, selected his corroborative detail with great care, and with an eye to its thematic relevance. Despite the length of the work (greater than that of *War and Peace*), each section or chapter is bound to every other by a series of tight and precise connections, and the dense nexus of relationships which results constitutes a series of variations on his central theme.

   Three themes in particular stand out in the chapter in question: social mobility, progress and money, and the three in combination give a misleadingly optimistic impression of the openness and flexibility of society. Baldomero Santa Cruz was in the 1790s a humble shop-assistant, but by dint of hard work managed to pass on to his son Baldomero II (the Don Baldomero of the novel) a solid and lucrative business. Don Baldomero in turn consolidated the enterprise so that by 1868 he was able to retire with a considerable fortune which freed his son Juanito from the necessity to work. The transition from white-collar worker to idle rich *señorito* is complete in a mere two generations.

   The relative flexibility of social categories means that people can move down the social scale as well as up.[3] Though Arnáiz *el gordo* is extremely wealthy, his kinsman Gumersindo Arnáiz comes close to financial ruin because of his father's bad management. Gumersindo's marriage to Isabel Cordero produces seven daughters, who remain a drain on the family's resources until they are married off. The three marriages recorded in the novel illustrate the varied range of class relationships in which members of the same family can become involved. Candelaria's husband is a shop-assistant, as are all his brothers; he has an uncle a pharmacist and a cousin a fishmonger. Benigna, on the other hand, marries the son of a wealthy banker, one of whose relations is a Marquess and another a tavern-keeper. Jacinta, for her part, marries the aforementioned *señorito*, Juanito Santa Cruz.

   Superficially, then, the chapter conveys the impression of a vital, entrepreneurial society, relatively free of snobbery, in which social status is determined by money and ability rather than birth, where the enterprising can pull themselves up by their own bootstraps, and where because of intermarriage family bonds transcend class divisions.[4] When we look more closely at the narrative presentation, however, a less optimistic picture emerges. As Geoffrey Ribbans has wisely pointed out,

By putting [the narrator of Part 1], however marginally, into the same environment as that of a group of his characters, the novelist endows him to some extent with the same preoccupations and prejudices, the same limited knowledge and the same liability to error as his fellows, while exempting the author *qua* author from identification with these views.[5]

This is surely well said, for the three themes I identified above are presented with perceptible ambiguity. Don Baldomero's understanding of progress, for example, entails rejecting his own strict upbringing and allowing Juanito to do as he pleases, a policy which has tragic consequences in Juanito's seduction of Fortunata. His adaptation of his business to modern needs, however, is reluctant, superficial, and dictated by his response to random and disruptive social change:

> Para que el progreso pusiera su mano en la obra de aquel hombre extraordinario . . . fue preciso que todo Madrid se transformase; que la desamortización edificara una ciudad nueva sobre los escombros de los conventos; que el marqués de Pontejos adecentase este lugarón; que las reformas arancelarias del 49 y del 68 pusieran patas arriba todo el comercio madrileño; que el grande ingenio de Salamanca idease los primeros ferrocarriles . . . y por fin, que hubiera muchas guerras y revoluciones y grandes trastornos en la riqueza individual (OC 5, 28).

> *(In order that progress should play its part in the work of that extraordinary man, Madrid had first to be transformed. It was a precondition that the disentailment of lands held in mortmain should build a new city on the rubble of the monasteries; that the Marqués de Pontejos should tidy up this scruffy town; that the tariff reforms of 1849 and 1868 should turn the whole commercial life of Madrid upside down; that the great brain of Salamanca should plan the first railways; and finally that there should be many wars and revolutions and great upheavals in individual wealth.)*

This is not a description of healthy growth or planned improvement, but of violence and instability. Furthermore, revolution has not changed the social and economic structure, but created *nouveaux riches*. The disentailment of church lands in 1837 failed in its avowed aim of creating a solid class of peasant proprietors, and instead consolidated the prosperity of bourgeois speculators like Salamanca.[6] The narrator, however, glosses over these facts because, as Ribbans has cogently suggested, he himself inhabits 'this prosperous commercial world, which is portrayed as natural and its values as self-evident'.[7] Nor is the narrator aware that the purely cosmetic transformation of Don Baldomero's establishment is characteristic of Restoration society as a whole, as the novel conclusively proves.

Identified as he is with the values of this 'mesocratic' society, as Galdós so often called it, the narrator takes it for granted that money is the principal motor of human relations. People can come to be considered as commodities.

As with so much else in Part 1 of *Fortunata y Jacinta*, this is made to emerge in spite of the narrator's easy-going acceptance of conventional values, by virtue of the author's manipulation of what James Whiston has called 'the half-conscious regions of metaphor'.[8] The most notable example is the way in which Isabel Cordero de Arnáiz hawks her seven unmarried daughters around like merchandise:

> A esta fatiga ruda del espionaje materno uníase el trabajo de exhibir y airear el muestrario, por ver si caía algún parroquiano o, por otro nombre, marido. Era forzoso *hacer el artículo* y aquella gran mujer, negociante en hijas, no tenía más remedio que vestirse y concurrir con su género a tal o cual tertulia de amigas (OC 5, 33).

> *(On top of this hard chore of maternal espionage, there was the work of displaying and airing the samples, in order to tempt some customer, in other words a husband. It was necessary to 'push the product', and that great woman, a merchant of daughters, had no choice but to put on her best dress and take her wares to this or that gathering of friends.)*

The complacent presentation of the commercial bourgeoisie in Chapter 2 prepares us for the way in which their self-satisfied assumptions will later be challenged by the earthy spontaneity of Fortunata. Galdós links the bourgeois and lower-class worlds with a transitional chapter centred on the figure of Estupiñá, who is not only a witness to the historical changes described in Chapter 2 but also functions at more than one social level. Though he regards himself as a cut above his neighbours in the Cava de San Miguel, he nevertheless stands close to Fortunata's world: it is in the tenement house where he lives that Juanito first meets Fortunata. On the other hand, as a former employee of Don Bonifacio Arnáiz, he holds a respected position in both the Arnáiz and Santa Cruz households. Indeed, because of what the narrator calls 'the democratic temper of the Spaniards' (OC 5, 65), and their 'mild and innocuous socialism' (*ibid.*), Estupiñá is virtually accepted as a member of the Santa Cruz family. However, though social distinctions are blurred, they are never completely abolished. Manuel Moreno-Isla, while allowing Estupiñá to embrace him after a long absence, speaks to him with 'that somewhat frigid benevolence employed by well-bred superiors' (OC 5, 318).

Estupiñá also embodies some of the opportunism and corruption which Galdós hinted at in his historical survey of the rise of the bourgeoisie. Despite his artisan origins, he survives economically not by hard work or rules of conduct, but by his contacts ('las relaciones') and by his gift of the gab. For all his honesty in matters of private property, he defrauds the Treasury on a large scale by his smuggling activities. He is skilful at bribing customs officials, and frequently helps prominent citizens to sort out their problems with the Finance Ministry. During his brief career as a cloth retailer, he is brusque with working-class customers, but 'very polite to ladies of distinction' (OC 5, 36). This sycophantic tendency reaches even greater proportions in his unconditional devotion to the Santa Cruz family. He goes shopping with Doña Barbarita to ensure that she always gets the best bargains. He spies on Juanito during the latter's first affair with Fortunata, but his loyalty to his adored 'Dauphin' later leads him to draw a wall of silence around Juanito's sexual proclivities. He treats Fortunata harshly after her return to the Cava de San Miguel because the official family view is that she is an enemy.[9]

The limits of benevolence: the 'Pituso' episode

Although Estupiñá provides a link between social classes, the adoption of the complacent, not-quite-reliable narrative perspective of Part 1 necessarily entails that, at least during that volume, Fortunata's world is seen from a great distance. Apart from a brief appearance when she and Juanito meet on the stairs of the tenement house in the Cava de San Miguel, where Juanito is visiting the ailing Estupiñá, Fortunata is perceived only indirectly and insofar as she impinges on the self-confident world of the Santa Cruz family. Thus, for example, Barbarita, during Juanito's first affair, observes her son's coarsening of language and behaviour. The most important episode, however, in which Fortunata is felt as a shadowy, distant presence is the affair of the false *Pituso* in Chapters 8, 9, and 10. José Ido del Sagrario tells Jacinta of the existence of a child of Fortunata's by Juanito, a boy of between two and three years old, usually called *el Pituso* from his mother's nickname *la Pitusa*. Jacinta's obsession with her own childlessness leads her impulsively to decide to adopt *el Pituso* in the hope that Juanito will acknowledge him, and that he will be incorporated into the family. To this end, she enlists the support of a family friend, Doña Guillermina Pacheco, who has a reputation for charitable works, but whose attitudes are unmistakably conditioned by class loyalties.[10] Characteristically, Guillermina bullies the child's uncle and guardian, José Izquierdo, into parting with the boy for less than a third of the 5,000 pesetas he had originally demanded, and stipulates to Jacinta that the balance of the total sum is to be contributed to an orphanage which Guillermina is building.

The matter, in other words, is approached essentially as a commercial transaction, and this is true of both Guillermina and Jacinta. Although in the main Jacinta is presented sympathetically,[11] she clearly belongs to the same class as Guillermina, and shares the same assumptions. Her attitude to the children she encounters in the poor quarter of Madrid where *el Pituso* lives is a blend of sentimentality and insensitivity. For example, she is drawn to Adoración because she is clean and well-behaved, but soon loses interest in her when she comes into possession of her 'toy', *el Pituso* (OC 5, 132).

Similar attitudes appear in accentuated form in the reactions of Barbarita and Don Baldomero. Barbarita, at first sceptical about the child's identity, is emotionally overwhelmed when she thinks she perceives a physical resemblance to Juanito. Don Baldomero, while trying to maintain a sober view of the affair, allows himself to be carried away to the extent of buying a toy accordeon for the child. In the last analysis, however, this sentimental kind of benevolence is inadequate to the facts of the case. Juanito confesses that Fortunata did bear him a child, but that the child died: el Pituso is not his son, so there is no question of his remaining in the Santa Cruz household. Now 'that precious little beast' can be thrown out, declares the ironically-named Benigna, conveniently forgetting that she herself has two step-children, whom she apparently had no difficulty in accepting. El Pituso therefore departs to Guillermina's orphanage to the accompaniment of the indefatigable geniality of Barbarita and Don Baldomero and the cheerful wheeze of the accordeon.

The ultimate effect of this episode is to demonstrate that however tolerant and flexible bourgeois society may appear on the surface, certain barriers are in the last analysis insurmountable.[12] Furthermore, the narrator unconsciously underlines the point by the bland and matter-of-fact tone in which he tells the story. When Jacinta listens at the door of Juanito's bedroom, when he and his father are discussing the child, she hears, not self-accusation or recrimination, but indulgent laughter. Barbarita's insensitive remark to Jacinta, that 'it really is a great pity, my dear, that you can't give us [a real grandson]' (OC 5, 148), is deeply wounding precisely because it reflects what Harriet Turner, in her brilliant analysis of this novel, has called the 'ambivalent good' of the family tie. Were Barbarita and Baldomero openly cruel, Jacinta could either try to resist or yield to force majeure. As it is, she can find no weapons to fight against decisions which appear to be well-meaning and practical, and which emanate from people for whom she feels only respect and affection. As Harriet Turner has expressed it, 'an appearance of "lo natural" becomes itself a tie that tyrannizes, binding things to the status quo, making them appear inevitable'.[13]

The significance of the false Pituso episode, and, indeed, of the whole of Part 1, is that they prefigure the experience of Fortunata in the remainder of the novel. She, too, finds the class barrier ultimately insurmountable. Like el Pituso, she is wrenched out of the social environment in which she feels most at home. She also falls foul of facile assumptions which the majority never thinks of questioning. Most tragic of all is the fact that, just as el Pituso's consignment to an orphanage seems 'natural' to nearly all those involved, so also Fortunata is led by her own moral confusion and the good intentions of others into a socially-sanctioned 'respectability' which proves disastrous.

The pursuit of respectability

Part 2 centres on Fortunata's unsuccessful marriage to Maximiliano Rubín, who when we first meet him is a pharmacy student of 25, ugly, sickly and of puny physique. This development of the plot brings us immediately out of the elegant salons of the Plaza de Pontejos, where the Santa Cruz family lives, into the drab world of the petty bourgeoisie. Apart from rounding out the picture of society, this is a necessary consequence of Galdós's thematic purpose. The social gulf between Fortunata and the Santa Cruz family is so obviously unbridgeable (at least while Fortunata is alive) that no-one thinks of attempting to cross it, except Juanito when he is in pursuit of his own pleasure. Entry into the petty bourgeoisie, however, though fraught with acute difficulties, is superficially more feasible, because the petty bourgeoisie's sense of its own identity is less concerned with money, status and elegant social forms than with respectability founded on moral earnestness. It is entirely in keeping with this that Maxi should propose marriage to Fortunata in order, as he sees it, to save her from the degradation in which she has been living since her abandonment by Juanito about four years previously. Despite Maxi's physical disadvantages and Fortunata's feelings of repugnance, his proposal is made to seem plausible because, in his section of society as much as in the *haute bourgeoisie*, marriage has less to do with instinctive affinity than with economic security and social respectability. It is on these grounds that Fortunata tries to persuade herself to accept the idea:

> ¡Casarme yo! . . . ¡Pa chasco! . . . ¡Y con este encanijado! . . . ¡Vivir siempre, siempre con él, todos los días . . . , de día y de noche! . . . ¡Pero calcula tú, mujer . . . , ser honrada, ser casada, señora de Tal . . . , persona decente! (OC 5, 180).

> *(Me marry? No bloomin' fear! And marry that weakling! Live with him all the time, all day every day, and all night as well! But just think, girl: to be a decent woman, married, Mrs. So-and-so, a respectable person!)*

In contemplating such a future, however, Fortunata has to contend with more than her reputation as a prostitute, for she brings to marriage with Maxi a passionate and unschooled nature. She is barely literate, and ignorant of a great deal of basic knowledge of the world around her: she does not even know the points of the compass, and thinks that Europe is a town. Of the Christian doctrine she learned as a child she retains hardly anything except the notion that salvation can be achieved by repentance. The one clear principle of conduct she adheres to is that 'despite what anyone said, nothing connected with love could possibly be sinful' (OC 5, 173). Yet she is far from being completely amoral, since she is neither mercenary nor sensual: indeed, as Montesinos remarks, 'her very lack of intelligence and refinement makes it difficult for her to give herself over to venal vice'.[14] When she is free from the dictation of men, she prefers to dress plainly, and Juanito complains that she does not practise the languid seductive movements of Villalonga's mistress Sofía la Ferrolana (OC 5, 322). Despite having passed through many hands, she has remained strangely untainted by her degraded life, and retains an unshakeable inward fidelity to Juanito.

This constancy gives her a firm conviction, albeit a somewhat confused and inarticulate one, that she is entitled to lay claim to a kind of moral integrity (*honradez*). However, precisely because her brand of *honradez* arises from her ignorant and unsophisticated nature, she cannot distinguish between her intuitive values and the more structured and socially sanctioned system of ideals which Maxi holds up for her guidance. That is why, despite her profound misgivings, she co-operates with an arrangement which seems to offer her the chance of having her *honradez* publicly validated. It is characteristic of her that she is readily moved to tears by Maxi's lofty sentiments, 'because she was very susceptible to emotion, and when anyone spoke to her solemnly and with magnanimous import she was moved, even though she might not understand certain concepts' (OC 5, 186).

The centre of Fortunata's tragic dilemma is surely here, for Maxi's petty bourgeois moral earnestness is totally detached from the legitimate demands of the body and of the individual's intuitive sympathies. His intense mental and emotional life, indeed, is in large measure a compensation for his physical inadequacies. Though his sexual impotence is hinted at rather than explicitly established, Galdós leaves us in no doubt that Maxi's aunt Doña Lupe, their mischievous scullery-maid Papitos and Fortunata herself are all convinced of his incapacity to consummate his marriage (OC 5, 181, 183, 186). Yet the intrinsic absurdity of his proposal is minimised by all those involved because his plan fits into a ready-made framework of shallow and ill-considered assumptions about 'regeneration' or 'expiation'. Though Maxi encounters an understandable initial resistance to his proposal on the part of his family, Doña Lupe and his priest brother Nicolás assume all too readily that if Fortunata undergoes a period of 'purification' in the Micaelas convent (an establishment maintained by the upper bourgeoisie for the reform of fallen women), the marriage will thereby cease to be absurd.[15] Maxi, in short, is as much a tragic victim of misguided idealism as Fortunata is, for his 'redemptorist' notions will later degenerate into insane messianic delusions. These delusions, however, are simply the intensification of notions which are accepted as normal and sensible by society at large, so that Maxi's madness, and his grotesque union with Fortunata, become a trenchant comment on the values of Church and society enshrined in institutions like the Micaelas convent.

Fortunata's dialectic

Predictably, Fortunata's stay in the Micaelas fails in its avowed object, not least because the nuns know little or nothing of 'the vast realm of the passions' (OC 5, 247). Worse still, it exposes her to influences which intensify both sides of her dilemma: her desire for respectability and her anarchic dedication to instinct. There can hardly be in all Galdós's work a more brilliant expression of emotional confusion than the scene in which Fortunata, towards the end of her period of 'purification', kneels before the exposed Sacrament in the convent chapel, experiencing, or believing herself to experience, 'a certain inner peace . . . resignation, and the conviction that we should take life as it comes . . . without aspiring to the complete and perfect fulfilment of our desires' (OC 5, 248). Even as she thinks this, however, she is gazing at the monstrance which, she now knows, Jacinta presented to the convent in thanksgiving for Juanito's recovery from a serious bout of pneumonia, that same illness brought on by his obsessive pursuit of Fortunata at the end of Part 1, when, hearing that she was back in Madrid, he searched for her night after night through the city streets. She has, by this time, actually seen Jacinta in the flesh for the first time, and, though at first jealous of the 'rival' who has 'stolen' Juanito from her, she soon feels 'an ardent desire . . . to have that same gentle and ladylike air' (OC 5, 243).

At the same time, the instinctive, lawless side of Fortunata's nature is being played upon by her contact with another of the inmates, Mauricia la Dura. Mauricia is an alcoholic, prone to violence when she has the craving, though gifted with 'a diabolical power for winning people's hearts' (OC 5, 245–6). Fortunata feels a mysterious attraction towards Mauricia, and this prompts an exchange of confidences, in which Mauricia reveals that Juanito knows where Fortunata is and has been prowling around the walls of the convent. At first, Fortunata tries to resist the prompting of her old passion for Juanito, but when Mauricia suggests that her forthcoming marriage will provide her with a cover for following her heart's desire, Fortunata feels that 'her friend's insinuations accorded with feelings of her own which she kept well hidden, as one would hide a dangerous weapon' (OC 5, 247).

In the light of this inner dialectic, it is not surprising that Fortunata's fragile religious discipline crumbles at the first trial: 'That shrine erected by dint of meditation and mental gymnastics split in two as if its foundations had been shaken' (OC 5, 265). On her wedding night, as Maxi lies incapacitated by an attack of migraine, she hears Juanito prowling on the landing outside their apartment. On the following day, she returns from an afternoon walk to find Juanito sitting on the sofa in her apartment, and with a wild shout of joy throws herself into his arms. Galdós describes this as 'a breaking-out of countless desires which were bottled up in her inmost being' (OC 5, 276), but although there is no doubt about the genuineness of Fortunata's outburst of feeling, we are not allowed to forget that her life has been irrevocably changed by her first seduction by Juanito four years previously, and by everything that has happened since. Galdós strategically places a reminder of this just before the joyful reunion. As Fortunata walks around the poorer suburbs of Madrid, earlier that same afternoon, she ponders on the disparity between her own life and that of the people she sees in the streets:

> Las mujeres mal vestidas que salían a las puertas y los chicos derrotados y sucios que jugaban en la calle atraían sus miradas, porque la existencia tranquila, aunque fuese oscura y con estrecheces, le causaba envidia. Semejante vida no podía ser para ella, porque estaba fuera de su centro natural. Había nacido para menestrala; no le importaba trabajar *como el obispo* con tal de poseer lo que por suyo tenía. Pero alguien la sacó de aquel su primer molde para lanzarla a vida distinta; después la trajeron y la llevaron diferentes manos. Y por fin, otras manos empeñáronse en convertirla en señora (OC 5, 275).

(She gazed longingly at the ill-dressed women who appeared at the doors, and the ragged and dirty children playing in the street, because she envied their quiet life, even if they lived in obscurity and straitened circumstances. Such a life was not for her, because she was out of her natural sphere. She was born to be a working girl. She did not mind working 'as hard as the bishop' so long as she could hold on to what was hers. But someone took her out of her original mould and launched her on a different life. Then she was dragged hither and thither by various hands. And finally other hands were determined to make a lady of her.)

Fortunata's joyful surrender to passion, then, does not inaugurate a new life of freedom from the trammels of conventional morality. Factitious and superficial as her 'reformation' may be, she has absorbed enough desire for order and a sufficient sense of right and wrong to be haunted immediately by the 'spectre of her perversity' (OC 5, 277). Within a very short time of renewing her liaison with Juanito, she experiences 'an intense desire to normalise her life without abandoning her overmastering passion' (OC 5, 289). Her inner dialectic, therefore, is not so much between good and evil as between two equally desirable goods which happen to be incompatible in her circumstances: her fidelity to her first love, Juanito, and her hunger for social acceptance, which shows itself above all in the need to have her unstructured moral values understood and in some way validated.[16]

The distortion of identity

Fortunata's tragedy is that the method by which she attempts to resolve this dilemma involves falsifying her own nature by accepting the standards imposed by others, and eventually brings about her death. When, for example, she sees the dedication with which Guillermina attends the dying Mauricia la Dura, she cannot help measuring in her mind the gulf which she believes to exist between herself and the 'saint' (OC 5, 368–9). Once again, however, she is the victim of her confused understanding of what constitutes virtue, for as Whiston has pointed out, Guillermina is presented in a critical light throughout this episode.[17] It is precisely this 'manía de imitación' (OC 5, 392) which leads her to try to vindicate herself by having another child by Juanito. Ironically, this final phase of the novel begins just at the point when Fortunata is most conscious, with a sense of joy and relief, that she is recovering her true identity as a woman of the people. As she helps out during Mauricia's last illness by making packed lunches for the menfolk to take to work, she reflects: '*This* is where I really belong, a working girl, married to an honest lump of a labourer who loves me! There's no two ways about it, girl, you were born an ordinary lass, and an ordinary lass you'll be all your life' (OC 5, 382–3).[18]

By an unfortunate coincidence, however, only a few minutes later, she meets Jacinta face to face for the first time, and her unschooled spontaneity gets the better of her to the point where she comes close to physical assault. This makes her simultaneously feel guilty and wish to justify herself, and when Guillermina later takes her to task for her aggressive behaviour, she defends herself by triumphantly asserting her superiority at the natural level: she can have children while Jacinta is barren. From now until the end of the novel, Fortunata's whole purpose in life is to achieve the social validation for which she still vaguely longs by exploiting this biological advantage, and when in due course Juanito's amorous dilettantism causes him to return to her, she seizes the opportunity to have another child. This is not to say that she is being cynical or manipulative: her moral confusion is too great for that, and in any case she is free of any mercenary aim, unlike Doña Lupe and her aunt Segunda, whose main thought is of the pension that she can extract from the Santa Cruz family (OC 5, 497–8, 535). Nevertheless, Galdós presents Fortunata's plan with a certain detachment. Her last liaison with Juanito is described as 'that third sally of the adventuress on to the field of her mad delusion' (OC 5, 428), and when, after her baby is born, she takes pleasure in the notion that she is the mother of the Santa Cruz heir, Galdós compares her toying with this idea to the senile Feijoo's childish game of *bilboquet* (OC 5, 505).

The purpose of this ironic detachment is to discourage the reader from adopting an oversimplified view of Fortunata's final 'vindication'. This is not to say that Galdós wishes us to take a coldly clinical attitude towards Fortunata's situation in the closing chapters. There can hardly be a more poignant moment in any Galdós novel than the moment when Fortunata, returning to the scene of her childhood in the Cava de San Miguel, plods wearily up the same stone staircase where she first met Juanito, saying to herself, 'How the world goes round! Who would have thought I'd finish up here again?' (OC 5, 477). As we have seen, however, she is not returning precisely to the point from which she started, for she has been changed irrevocably by the experience of the intervening years. 'Now I realise,' she goes on, 'that something of my betters has rubbed off on me, however little. I look at all this with affection; but it seems so common now!' (*ibid.*).[19] Despite the poignancy of the ending, however, there can be no doubt that Fortunata brings about her own death by allowing her old passionate spontaneity to get the better of her once more. Outraged by the perfidy of her friend Aurora, who is now Juanito's mistress, Fortunata, very soon after the birth of her baby, rises from her bed to attack her rival, and as a result has a fatal haemorrhage. The certainty of approaching death produces a change in her attitude towards Jacinta. Whereas only a few days previously she was gleefully nursing the thought of Jacinta's rage and envy at her becoming the mother of the Santa Cruz heir, she now decides to make her a free gift of the child, convinced in her own mind that this is her ultimate vindication:

> En aquella idea vaciaba como en un molde todo lo bueno que ella podía pensar y sentir, en aquella estampaba con sencilla fórmula el perfil más hermoso *y quizá menos humano* de su carácter, para dejar tras sí una impresión clara y enérgica de él. . . .
> '¡Ah!, qué idea tan repreciosa . . . Con ella no necesito Sacramentos; claro, como que me lo han dicho de arriba' (OC 5, 536 [*my emphasis*]).

(Into that idea she poured, as into a mould, the best that she could think and feel. On it she imprinted with one simple operation the most beautiful and also perhaps the least human trait of her character, so as to leave behind a strong and vigorous impression of it.
'Oh, what a really lovely idea! Having it, I don't need sacraments. Why should I, since it has been given me from above?' [my emphasis]).

Similarly, Jacinta's old hostility towards Fortunata gives way to something akin to understanding:

Con la muerte de por medio, la una en la vida visible y la otra en la invisible, *bien podría ser* que las dos mujeres se miraran de orilla a orilla, con intención y deseos de darse un abrazo (OC 5, 542 [*my emphasis*])

(With death coming between them, leaving one in the visible world and the other in the invisible, it could well be that the two women gazed at each other from opposite shores, intending and wanting to exchange an embrace [my emphasis]).

There is no doubt about the genuineness either of Fortunata's serenity or of Jacinta's movement of sympathy towards her rival, but, as the emphasised passages in the above quotations suggest, the language in which Galdós chooses to present the change in their feelings towards each other is studiously non-committal. The effect of this is that we cannot be sure that the author either shares or wishes us to share the two women's view of their situation. To do so, indeed, would be to opt for a more optimistic reading of the ending of the novel than the evidence appears to warrant. True, many critics do read the ending optimistically, arguing that the child of Fortunata and Juanito will help to revitalise the bourgeoisie with the blood of the common people, the *pueblo*.[20] To interpret the ending in this way, however, is to assume that Galdós had more faith in the capacity of the middle class to learn from experience than the novel itself suggests. Jacinta's sympathy for Fortunata stands out as an exception: by contrast, Guillermina, in her trite insistence that the dying Fortunata 'purify' herself and reject 'worldly' ideas, articulates more authentically the conventional views of society at large. None of the Santa Cruz family attends Fortunata's funeral, though characteristically they pay for an absurdly lavish one. The social and moral barriers which determine the whole direction of the plot of *Fortunata y Jacinta* and the destinies of the characters remain, in the end, as insurmountable as ever: the bourgeoisie finally emerges victorious, and Fortunata's son will be brought up much like his father.[21] Peter Bly draws attention to the telling detail of Estupiñá carrying the baby off in his basket, 'as agitated as if he were a thief or a smuggler' (OC 5, 538), which reminds us not only of Estupiñá's smuggling past and his long years of toadying to the bourgeoisie, but also of Juanito's callous reaction to his wife's involvement with the false *Pituso* three years earlier: 'You don't suppose Estupiñá brings babies in under his cloak, like a box of cigars?' (OC 5, 145). Just as the false *Pituso* was taken from Jacinta's arms and put in an orphanage, so the true one is taken from his mother, to receive quite different treatment.

The optimistic 'social-regenerationist' reading of the ending would be easier to sustain if the novel as a whole displayed a definite preference for the values and attitudes of the *pueblo*, but there is little evidence of such a preference. It is true that on one occasion the more omniscient narrator of Part 3 (whose voice at this moment seems virtually indistinguishable from the author's) expresses the view that 'el pueblo posee las verdades grandes y en bloque, y a él acude la civilización conforme se le van gastando las menudas, de que vive' (OC 5, 407) (The *pueblo* possesses the great truths in their primitive state, and civilisation goes to the *pueblo* as the little truths by which [society] lives become threadbare). But such comments are notable for their rarity: on other occasions, these sentiments are more usually found in the mouth of Juanito Santa Cruz, and constitute one of the sophistries by which he seeks to cover up his moral instability.[22] Besides, the narrator almost immediately follows up this remark with a reference to 'the rage, the passion, the uncouthness of the *pueblo*' (OC 5, 408), qualities which bulk as large in the novel as the *pueblo*'s vitality and spontaneity. Indeed, Fortunata herself recoils from the squalor and coarseness which she encounters on her return to the Cava de San Miguel (OC 5, 477).

The other main difficulty in the way of an optimistic reading of the novel is the character of Fortunata herself. She has been described as 'a monumental figure' who breaks through the barriers of class,[23] and as 'a champion of invisible consciousness at war with "race, milieu et moment" and, in ultimate victory, an avenging angel who renders them impotent'.[24] If these statements were true, we would expect Fortunata to be much less passive and bewildered than in fact she is for most of the novel: 'She felt like a living puppet, played with by an unknown, invisible entity, on whom she could not put a name' (OC 5, 275). Nor will it do to regard Fortunata as the victorious champion of natural, spontaneous feeling. It is true that what Gilman calls her 'oral integrity'[25] enables her to expose the hypocrisy of bourgeois society, but Galdós provides us with no grounds for believing that a society founded on instinct alone would actually work. Even if Fortunata had achieved her ideal of marriage to a person of her own class whom she loved, even if Juanito were a humble bricklayer, as she often wished, she would still have had to function within some framework of social and moral convention. As has been well said, 'to renounce societal organization and order is a repudiation and humiliation of man and points out his enslavement to instinct only'.[26] This is surely borne out by the evidence of the novel, for spontaneous outbursts of feeling are more often than not shown to be destructive in their effects.[27]

The overall import of the novel is therefore not optimistic and regeneration-ist, but pessimistic and conservative. Fortunata's tragedy is the tragedy of a passionate and unsophisticated individual who is wrenched out of her natural environment by the selfish intervention of someone from another social sphere, and who is then made to function in the corrupt and artificial world of petty bourgeois convention, to which she is temperamentally quite unsuited.[28] The clear implication is that, given the way in which society is structured, Fortunata could only have achieved happiness by remaining in her true sphere, where her earthy spontaneity, instead of wasting itself in conflict with the inevitability of given circumstances, could have enriched her life by being channelled productively within a socially unpretentious and morally sanctioned relationship. As it is, the final impression which we take away from a reading of the novel is of the needless waste of a life.[29]

To say that given circumstances are inevitable is not, however, to concede that the existing structure of society is in any way normative. If we call the ending tragic, we imply that the protagonist, in other, more ideal circumstances, would, instead of suffering, have received the reward due to her excellent qualities. As John Macklin has judiciously expressed it, 'the criteria by which [Fortunata's claim to be an angel] can be tested are not of this world'.[30] Though Galdós does not categorically endorse her assertion that she is the equal of Jacinta, though our sense of tragic waste arises primarily from the spectacle of Fortunata naively pursuing mistaken goals, the novel, if it is to make sense, must surely imply that what Ribbans has called her 'honest consistency' is wholly admirable, not least because of the way in which it stands out in shining contrast to the hypocrisy of society. In concentrating, as I have in this chapter, on Galdós's new awareness of the class structure of society, I am far from suggesting that he has abandoned his characteristic moral idealism. On the contrary, Fortunata's passionate belief in love and Maxi's visionary generosity, both unquestionably genuine even if misguided, suggest that spiritual values can be found in the midst of the drab greyness of everyday life, and even in the midst of madness.

In *Fortunata y Jacinta*, in other words, Galdós has finally brought to fruition the possibility, adumbrated six years earlier in *La desheredada*, of combining what is best in Realism and Naturalism with his belief in universal values. The title of Chapter 6 of Part 3, indeed, 'Spiritual Naturalism', provides a convenient label for a literary procedure which is characteristic of the novel as a whole. The chapter centres on the death of Mauricia la Dura who, in the midst of her alcoholic ravings, shows remorse for her past life, and a capacity for friendship which moves Fortunata deeply. Conversely, Guillermina's fussy activity in preparing Mauricia to receive Holy Communion, and her domineering attitude towards those around her, forms an ironic counterpoint to her own professed concern for spiritual matters (OC 5, 370–75). Doña Lupe, for her part, practises 'charity' primarily to gain the approval of Guillermina and the other distinguished ladies who, according to press reports, are alleged to accompany her on such occasions. As James Whiston has shrewdly remarked, the language of altruism often 'evokes more the naturalistic atmosphere of the struggle for life than any religious sentiment'.[31]

'Spiritual Naturalism', therefore, entails recognising the essentially ambiguous nature of reality, in which good and evil are so inextricably bound up with each other that it is virtually impossible to pursue one without the other. This I take to be the essence of Galdós's conception of realism as it developed in the mid-1880s, determining not only his view of life but his techniques of presentation. It is because he believes in what he once called the 'chiaroscuro' of life (OC 4, 1152) that he can, on the one hand, wax gently ironic at Maxi's melodramatic outbursts of jealousy and Fortunata's 'sally into the field of her delusion', and, on the other, present Maxi's suffering with great compassion and confer a poignant lyrical intensity on Fortunata's death scene and on the whole closing section of the novel. There is, in short, a much better balance than in *La desheredada* between social and moral criticism and sympathetic involvement in the human dilemmas of the characters. Precisely because of the larger scope of *Fortunata y Jacinta*, and the skill with which the moral quality of Restoration society is revealed, Galdós successfully persuades us of the magnitude of the issues he is treating, without needing to resort to the strained lyricism of *Gloria* or the sometimes harsh satire of parts of *La desheredada*. Moreover, because he is concerned not solely with the external social world but with the intense inner life of his characters and with the conflict between this inner life and social realities, he cannot afford to pin his faith exclusively to the external observation and analysis favoured by the Naturalists. As Zahareas has aptly expressed it,

> Galdós is not against reason in *Fortunata*, but shows that the strict objectivation of life (as naturalists conceived it) fails to solve one single spiritual problem, that the spiritual life of man can at times be deformed, but not easily rationalized. In fact, the attempts to regulate spiritual life (as with Fortunata or with Jacinta and Maxi) merely intensify the tragic conflict between the personality and the surrounding world, whether societal or religious.[32]

In a sense, therefore, Galdós has, with *Fortunata y Jacinta*, come full circle, for in this novel he is implicitly reasserting what he already knew at the very outset of his career, that external observation only reveals phenomena, not ultimate truths. In another sense, however, he has travelled far along a difficult and tortuous road, passing through the phases of confident reformist enthusiasm and austere social criticism to a realisation that the novel can best fulfil its cognitive function by dramatising the intractable ambiguity of reality, and the interplay between reason and instinct, between abstract principle and the sheer unruliness of life, which make up both the glory and the pain of human existence.

Notes to Chapter 9

1. *Galdós* (Madrid, 1912), p. 156. Galdós himself seems to have felt uneasy about the sheer bulk of *Fortunata y Jacinta*, to judge from his remark, in a letter of 9 April 1887 to Narcís Oller, that 'considero calamidad irreparable para mí haber hecho una obra tan larga, en la cual seguramente la sustancia no ha de corresponder a las dimensiones' (William H. Shoemaker,

'Una amistad literaria: La correspondencia epistolar entre Galdós y Narciso Oller', *Boletín de la Real Academia de Bellas Letras de Barcelona*, 30 [1963–4], p. 282).

2. *On Realism* (London, 1973), p. 112.
3. Cf. Sherman H. Eoff, *The Novels of Pérez Galdós*, (Washington University Studies, St. Louis, 1954), p. 101.
4. Cf. Geoffrey Ribbans, *Pérez Galdós, 'Fortunata y Jacinta'* (Critical Guides to Spanish Texts, no. 21, London, Grant & Cutler, 1977), p. 69.
5. *op. cit.*, p. 38.
6. Carr, *Spain 1808–1939* (Oxford, 1966), pp. 175–6.
7. *op. cit.*, pp. 39–40.
8. James Whiston, 'Language and situation in Part I of *Fortunata y Jacinta*', *Anales Galdosianos*, 7 (1972), p. 79.
9. Cf. Peter A. Bly, 'Fortunata and No. 11, Cava de San Miguel', *Hispanófila*, No. 59 (1977), pp. 46–7.
10. See J. L. Brooks, 'The character of Doña Guillermina Pacheco in Galdós's novel *Fortunata y Jacinta*', *Bulletin of Hispanic Studies*, 38 (1961), p. 94. See also James Whiston, 'The materialism of life: religion in *Fortunata y Jacinta*', *Anales Galdosianos*, 14 (1979), pp. 70–71. For a contrasting view, see Juan Menéndez y Arranz, *Un aspecto de la novela 'Fortunata y Jacinta'* (Madrid, 1952), p. 49.
11. See Harriet S. Turner, 'Family ties and tyrannies: a reassessment of Jacinta', *Hispanic Review*, 51 (1983), pp. 1–22.
12. Contrast Eoff, *op. cit.*, p. 112.
13. *art. cit.*, p. 4.
14. *op. cit.*, vol. 2, p. 230. Peter Goldman, in claiming that 'Fortunata's social pretensions have taken root if Villalonga's description of her clothing and jewelry [at the end of Part 1] is to be believed', overlooks the fact that Fortunata has almost certainly been obliged to dress elegantly by the man with whom she is then living. Though Goldman is right to point out that Fortunata has risen far enough in the social scale to view with distaste her old haunts in the Cava de San Miguel, it seems to me illogical to conclude, as he does, that her eventual reversion to her original working-class speech-habits is evidence of her 'definitive rise' ('Feijoo and the failed revolution: A dialectical inquiry into *Fortunata y Jacinta* and the poetics of ambiguity', in Peter B. Goldman, ed., *Conflicting Realities: Four Readings of a Chapter by Pérez Galdós* [*Fortunata y Jacinta, Part III, Chapter IV*], [London, Támesis, 1984], pp. 112–113).
15. '... the operation is viable ... so long as Fortunata is educated ... with the rigour and discipline needed to subjugate both [her] libertarian bent and the bad habits she has acquired during her years of disorder and moral anarchy' (Carlos Blanco Aguinaga, 'Having no option: The restoration of order and the education of Fortunata', in Goldman, *op. cit.*, p. 25.).
16. See Anthony N. Zahareas, 'The tragic sense in *Fortunata y Jacinta*', *Symposium*, 19 (1965), pp. 39, 46.
17. 'Materialism', p. 74.
18. It is in the context of Fortunata's periodic search for authenticity that we must understand the important episode analysed by the four contributors to Goldman. ed., *Conflicting Realities* (which for reasons of space I have not dealt with in this chapter), in which the retired colonel Evaristo Feijoo becomes Fortunata's mentor and lover for a short period after one of her separations from Juanito. Goldman takes the view that Feijoo's attempt to educate Fortunata in 'practical philosophy' fails 'because she is too self-centred, a sentimental bourgeois [*sic*], an "apasionada" like Maxi' (*op. cit.*, p. 98). But Fortunata's passionate nature is clearly presented in the novel as characteristic of the *salvajismo* of the *pueblo*. See also note 14 above.
19. Cf. Bly, *art. cit.*, p. 47.
20. See, e.g., Eoff, *op. cit.*, p. 99. Also John H. Sinnigen, 'Individual, class and society in *Fortunata y Jacinta*', in Robert J. Weber, ed., *Galdós Studies II* (London, Támesis, 1974), p. 65. Also Ribbans, *op. cit.*, p. 70.
21. Among the many critics who subscribe to this view are Ricardo Gullón, in *Técnicas de Galdós* (Madrid, 1970), p. 147. See also Julio Rodríguez-Puértolas, *Galdós, burguesía y revolución*

(Madrid, 1975), pp. 55, 58; Bly, *art. cit.*, pp. 44–5; John J. Macklin, 'Benito Pérez Galdós: *Fortunata y Jacinta*', in D. A. Williams, ed., *The Monster in the Mirror: Studies in Nineteenth-Century Realism* (Oxford University Press, 1978), p. 201; Stephen Gilman, *Galdós and the Art of the European Novel: 1967–1887* (Princeton University Press, 1981), p. 245.

22. Peter Goldman is undoubtedly right up to a point to claim that 'Juanito has a certain vision of social realities which frequently is lucid and accurate', but in my view he underestimates the extent to which the reader's judgement of Juanito's reliability as a witness is bound to be affected by his reaction towards his moral corruption (*op. cit.*, p. 103). Other contributors to the Goldman volume assert with some justification that the narrator's reliability is compromised by his identification with the complacent bourgeoisie, but they fail to distinguish clearly enough between the partially-reliable narrator of Part 1 and the more omniscient narrator of the remainder of the novel. For example, most of the evidence which Carlos Blanco draws on in attempting to make his case that the narrator *throughout* the novel 'reflects the ideology of the new ruling class' is drawn from Part 1 (Goldman, *op. cit.*, pp. 34–7). John Kronik, in claiming that 'the reader whom the narrative engages in its shiftiness is brought to an awareness, not of the veracity of the account, but of the mechanism adduced to effect the illusion of verisimilitude, hence of its falseness' (Goldman, *op. cit.*, p. 50) underestimates the degree to which Galdós exploits a very complex narrative perspective so as to enable us to distinguish between the falsity of some accounts of reality and the veracity of others. The truth of the matter is that Galdós moves at will in and out of various narrative modes, no one of which can be taken as a basis for a generalisation about the novel as a whole, though, to be sure, different modes predominate proportionally in different parts of the novel. The best accounts of narrative perspective in this novel are to be found in James Whiston, 'Language and situation in Part I of *Fortunata y Jacinta*', *Anales Galdosianos*, 7 (1972), pp. 79–91, and Geoffrey Ribbans, *op. cit.*, pp. 37–70.

23. Sinnigen, *art. cit.*, p. 65.

24. Gilman, *op. cit.*, p. 324.

25. *op. cit.*, p. 273.

26. Zahareas, *art. cit.*, p. 43.

27. Nor is this confined to the *pueblo*, for the elegant and misanthropic aristocrat Manuel Moreno-Isla almost certainly brings about his own death by the emotional strain arising from his hopeless infatuation with Jacinta. Harriet Turner has persuasively suggested that Moreno-Isla and Fortunata are simultaneously destroyed and redeemed by their capacity for feeling ('Strategies in narrative point of view: On meaning and morality in the Galdós novel', in B. Brancaforte, E. R. Mulvihill and R. G. Sánchez, eds., *Homenaje a Antonio Sánchez-Barbudo* [Madison, University of Wisconsin, 1981], p. 75).

28. As Stephen Miller has cogently expressed it, Galdós is primarily concerned, in the novels of the mid-1880s, with 'la podredumbre moral que hace vano cualquier proyecto de regeneración política o económica a nivel nacional' (*El mundo de Galdós* [Santander, 1983], p. 111).

29. See Anthony N. Zahareas, 'El sentido de la tragedia en *Fortunata y Jacinta*', *Anales Galdosianos*, 3 (1968), p. 26 (a revised and expanded version of his 1965 article). See also Turner, 'Strategies', p. 76.

30. *art. cit.*, p. 202.

31. 'Materialism', p. 68.

32. 'Tragic sense', p. 47.

10

The Realism of Galdós

Galdós and the Spanish novel of the nineteenth century

Although in this study we have examined only some of the novels written during the first half of Galdós's career, this nevertheless gives us a basis for an overall assessment of his literary significance. By any standards, the sheer scale of his output earns him a place on the map of European literature: 31 novels, of which perhaps a dozen can stand comparison with the best in any language; 46 *Episodios Nacionales*, which gained him considerable popularity in his lifetime and are still widely read; 15 original plays; and a very large body of political and literary journalism.

Galdós's real importance, however, lies in the fact that he established the modern realist novel in Spain virtually single-handed. Among his contemporaries, only Leopoldo Alas can compare with Galdós in the subtlety, complexity and comprehensiveness of his vision of society. Alas's reputation, however, is based mainly on one work, *La Regenta* (1884–5), and to a lesser extent on *Su único hijo* (1890), and in any case Alas was able to benefit considerably from the fact that Galdós had already established a climate of critical acceptance for the serious novel. Galdós, however, had had to struggle against much greater odds at the outset of his writing career. The reading public was sparse and uneducated, there were no suitable Spanish models on which to build, and there were commercial obstacles to the publication of serious fiction: according to Berkowitz, publication of *La Fontana de Oro* had to be privately financed by Galdós's sister-in-law.[1]

There seems, then, ample justification for the view of contemporary critics such as Manuel de la Revilla and Alas that Galdós was the creator of Spanish realism. As we saw in Chapters 2 and 3, the debate on realism in Spain in the 1860s and early 1870s was largely conducted at the level of abstraction, since there were no contemporary Spanish works which could be cited as examples of the new tendency. By the late 1870s, however, the general understanding of realism in Spain was much clearer and more coherent, and this was in no small measure due to the fact that by then Galdós's novels had come to be accepted by wide sections of critical opinion as the best exemplars of a type of realism which sought to be faithful to the national literary tradition, to give due weight to the accurate representation of the world, and at the same time to preserve some sense both of ideal transcendence and of civic responsibility. Revilla, writing in 1878, declared that Galdós's novels were 'models of perfect realism' because 'without going beyond the limits of truth, he knows how to idealise, judiciously and subtly, the data that external reality offers us'.[2] In another essay, written in the following year, Revilla gives a definition of realism, largely derived from his reflections on Galdós's novels, which is remarkably similar in its comprehensiveness to that of de Vogüé, which I quoted in Chapter 3:

El arte no es, pues, mera idealidad ni copia servil de lo real: es idealización de lo real por la fantasía creadora, la emoción viva e intensa y la personalidad activa y vigorosa del artista, y también realización sensible de lo ideal que el artista, con mirada escrutadora, sabe adivinar en el seno mismo de la realidad.[3]

(Art is not, then, mere idealism, or a slavish copy of [external] reality. It is the idealisation of the real by the artist's creative imagination, his lively and intense emotion, and his active and vigorous personality. It is also the tangible realisation of the ideal quality which the artist, with his penetrating vision, can glimpse at the heart of [external] reality.)

This definition, of course, makes Galdós seem more old-fashioned than our exploration of his work has shown him to be, and had Revilla lived (he died in 1881 at the age of 35), he would probably have modified his description in the light of Galdós's later practice. In the event, it fell to Leopoldo Alas to develop the theory of realism in Spain in response to Galdós's novels of the 1880s. Significantly, Alas's most influential critical writings were published in the years 1881–3, largely under the impact of the shift in Galdós's style and interests represented by *La desheredada*. In an essay on that novel, published in *La literatura en 1881* (a survey written in 1882, in collaboration with Armando Palacio Valdés), Alas hailed Galdós not only as the most significant novelist to emerge in the wake of the Revolution of 1868 but also as the harbinger of a revolution in literature which would parallel the progress achieved in the political sphere.[4] A similar notion is expressed in his 1881 essay 'El libre examen y nuestra literatura presente' ('Free enquiry and contemporary Spanish literature').[5] Galdós's novels, particularly *La desheredada*, were also the principal inspiration for two important series of articles which Alas wrote at this time, that on Naturalism in *La Diana* in 1882, and that on style in the novel in *Arte y Letras* between July 1882 and December 1883.[6]

Although Alas's criticism sometimes reveals the limitations of its journalistic, often polemical form, he correctly identified most of the main constituents of Galdós's realism which we have been examining in this study: his educational mission, his cultural nationalism, and his comprehensive view of reality as embracing both the material and non-material. His view of Galdós may therefore appropriately stand as a conclusion to this study. Alas's deep intuitive understanding of what Galdós was trying to achieve arose in part from the fact that both men had been exposed to very similar intellectual influences during their education. Alas's teachers at the University of Madrid during the early 1870s included Krausists who were pupils of those who had taught Galdós ten years before. His doctoral thesis was supervised by Francisco Giner de los Ríos, who, as we saw in Chapter 2, greatly influenced the development of Galdós's literary theory at the beginning of his career. Like Galdós, Alas appears to have absorbed at an early stage the Krausist-enlightenment conception of literature as a means of moral and intellectual regeneration.[7] Consequently, when he first met Galdós at some time around 1874 (significantly, in that powerhouse of Krausist culture, the Ateneo), Alas quickly identified him as the person best qualified to carry out the much-needed revitalisation of the novel. Not surprisingly, therefore, Alas's first major piece of criticism on the novel was his review of *Gloria* in the *Revista Europea* in February 1877. Alas welcomed the novel warmly because he saw it as contributing to the spread of enlightenment:

> Algunos autores ... sintiéndose llenos de fuerzas adecuadas, han emprendido la meritoria empresa de remover y conmover la conciencia nacional, y hablando a la fantasía de nuestro pueblo con poderosas imágenes, llenas de frescura, originalidad y *sabor de patria*, despiertan en él los dormidos gérmenes del pensamiento reflexivo de un sueño de siglos.[8]

> *(Some authors, feeling that they have the requisite energy, have undertaken the meritorious task of shaking and stirring up the consciousness of the nation, and, by speaking to the imagination of our people with powerful images full of freshness, originality and the authentic flavour of the fatherland, awaken in them the dormant seeds of reflective thought, which have been asleep for centuries.)*

With the same enthusiasm with which he had declared in his review of *Gloria* that 'the tendentious or philosophical novel is particularly opportune in our country at the present time', Alas hailed Galdós's move towards Naturalism in 1881. There was no real inconsistency in this, for Alas's literary theory, like that of Galdós and their common mentor, Francisco Giner, was unified by the Krausist-enlightenment notion of progress, which meant, among other things, that literature and history advanced *pari passu* and obeyed similar laws. Thus, in his essay on *La desheredada*, Alas wrote of the contemporary development of literature as taking the direction 'determined by the laws common to all elements of civilisation',[9] an idea frequently reiterated in his critical writings of the period 1881–3. The main reason, therefore, for Alas's approval of Galdós's openness towards Naturalism was that Naturalism offered the opportunity for the novel to become a serious, objective study of society, which would yield greater understanding and thereby contribute to the advancement of reform. The aim of Naturalism, Alas wrote in 1882, was 'that art should, more effectively than hitherto, subserve the general interests of human life, and enter seriously, in a central role, into the progressive activity of peoples'.[10]

The nature of Galdós's commitment

Alas, then, understood very well that, as I have tried to argue in this book, Galdós's artistic imperative to create was inseparable from what he saw as his duty to criticise, increase understanding and thereby foster intellectual progress. In emphasising, however, the essential continuity of Galdós's work, from the novels of the 1870s to *La desheredada* and beyond, Alas, in my view, underestimated the significance of the shift towards a denser, more complex realism which took place in the years 1880–84. Not only does Galdós continue to be concerned, as before, with the way in which ideals and fantasies conflict with reality, but he shows a new awareness of the interplay of social and economic forces. His ethical concerns remain paramount, to be sure, but in novels like *Tormento* and *Fortunata y Jacinta* individual ethical dilemmas appear as concrete manifestations of the social tensions and collective relationships which make moral decisions more complicated. This, in my view, strengthens Galdós's claim to a place in the mainstream of the European novel, for in a sense he combines successfully within one body of work the Enlightenment and Realist perspectives which Lukács associates respectively with Stendhal and Balzac.

In the particular circumstances of nineteenth-century Spain, however, the balance between the Realist and reformist imperatives was potentially very fragile. If the great novels of the 1880s and 1890s have a certain weight and texture, it is due in no small measure to the relatively crisis-free atmosphere of Galdós's middle period, which made it easier to explore issues from all possible sides, and to show the variety and complexity of human experience and motivation. There were, however, moments in his life when the pressure of contemporary events forced him, as he wrote to Pereda in 1877, to be either a *tirio* or a *troyano*, i.e., to take sides, to stand up and be counted.[11] One such moment had occurred in the 1870s, another was to come in the latter years of his career. For in 1897, Cánovas del Castillo was assassinated, and although the political system associated with his name remained theoretically in being until 1923, its continued viability as a working compromise was decisively impaired. In the following year, Spain became involved in war with the United States over Cuba, suffering a humiliating defeat which entailed the loss of the final remnants of the once-great Spanish empire. Among writers and intellectuals of all kinds, this event was seen as a major psychological cataclysm, raising fundamental questions about Spanish national identity and Spain's future role in the world. Even before this, however, in 1893, Galdós had expressed in one of his *La Prensa* articles considerable pessimism about what he saw as a deep-seated malaise afflicting contemporary society:

¿No advertís en nuestra pobre humanidad una desasosiego alarmante? ¿Es resultado de la desilusión religiosa, seguida de la desilusión filosófica? ¿Es el desencanto político, seguido del desencanto social? Empezamos el siglo luchando por las libertades políticas. Conseguimos las libertades, y los pueblos no son felices, ni sus sociedades adquieren asiento y robustez. Los ideales religiosos se ajan como flores arrancadas del tallo . . . el siglo acaba en medio de una confusión semejante a la de la torre de Babel (Ined 2, 186).

(Do you not perceive in our poor humanity an alarming uneasiness? Does it arise from religious disillusionment, followed by philosophical disillusion-ment? Is it disenchantment with politics, followed by disenchantment in the social sphere? We began the century by fighting for political liberty. We won liberty, and yet people are not happy, nor has society acquired stability and robustness. Religious ideals wilt like flowers plucked from the stem. The century is coming to an end amid a confusion similar to that of the tower of Babel.)

By 1897–8, this uneasiness had crystallised into a conviction that the crisis of the end of the century arose from long-standing problems which the politicians of the Restoration had failed to solve, especially the continued power of the Church. Such gains as the Restoration had brought in its train now seemed illusory, a view reflected in Galdós's speech of reception into the Royal Spanish Academy in 1897, when he declared gloomily that 'the so-called middle class doesn't yet effectively exist'.[12] Having advocated for many years a policy of tolerance and compromise, Galdós began to display some of the vehemence characteristic of a person from whose eyes the scales have recently fallen. His moral vision became as simple and as sharply defined as it had been in the 1870s, and the presentation of reality in his novels tended once more towards the didactic and the schematic. From the mid-1890s on, he had found a more suitable vehicle for his increasingly polemical statements in the theatre: *Doña Perfecta* was adapted for the stage in 1896, and in 1901 Galdós scored a notable *succès de scandale* with his anti-clerical play *Electra*.[13] Not only did Galdós begin once more in 1898 to produce new *Episodios Nacionales* but in his other novels, he tried to grapple with the problem of revealing 'the essential Spain' through the use of large-scale allegory such as that employed in *El caballero encantado* (1909), to which he deliberately gave the sub-title 'Cuento real . . . inverosímil'. We should not, however, regard this more *engagé* stance as an aberration, for as we have seen throughout this study, Galdós's *prurito de enseñanza*, his overriding concern with conveying a message, underlies all his work. The content and tone of the message changed in response to prevailing circumstances, but he always wrote as his sense of social and moral mission dictated at any one time.

Far from impairing the complexity and sophistication of his work, this moralistic focus enhances it, at least in the major novels of the 1880s and 1890s. This is because the kind of issue with which Galdós is primarily concerned is closely bound up with the work of the imagination, whether literary or otherwise. We saw from the very outset of this study that Galdós's perception of the task which awaited him as he embarked on his literary career had two elements: the urge to combat the dominance of trivial and meretricious novels, and the desire to contribute to national regeneration. Throughout his career, the re-education of the taste of the reading public towards sound literature and the improvement of its moral and intellectual health went hand in hand. Galdós is concerned, in other words, not only to express a clear and cogent criticism of everything that he believes to be wrong with contemporary Spanish society, but also to demonstrate the partial, problematical and potentially misleading character of conventional constructs of the human mind, whether in the area of public institutions, private motivation, or, most important of all, artistic expression.

It follows that if we are to avoid misreading Galdós's novels as we misread other literature and the world around us, we must pay attention to the various clues and patterns of significance (e.g., ironic overtones, juxtapositions, and frameworks of analogy and imagery) whereby he encourages us to distinguish between true and false perception, true and false values. We must, in short, read with the maximum of moral discernment, imaginative sympathy and intellectual rigour which we can muster. As Monroe Z. Hafter has expressed it in his excellent study of *Angel Guerra*, 'Galdós's art regularly seeks to foster judgement':[14] in the first instance, the reader's judgement of the reality presented; but also the judgement which the novel passes on the reader, who, at least at the time of the original publication of the novels, belonged to the very society which Galdós was striving to re-educate towards a more critical, lucid and sober view of itself. The ultimate source of Galdós's realism surely lies here, for the ethical problems which life in Restoration society posed day by day could only be actualised in the vivid portray of social, political and economic reality. To us, a hundred years later, Galdós's novels not only re-present the essence of that reality, but can also, if we read them aright, lead us to a better understanding of the meanness and folly, but also some of the triumphs, of our common humanity.

Notes to Chapter 10

1. *Benito Pérez Galdós, Spanish Liberal Crusader* (Madison, University of Wisconsin Press, 1948), p. 85.
2. 'Bocetos literarios: Don Benito Pérez Galdós', *Revista Contemporánea*, 14 (1878), p. 123.
3. *Obras* (Madrid, 1883), p. 161. This text may also be found in Juan López-Morillas, ed., *Krausismo: Estética y literatura* (Barcelona, 1973), pp. 177–8.
4. *Galdós* (Madrid, 1912), pp. 94–5.
5. *Solos de Clarín* (Madrid, Alianza Editorial, 1971), pp. 72–3.
6. Parts of these series may be consulted in Leopoldo Alas, *Teoría y crítica de la novela española*, ed. by Sergio Beser (Barcelona, 1972), pp. 51–86, 108–149.
7. See John W. Kronik, 'Leopoldo Alas, Krausism and the plight of the humanities in Spain', *Modern Language Studies*, 11, no. 3 (Fall 1981), pp. 3–15.

8. *Galdós*, pp. 41–2. Also in *Solos de Clarín* (1971), p. 340.
9. *Galdós*, p. 95; *Teoría*, p. 225.
10. *Teoría*, p. 127.
11. Carmen Bravo-Villasante, 'Veintiocho cartas de Galdós a Pereda', *Cuadernos Hispanoamericanos nos.* 250–252 (Oct. 1970–Jan. 1971), p. 18.
12. Menéndez y Pelayo — Pereda — Pérez Galdós, *Discursos leídos ante la Real Academia Española en las recepciones públicas del 7 y 21 de febrero de 1897* (Madrid, 1897), p. 18. This text may also be found in Benito Pérez Galdós, *Ensayos de crítica literaria*, ed. Laureano Bonet (Barcelona, 1972), p. 178.
13. Interestingly, Galdós began to reiterate around this time the ideas about the close affinity between the novel and drama which he had expressed to Mesonero Romanos in 1877 (Stephen Miller, *El mundo de Galdós* [Santander, 1983], pp. 34–5; see also note 24 to Chapter 5 above).
14. 'Bálsamo contra bálsamo in *Angel Guerra*', *Anales Galdosianos*, 4 (1969), p. 39.

Select Bibliography

As its title suggests, this bibliography does not aim to be exhaustive, but is intended to help the student who wants to pursue his investigation of Galdós and/or the nineteenth-century Spanish novel. Apart from a few classics of Galdós criticism, most of the items mentioned are relatively recent, and should be reasonably accessible. Studies of specific novels are limited to those analysed in this book.

General: Theory of the novel

Auerbach, Erich, *Mimesis*, tr. Willard Trask (Garden City, New York, 1957). First English ed., Princeton University Press, 1953. First German ed., Berne, 1946.

Balzac, Honoré de, 'Avant-Propos' to *La Comédie humaine*, vol. 1 (Paris, Pléiade, 1962).

Becker, George J., ed., *Documents of Modern Literary Realism* (Princeton University Press, 1963).

Bergonzi, Bernard, *The Situation of the Novel* (Harmondsworth, Penguin Books, 1972).

Booth, Wayne C., *The Rhetoric of Fiction* (Chicago University Press, 1961).

Furst, Lilian R., and Skrine, Peter N., *Naturalism* (London, Methuen Critical Idiom Series, no. 18, 1971).

Grant, Damian, *Realism* (London, Methuen Critical Idiom Series, no. 9, 1970).

Levin, Harry, *Contexts of Criticism* (Harvard University Press, 1957).

Levin, Harry, *The Gates of Horn* (New York, Oxford University Press, 1966). First ed. 1963.

Lodge, David, *Language of Fiction* (London, 1966).

Lukács, Georg, *Studies in European Realism* (London, 1950).

Maupassant, Guy de, Preface to *Pierre et Jean* (1888).

Salvan, Albert, 'L'essence du réalisme français', *Comparative Literature*, 3 (1951), pp. 218–33.

Stern, J. P., *On Realism* (London, 1973).

Stevick, Philip, ed., *The Theory of the Novel* (New York, 1967).

Watt, Ian, *The Rise of the Novel* (London, 1957).

Williams, D. A., ed., *The Monster in the Mirror: Studies in Nineteenth-Century Realism* (Oxford University Press, 1978).

Emile Zola, *Le Roman expérimental* (Paris, Charpentier, 1923). First published 1880.

Nineteenth-century Spain: General History

Aranguren, José-Luis L., *Moral y sociedad: La moral social española en el siglo XIX* (Madrid, 1966).

Brenan, Gerald, *The Spanish Labyrinth* (Cambridge University Press, 1943).

Carr, Raymond, *Spain 1808–1975* (Oxford, 1982). First published as *Spain 1808–1939* (Oxford, 1966).

Hennessy, C. A. M., *Modern Spain* (London, The Historical Association, 1965).

Jutglar, Antoni, *Ideologías y clases en la España contemporánea*, 2 vols. (Madrid, 1968).
Palacio Atard, V., *La España del siglo XIX (1808–1898): Introducción a la España contemporánea* (Madrid, Espasa-Calpe, 1978).
Trend, J. B., *The Origins of Modern Spain* (London, Cambridge University Press, 1934).

Nineteenth-century Spain: Intellectual History

Azcárate, Gumersindo de, *Minuta de un testamento*, ed. by Elías Díaz (Barcelona, 1967). First published 1876.
Castro, Fernando de, *Memoria testamentaria*, ed. José Luis Abellán (Madrid, 1975). First published 1874.
Díaz, Elías, *La filosofía social del krausismo español* (Madrid, 1973).
Giner de los Ríos, Francisco, *Ensayos* (Madrid, Alianza Editorial, 1969).
Jobit, Pierre, *Les Educateurs de l'Espagne contemporaine*, vol. 1, *Les Krausistes* (Bordeaux and Paris, 1936).
Kronik, John W., 'Leopoldo Alas, Krausism and the plight of the humanities in Spain', *Modern Language Studies*, 11, no. 3 (Fall 1981), pp. 3–15.
López-Morillas, Juan, *El krausismo español*, 2nd ed., (Mexico–Madrid–Buenos Aires, 1980). First ed. Mexico, 1956.
López-Morillas, Juan, *Hacia el 98: Literatura, sociedad, ideología* (Barcelona, Ariel, 1972).
Ruiz Salvador, Antonio, *El Ateneo Científico, Literario y Artístico de Madrid (1835–1885)* (London, Támesis, 1971).
Sanz del Río, Julián, *Textos escogidos*, ed. by Eloy Terrón (Barcelona, 1968).

Nineteenth-century Spain: Literary Theory

Alas, Leopoldo, *Solos de Clarín* (Madrid, Alianza Editorial, 1971).
Alas, Leopoldo, *Teoría y crítica de la novela española*, ed. Sergio Beser (Barcelona, Laia, 1972).
Blanco García, Francisco, *La literatura española en el siglo XIX*, Parte 1a, vol. 2 (Madrid, 1891).
Castillo y Soriano, José del, 'García Gutiérrez', *Revista Contemporánea*, vol. 25 (1880).
Davis, Gifford, 'The Spanish debate over Idealism and Realism before the impact of Zola's Naturalism', *PMLA*, 84 (1969), pp. 1649–56.
Discursos leídos ante la Real Academia Española en la recepción pública de don Cándido Nocedal (Madrid, 1860).
Eoff, Sherman H., 'The Spanish novel of "ideas": Critical opinion', *PMLA*, 55 (1940), pp. 531–58.
Gil y Zárate, Antonio, *Manual de literatura. Primera parte: Principios generales de Poética y Retórica* (Madrid, 1842).
Giner de los Ríos, Francisco, *Estudios de literatura y arte* (Madrid, 1876).
González Serrano, Urbano, *Cuestiones contemporáneas* (Madrid, 1883).
Gullón, Germán, *El narrador en la novela del siglo XIX* (Madrid, Taurus, 1976).
Lista, Alberto, *Ensayos literarios y críticos* (Madrid, 1844).
Livingstone, Leon, 'Interior duplication and the problem of form in the modern Spanish novel', *PMLA*, 73 (1958), pp. 393–406.
López-Morillas, Juan, ed., *Krausismo: Estética y literatura* (Barcelona, Labor, 1973).
Menéndez y Pelayo — Pereda — Pérez Galdós, *Discursos leídos ante la Real Academia Española en las recepciones públicas del 7 y 21 de febrero de 1897* (Madrid, 1897).
Miller, Stephen, 'Mesonero Romanos y la novela moderna en España', *Insula*, no. 407 (October 1980).
Navarrete, Ramón de, 'La novela española', *El Semanario Pintoresco Español*, 2a serie, 12 (1847), pp. 82–4, 117–19, 130–31.
Navas-Ruiz, Ricardo, ed., *El romanticismo español: Documentos* (Salamanca, Anaya, 1971).

Olguín, Manuel, *Marcelino Menéndez Pelayo's Theory of Art, Aesthetics and Criticism* (University of California Publications in Modern Philology, vol. 28, no. 6, 1950).

Olguín, Manuel, 'The theory of Spanish realism in Milá and Revilla', *Modern Language Quarterly*, 14 (1953), pp. 298–310.

Osborne, Robert E., 'The aesthetic ideas of Emilia Pardo Bazán', *Modern Language Quarterly*, 11 (1950), pp. 98– 104.

Pardo Bazán, Emilia, Preface to *Un viaje de novios* (1881), in *Obras completas*, vol. 3 (Madrid, Aguilar, 1973), pp. 571–3.

Pardo Bazán, Emilia, *La cuestión palpitante* (1883), in *Obras completas*, vol. 3 (Madrid, Aguilar, 1973), pp. 574–647.

Pardo Bazán, Emilia, 'Coletilla a "La cuestión palpitante"', in *Obras completas*, vol. 3 (Madrid, Aguilar, 1973), pp. 648–660.

Pattison, Walter T., *El naturalismo español* (Madrid, 1965).

Pérez Galdós, Benito, *Ensayos de crítica literaria*, ed. Laureano Bonet (Barcelona, 1972).

Revilla, Manuel de la, 'Bocetos literarios: Don Benito Pérez Galdós', *Revista Contemporánea*, 14 (1878), pp. 117–24.

Revilla, Manuel de la, *Obras* (Madrid, 1883).

Ruiz Aguilera, Ventura, 'Prólogo' to vol. 1 of *Proverbios ejemplares*, 2 vols. (Madrid, 1864).

Valera, Juan, 'Apuntes sobre el nuevo arte de escribir novelas' (1886–7), in *Obras completas*, vol. 2 (Madrid, Aguilar, 1949), pp. 622–711.

Zavala, Iris M., 'El triunfo del canónigo: Teoría y novela en la España del siglo XIX', in Santos Sanz Villanueva and Carlos J. Barbachano, *Teoría de la novela* (Madrid, 1976), pp. 93–139.

Nineteenth-century Spain: General Literary History

González Herrán, José Manuel, *La obra de Pereda ante la crítica literaria de su tiempo* (Santander, 1983).

Romero Tobar, Leonardo, *La novela popular española del siglo XIX* (Barcelona, 1976).

Shaw, Donald L., 'The anti-Romantic reaction in Spain', *Modern Language Review*, 63 (1968), pp. 606–11.

Shaw, Donald L., *A Literary History of Spain: The Nineteenth Century*, (London and New York, 1972).

Zulueta, E. de, *Historia de la crítica española contemporánea* (Madrid, 1966).

Galdós: Bibliographies

Hernández Suárez, Manuel, *Bibliografía de Galdós*, vol. 1 (Ediciones del Excmo. Cabildo Insular de Gran Canaria, 1972) (A bibliography of primary sources. A further volume on secondary sources was planned, but has not to date appeared. Readers may consult Sr. Hernández Suárez's cumulative bibliography of secondary material in *Anales Galdosianos*, vols. 3 (1968), 4 (1969), 6 (1971), 7 (1972) and 9 (1974).

Sackett, Theodore A., *Pérez Galdós, an Annotated Bibliography* (Albuquerque, 1968).

Woodbridge, Hensley C., *Pérez Galdós: A Selective Annotated Bibliography* (Metuchen, New Jersey, 1975).

Galdós: Editions of Manuscripts and Studies of Textual Problems

Gimeno Casalduero, Joaquín, 'Los dos desenlaces de *La Fontana de Oro*: Origen y significado', *Anejo de Anales Galdosianos* (Los Angeles, Del Amo Foundation, 1978), pp. 55–69.

Jones, C. A., 'Galdós's second thoughts on *Doña Perfecta*', *Modern Language Review*, 54 (1959), pp. 570–3.

Pattison, Walter T., *Etapas preliminares de 'Gloria'* (Barcelona, 1979).

Pattison, Walter T., '*La Fontana de Oro*: Its early history', *Anales Galdosianos*, 15 (1980), pp. 5–9.
Smieja, Florian, 'An alternative ending of *La Fontana de Oro*', *Modern Language Review*, 61 (1966), pp. 426–33.
Weber, Robert J., *The Miau Manuscript of Benito Pérez Galdós: A Critical Study* (University of California Press, Berkeley and Los Angeles, 1964).
Whiston, James, 'Las pruebas corregidas de *Fortunata y Jacinta*', *Actas del Segundo Congreso Internacional de Estudios Galdosianos*, 2 vols. (Ediciones del Excmo. Cabildo Insular de Gran Canaria, 1978 and 1980), vol. 1, pp. 258–65.
Whiston, James, *The Early Stages of Composition of Galdós's 'Lo prohibido'* (London, Támesis, 1983).

Galdós: Editions of his Journalistic and Occasional Writings

Pérez Galdós, B., *Obras inéditas*, ed. by Alberto Ghiraldo, 16 vols. (Madrid, 1923–30).
Pérez Galdós, B., *Crónica de Madrid (1865–1866)*, ed. by Alberto Ghiraldo (Madrid, 1933).
Pérez Galdós, B., *Crónica de la quincena*, ed. William H. Shoemaker (Princeton, 1948).
Pérez Galdós, Benito, *Los artículos políticos en la 'Revista de España', 1871–1872*, ed. Brian J. Dendle and Joseph Schraibman (Lexington, Kentucky, 1982).
Shoemaker, William H., ed., *Los prólogos de Galdós* (Mexico, 1962).
Shoemaker, William H., ed., *Los artículos de Galdós en 'La Nación'* (Madrid, 1972).
Shoemaker, William H., ed., *Las cartas desconocidas de Galdós en 'La Prensa' de Buenos Aires* (Madrid, 1973).

Galdós: Published Correspondence

Bravo-Villasante, Carmen, 'Veintiocho cartas de Galdós a Pereda', *Cuadernos Hispanoamericanos*, nos. 250–252 (Oct. 1970–Jan. 1971), pp. 9–51.
Cossío, M. B., 'Galdós y Giner: Una carta de Galdós', *Boletín de la Institución Libre de Enseñanza*, no. 719 (29 February 1920), pp. 60–62.
de la Nuez, Sebastián, and Schraibman, José, eds., *Cartas del archivo de Galdós* (Madrid, Taurus, 1967).
Ortega, Soledad, ed., *Cartas a Galdós* (Madrid, 1964).
Pardo Bazán, Emilia, *Cartas a Benito Pérez Galdós (1889–1890)*, ed. by Carmen Bravo-Villasante (Madrid, 1975).
Shoemaker, W. H., 'Una amistad literaria: La correspondencia epistolar entre Galdós y Narciso Oller', *Boletín de la Real Academia de Buenas Letras de Barcelona*, 30 (1963–4), pp. 247–306.
Shoemaker, W. H., 'Sol y sombra de Giner en Galdós', in *Homenaje a Rodríguez-Moñino*, vol. 2 (Madrid, 1966), pp. 213–225.
Smith, Gilbert, 'Galdós's *Tristana*, and letters from Concha-Ruth Morell', *Anales Galdosianos*, 10 (1975), pp. 91–120.

Galdós: Biography

Berkowitz, H. Chonon, *Pérez Galdós, Spanish Liberal Crusader* (Madison, 1948).
Estébanez Calderón, Demetrio, 'Evolución política de Galdós y su repercusión en la obra literaria', *Anales Galdosianos*, 17 (1982), pp. 7–23.
Lambert, A. F., 'Galdós and Concha-Ruth Morell', *Anales Galdosianos*, 8 (1973), pp. 33–49.
Pattison, Walter. T., 'Two women in the life of Galdós', *Anales Galdosianos*, 8 (1973), pp. 23–31.
Shoemaker, W. H., '¿Cómo era Galdós?', *Anales Galdosianos*, 8 (1973), pp. 5–21.

Galdós: Collections of Critical Articles on his Work

Rogers, Douglass M., ed., *Benito Pérez Galdós* (Madrid, Taurus, 1973).
Varey, J. E., ed., *Galdós Studies I* (London, Támesis, 1970).
Weber, Robert J., ed., *Galdós Studies II* (London, Támesis, 1974).

Galdós: General Studies of his Works and Technique

Alas, Leopoldo, *Galdós* (Madrid, 1912).
Andreu, Alicia, *Galdós y la literatura popular* (Madrid, SGEL, 1982).
Berkowitz, H. C., *La biblioteca de Benito Pérez Galdós* (Las Palmas, 1951).
Beyrie, Jacques, *Galdós et son mythe*, 3 vols. (Université de Lille III, 1980).
Blanco Aguinaga, Carlos, *La historia y el texto literario: Tres novelas de Galdós* (Madrid, 1978).
Bly, Peter A., *Galdós's Novel of the Historical Imagination* (Liverpool, 1983).
Brown, Reginald F., 'Una relación literaria y cordial: Benito Pérez Galdós y Ventura Ruiz Aguilera', *Actas del V Congreso Internacional de Hispanistas*, 2 vols. (Bordeaux, 1977), vol. 1, pp. 223–33.
Cardwell, R. A., 'Galdós's early novels and the *segunda manera*: A case for a total view', *Renaissance and Modern Studies* (Nottingham), 14 (1971), pp. 44–62.
Casalduero, Joaquín, *Vida y obra de Galdós* (Madrid, Gredos, 1961). First ed. 1943.
Eoff, Sherman H., *The Novels of Pérez Galdós* (Washington University Studies, St. Louis, 1954).
Eoff, Sherman H., 'Galdós y los impedimentos del realismo', *Hispanófila*, no. 24 (May 1965), pp. 25–34.
Gilman, Stephen, *Galdós and the Art of the European Novel, 1867–1887* (Princeton University Press, 1981).
Goldman, Peter B., 'Galdós and the politics of conciliation', *Anales Galdosianos*, 4 (1969), pp. 73–87.
Goldman, Peter B., 'Historical perspective and political bias: Comments on recent Galdós criticism', *Anales Galdosianos*, 6 (1971), pp. 113–24.
Gullón, Ricardo, *Galdós, novelista moderno* (Madrid, Taurus, 1960).
Gullón, Ricardo, *Técnicas de Galdós* (Madrid, Taurus, 1970).
Hafter, Monroe Z., 'Ironic reprise in Galdós's novels', *PMLA*, 76 (1961), pp. 233–39.
Hilt, Douglas, 'Galdós and Spain: The novelist as historian', *History Today*, May 1974, pp. 315–25.
Miller, Stephen, *El mundo de Galdós* (Santander, Sociedad Menéndez Pelayo, 1983).
Montesinos, José F., *Galdós*, 3 vols. (Madrid, Castalia, 1968–73).
Nimetz, M., *Humor in Galdós* (New Haven and London, Yale University Press, 1968).
Olmet, Luis Antón del and García Carraffa, Arturo, *Galdós* (Madrid, 1912).
Pattison, Walter T., *Benito Pérez Galdós and the Creative Process* (Minneapolis, University of Minnesota Press, 1954).
Ricard, Robert, *Galdós et ses romans* (Paris, 1961).
Ricard, Robert, *Aspects de Galdós* (Paris, 1963).
Risley, William R., '"Narrative overture" in Galdós's early *Novelas españolas contemporáneas*', *Kentucky Romance Quarterly*, 31 (1984), pp. 135–146.
Rodríguez-Puértolas, Julio, *Galdós, burguesía y revolución* (Madrid, 1975).
Santaló, Joaquín, *The Tragic Import in the Novels of Pérez Galdós* (Madrid, 1973).
Turner, Harriet S., 'Strategies in narrative point of view: On meaning and morality in the Galdós novel', in B. Brancaforte, E. R. Mulvihill and R. G. Sánchez, eds., *Homenaje a Antonio Sánchez-Barbudo* (Madison, University of Wisconsin, 1981), pp. 61–77.
Urey, Diane, *Galdós and the Irony of Language* (Cambridge, 1982).

Galdós: Studies of Specific Novels

La sombra

Austin, Karen, 'Don Anselmo and the author's role', *Anales Galdosianos*, 18 (1983), pp. 39–47.
Bosch, R., '*La sombra* y la psicopatología de Galdós', *Anales Galdosianos*, 6 (1971), pp. 21–42.
Cardona, Rodolfo, 'Introducción a *La sombra*', in Douglass M. Rogers, ed., *Benito Pérez Galdós* (Madrid, Taurus, 1973), pp. 247–55.
Casalduero, Joaquín, '*La sombra*', *Anales Galdosianos*, 1 (1966), pp. 33–8.
de la Nuez, Sebastián, '*La sombra*, primera novela de Galdós', *Letras de Deusto*, 4 (1974), pp. 135–59.
Turner, Harriet S., 'Rhetoric in *La sombra*: The author and his story', *Anales Galdosianos*, 6 (1971), pp. 5–19.

'La novela en el tranvía'

Oliver, Walter, 'Galdós's "La novela en el tranvía": Fantasy and the art of realistic narration', *Modern Language Notes*, 88 (1973), pp. 249–63.

La Fontana de Oro

Alcalá Galiano, José, '*La Fontana de Oro*, de Pérez Galdós', *Revista de España*, 20 (1871), pp. 148–58.
García Barrón, Carlos, 'Antonio Alcalá Galiano y la Fontana de Oro', *Hispania*, 47 (1964), pp. 91–94.
Gilman, Stephen, 'History as news in *La Fontana de Oro*', in *Estudios dedicados a Helmut Hatzfeld* (Barcelona, 1974).
Gilman, Stephen, '*La Fontana de Oro*: Historical fable or historical prophecy?', in *Les Cultures ibériques en devenir: Essais publiés en hommage à la mémoire de Marcel Bataillon (1895–1977) par la Fondation Singer-Polignac* (Paris, 1979), pp. 135–39.
Gimeno Casalduero, Joaquín, 'Los dos desenlaces de *La Fontana de Oro*: Origen y significado', *Anejo de Anales Galdosianos* (Los Angeles, Del Amo Foundation, 1978), pp. 55–69.
Pattison, Walter T., '*La Fontana de Oro*: Its early history', *Anales Galdosianos*, 15 (1980), pp. 5–9.
Petit, Marie-Claire, *Galdós et 'La Fontana de Oro': Genèse de l'oeuvre d'un romancier* (Paris, 1972).
Smieja, Florian, 'An alternative ending of *La Fontana de Oro*', *Modern Language Review*, 61 (1966), pp. 426–33.

Doña Perfecta

Blanquat, Josette, 'De l'Histoire au roman *Doña Perfecta*: Approche méthodologique', in *Actes du VIe Congrès National des Hispanistes Français de l'Enseignement Supérieur* (Annales Littéraires de l'Université de Besançon, no. 126, 1972), pp. 59–71.
Cardwell, Richard A., 'Galdós's *Doña Perfecta*: Art or argument?', *Anales Galdosianos*, 7 (1972), pp. 29–47.
Estébanez Calderón, Demetrio, '*Doña Perfecta*, de B. P. Galdós, como novela de tesis', *Boletín de la Biblioteca de Menéndez Pelayo*, 55 (1979), pp. 107–46.
Jones, C. A., 'Galdós's second thoughts on *Doña Perfecta*', *Modern Language Review*, 54 (1959), pp. 570–3.
Penuel, Arnold M., 'The problem of ambiguity in Galdós's *Doña Perfecta*', *Anales Galdosianos*, 11 (1976), pp. 71–88.
Standish, Peter, 'Theatricality and humour: Galdós's technique in *Doña Perfecta*', *Bulletin of Hispanic Studies*, 54 (1977), pp. 223–31.

Turner, Harriet, 'The shape of deception in *Doña Perfecta*', *Kentucky Romance Quarterly*, 31 (1984), pp. 125–34.

Varey, J. E., *Pérez Galdós, 'Doña Perfecta'* (Critical Guides to Spanish Texts, no. 1, London, Grant & Cutler, 1971).

Zahareas, Anthony, 'Galdós's *Doña Perfecta*: Fiction, history and ideology', *Anales Galdosianos*, 11 (1976), pp. 29– 58.

Zappala, Michael, 'Classical darkness and Prometheus in *Doña Perfecta*', *Revista Hispánica Moderna*, 40 (1978–9), pp. 35–41.

Gloria

Rodgers, E. J., 'Religious conflict and didacticism in *Gloria*', *Anales Galdosianos*, 1 (1966), pp. 39–51.

Shoemaker, W. H., 'A note on Galdós's religion in *Gloria*', *Anales Galdosianos*, 11 (1976), pp. 109–18.

Marianela

Bly, Peter, 'Egotism and charity in *Marianela*', *Anales Galdosianos*, 7 (1972), pp. 49–66.

Dendle, Brian J., 'Galdós, Ayguals de Izco and the Hellenic inspiration of *Marianela*', in Robert J. Weber, ed., *Galdós Studies II* (London, Támesis, 1974), pp. 1–11.

Wellington, Marie A., '*Marianela*: Nuevas dimensiones', *Hispania*, 51 (1968), pp. 38–48.

Wellington, Marie A., '*Marianela* de Galdós y Diderot', *Cuadernos Hispanoamericanos*, no. 324 (June 1977), pp. 558–69.

La desheredada

Bravo-Villasante, Carmen, 'El naturalismo de Galdós y el mundo de *La desheredada*', *Cuadernos Hispanoamericanos*, no. 230 (Feb. 1969), pp. 479–86.

Durand, Frank, 'The reality of illusion: *La desheredada*', *Modern Language Notes*, 89 (1974), pp. 191–201.

Engler, Kay, 'Linguistic determination of point of view: *La desheredada*', *Anales Galdosianos*, 5 (1970), pp. 67–73.

Gordon, Michael, 'The medical background to Galdós's *La desheredada*', *Anales Galdosianos*, 7 (1972), pp. 67–77.

Gordon, Michael, '"Lo que le falta a un enfermo le sobra a otro": Galdós's conception of humanity in *La desheredada*', *Anales Galdosianos*, 12 (1977), pp. 29–37.

Risley, William R., 'Setting in the Galdós novel, 1881–1885', *Hispanic Review*, 46 (1978), pp. 23–40.

Robin, C.-N., *Le Naturalisme dans 'La desheredada' de Pérez Galdós* (Annales Littéraires de l'Université de Besançon, Paris, 1976).

Ruiz Salvador, Antonio, 'La función del trasfondo histórico en *La desheredada*', *Anales Galdosianos*, 1 (1966), pp. 53–62.

El amigo Manso

Blanquat, Josette, 'Le Naturalisme espagnol en 1882: *El amigo Manso* de Galdós', *Bulletin Hispanique*, 64 bis (1962) (Hommage à Marcel Bataillon), pp. 318–335.

Davies, Gareth A., 'Galdós's *El amigo Manso*, an experiment in didactic method', *Bulletin of Hispanic Studies*, 39 (1962), pp. 16–30.

Kronik, John W., '*El amigo Manso* and the game of fictive autonomy', *Anales Galdosianos*, 12 (1977), pp. 71–94.

Russell, Robert H., '*El amigo Manso*: Galdós with a mirror', *Modern Language Notes*, 88 (1963), pp. 161–8.

Tormento

Durand, Frank, 'Two problems in Galdós's *Tormento*', *Modern Language Notes*, 79 (1964), pp. 513–25.
Gullón, Germán, 'Tres narradores en busca de un lector', *Anales Galdosianos*, 5 (1970), pp. 75–80.
Rodgers, Eamonn, 'The appearance-reality contrast in Galdós's *Tormento*', *Forum for Modern Language Studies*, 6 (1970), pp. 382–98.
Sinnigen, John H., 'Ideología, reflejo y estructuras literarias en Galdós: El ejemplo de *Tormento*', *Actas del VI Congreso Internacional de Hispanistas* (Toronto, 1980), pp. 711–13.

Fortunata y Jacinta

Bacarisse, S., 'The realism of Galdós: Some reflections on language and the perception of reality', *Bulletin of Hispanic Studies*, 42 (1965), pp. 239–50.
Blanco-Aguinaga, Carlos, 'On "The birth of Fortunata"', *Anales Galdosianos*, 3 (1968), pp. 13–24.
Bly, Peter A., 'Fortunata and No. 11, Cava de San Miguel', *Hispanófila*, No. 59 (1977), pp. 31–48.
Braun, Lucille V., 'Galdós's recreation of Ernestina Manuel de Villena as Guillermina Pacheco', *Hispanic Review*, 38 (1970), pp. 32–55.
Brooks, J. L., 'The character of Doña Guillermina Pacheco in Galdós's novel *Fortunata y Jacinta*', *Bulletin of Hispanic Studies*, 38 (1961), pp. 86–94.
Eoff, Sherman H., 'The treatment of individual personality in *Fortunata y Jacinta*', *Hispanic Review*, 17 (1949), pp. 269–89.
Goldman, Peter B., ed., *Conflicting Realities: Four Readings of a Chapter by Pérez Galdós (Fortunata y Jacinta, Part III, Chapter IV)* (London, Támesis, 1984).
Holmberg, A. C., 'Louis Lambert and Maximiliano Rubín: The inner vision and the outer man', *Hispanic Review*, 46 (1978), pp. 119–36.
Macklin, John J., 'Benito Pérez Galdós: *Fortunata y Jacinta*', in D. A. Williams, ed., *The Monster in the Mirror: Studies in Nineteenth-Century Realism* (Oxford University Press, 1978), pp. 179–203.
Menéndez y Arranz, Juan, *Un aspecto de la novela 'Fortunata y Jacinta'* (Madrid, 1952).
Raphael, S., 'Un extraño viaje de novios', *Anales Galdosianos*, 3 (1968), pp. 35–49.
Ribbans, Geoffrey, 'Contemporary history in the structure and characterisation of *Fortunata y Jacinta*', in J. E. Varey, ed., *Galdós Studies I* (London, Támesis, 1970), pp. 90–113.
Ribbans, Geoffrey, 'El carácter de Mauricia "la Dura" en la estructura de *Fortunata y Jacinta*', *Actas del V Congreso Internacional de Hispanistas* (Bordeaux, 1977), vol. 2, pp. 713–21.
Ribbans, Geoffrey, *Pérez Galdós, 'Fortunata y Jacinta'* (Critical Guides to Spanish Texts, no. 21, London, Grant & Cutler, 1977).
Sinnigen, John H., 'Individual, class and society in *Fortunata y Jacinta*', in Robert J. Weber, ed., *Galdós Studies II* (London, Támesis, 1974), pp. 49–68.
Turner, Harriet S., 'Family ties and tyrannies: a reassessment of Jacinta', *Hispanic Review*, 51 (1983), pp. 1–22.
Whiston, James, 'Language and situation in Part I of *Fortunata y Jacinta*', *Anales Galdosianos*, 7 (1972), pp. 79–91.
Whiston, James, 'The materialism of life: religion in *Fortunata y Jacinta*', *Anales Galdosianos*, 14 (1979), pp. 65–81.
Zahareas, Anthony N., 'The tragic sense in *Fortunata y Jacinta*', *Symposium*, 19 (1965), pp. 38–49.
Zahareas, Anthony N., 'El sentido de la tragedia en *Fortunata y Jacinta*', *Anales Galdosianos*, 3 (1968), pp. 25–34 (a revised and expanded version of the previous article).